MEMES FOR MUMMYJI

Advance Praise for *Memes for Mummyji*

'Santosh Desai provides penetrating insights into our sense of self. His writing is accessible but deep. He has turned the observation of society into a gentle art form. With great subtlety he uncovers the ways in which the new information order and social forces are transforming us.'

– **Pratap Bhanu Mehta**, academic and public intellectual

'Santosh Desai is the prose laureate of India's hybrid modernity. No one has explained the everyday transitions in desi life with such empathy, lucidity and grace. Memes for Mummyji is required reading for anyone trying to get a handle on Hindustan.'

– **Mukul Kesavan**, writer

'Santosh Desai's book is a triumph of opinion journalism; he is one of the very few columnists who are interesting and memorable. He gets into the mind of India and tells us clearly what he sees.'

– **Manu Joseph**, author of *Why the Poor Don't Kill Us*

'Brilliant and unparalleled sensemaking of the chaos and contradictions when new and old India collide! The profound insights and humorous observations make this book a delightful and valuable read.'

– **Rama Bijapurkar**, author of *We Are Like That Only* and *Lilliput Land*

SANTOSH DESAI

MEMES FOR MUMMYJI

Making Sense of Post-Smartphone India

HarperCollins *Publishers* India

First published in India by HarperCollins *Publishers* 2025
HarperCollins *Publishers* India, Cyber City,
Building 10-A, Gurugram, Haryana – 122002, India
www.harpercollins.co.in

2 4 6 8 10 9 7 5 3 1

P-ISBN: 978-93-7307-109-1
E-ISBN: 978-93-7307-870-0

Typeset in 11/13.7 Berling LT Std
by HarperCollins *Publishers* India Pvt. Ltd

Printed and bound at
Nutech Print Services Pvt. Ltd.

This book is printed on FSC® certified paper
which ensures responsible forest management.

HarperCollins *Publishers*, Macken House, 39/40 Mayor Street Upper,
Dublin 1, D01 C9W8, Ireland

CONTENTS

CHAPTER 9

ACKNOWLEDGEMENTS

THIS BOOK IS AN ATTEMPT to bring together and reflect upon the ideas that have shaped my column in *The Times of India*, which I have been writing for the last twenty-one years. Getting a weekly platform in a paper like the TOI is a unique opportunity and a special privilege, for which I am truly grateful. I am especially grateful to the TOI for the kind permission to use the material that has appeared in its pages.

This book would not have been possible without the gentle but persistent efforts of my editor Amit Agarwal. He has been a champion of the book, and has played an invaluable role in helping put it together in his trademark gentlemanly manner.

I have been fortunate enough to work in close proximity with Kishore Biyani, who is an original and provocative thinker about India. Conversations with him have challenged and informed my ideas about how India is dealing with change. My gratitude also to my colleagues, past and present, at Futurebrands; much of this book is an outcome of their work. I couldn't have done this without their input and provocation. Anirban Mukerjee, Lipika Kumaran, Samit Mehrotra, Sunil Vashishth and Sraboni Bhaduri have all been fellow travellers in this journey to make sense of India.

My family has provided active support, without which this book would have been impossible to conceive. Writing a weekly column can sometimes take a toll on them as many plans revolve around my constraints. But more significantly, they have been my first readers – each piece has had to earn their approval before reaching anyone else. My ninety-year-old dad, who passionately follows my writing; wife, Vibha; and my daughters, Pallavi and Ketaki, are all vital elements of my support system.

My younger daughter Ketaki, who is a writer and a journalist, played a special role, going over the drafts and editing my work with a sternly critical eye. A tyrant in the making, she pushed me relentlessly when my efforts flagged.

The list would not be complete without the readers of my column, who have been a constant source of encouragement, both in terms of appreciation and criticism. I hope that this effort offers something in return.

INTRODUCTION

The mobile phone changed everything. This is not a particularly original observation, but sometimes a cliché is only the residue of a truth we haven't yet fully absorbed. We know that life has changed, we say it often, we nod sagely when someone else says it, and yet we rarely stop to look at how exactly it has changed. This book is an attempt to do that. Not by charting data curves or tracking policy implications, but by standing at street corners, inside living rooms, under flyovers, and inside WhatsApp groups – where the real transformation has been quietly underway.

The mobile phone – more accurately, the smartphone – didn't just give us access to the world. It allowed us to rebuild the world around ourselves. We are no longer merely in the world; we carry it with us. A little slab of glass and metal is now our camera, our calendar, our confessional, our shopping mall, our protest poster, our mirror. It is also our memory, our boredom killer, our ego amplifier, and often, our reality. We once looked at our phones. Now we live inside them.

This book is about that shift. About the times we live in. About the post-mobile-phone era and its distinctive grammar.

More specifically, it is about what this shift has done to us – not just to our habits but to our ideas of the self, of the social, of meaning. We are watching, perhaps without quite knowing it, the quiet rearrangement of Indian society – not in large, dramatic ruptures, but in the small frictions of daily life. A mother sends good-morning messages on thirty WhatsApp groups. A teenager in Rajkot changes his SIM cards to toggle between three girlfriends. A cab driver in Mumbai doesn't know the city but knows the GPS intimately. A child learns to fold clothes from YouTube, while her father watches reels on how to raise children.

Something profound is happening here. And it is happening not just in metros or elite drawing rooms, but in Tier-2 towns, in government housing colonies, in wedding halls and traffic jams. The old structures of Indian life – family, caste, geography, hierarchy – are not being erased. They are being remixed. The mobile phone is not a disruptive force in the conventional Silicon Valley sense. In India, it is a sneaky intruder and a loyal accomplice. It creates new openings, new performances, new desires – but always within an ecology of the familiar.

We are still getting married the old way, but now the 'haldi' ceremony has a hashtag. We still value family, but we do so while being silently glued to separate screens. The individual, once submerged under layers of 'we', is now assertive, visible, marketable – and yet still tethered to the collective.

Modernity, as always in India, arrives not as a clean slate but as a noisy negotiation.

And it is not just the minutiae of life; politics and media, too, look completely different. The current discourse would be unrecognizable to someone from 2010, and it didn't look too rosy even then. Our public lives seem framed by a sense of anger, that we direct towards each other across a variety of subjects.

The chapters that follow are drawn from years of weekly columns – essays written in real time as India navigated its smartphone adolescence. Each piece has been updated to reflect the present moment. Outdated references have been deleted, and recent shifts in Indian life and culture have been woven in. The pieces are grouped not by chronology but by theme: Digital culture, changing social norms, the body and leisure, work, urban space, outrage and politics. Each theme holds up a mirror to the ways in which this era has reshaped our inner lives and outer rituals.

Some of these changes are exhilarating. A young woman in a small town can now start a business from her phone, learn photography, fall in love, or fight for her rights – all without leaving her room. Others are more insidious. The same phone that empowers her also surveils her. It subjects her to anonymous judgement, algorithmic scrutiny, and the invisible enforcement of community values. Privacy is shrinking, the self is always being performed, and outrage is a form of participation. We have gained access to the world and lost the ability to stay still.

This book is not a lament. Nor is it a celebration. It is a series of attempts to notice – to pause and peer into the ordinary and find in it the tectonic shifts that define our moment. It is written in a tone that deliberately resists grand narratives and sweeping claims. For the truth is that the biggest shifts often manifest as the smallest habits: how we type, how we pose, how we forward jokes, how we measure love in message counts, how we consume food, music, politics, and each other.

There are new archetypes now: the influencer, the gamer, the unboxer, the keyboard warrior, the lurking uncle. There are new rituals: group exit dramas, good-morning flower bombs, Instagrammable meals, sleepy Zoom calls, outraged comment threads. The sacred and the trivial now share a screen.

But even more interesting are the subtler shifts. How time is experienced more horizontally, with all our apps running parallel lives. How emotion is outsourced to emojis. How the very idea of the self is being overdocumented, annotated, edited, filtered, tracked. We are living in a state of constant presence, and yet we feel curiously absent from ourselves. We are the most connected generation, and perhaps the loneliest.

This book attempts to track these ironies. How we are freer but more anxious. More expressive, yet less reflective. More seen, yet less known. Each essay tries to capture not just what is changing, but how it, in turn, changes us – what it feels like to live through a shift that is still ongoing.

If my earlier book, *Mother Pious Lady*, tried to understand India through the lens of tradition adapting to modernity, *Memes for Mummyji* explores what happens when that very modernity becomes tradition. When the digital is not a novelty but a habitat. When being online is not an activity but a default condition.

The title – *Memes for Mummyji* – is both affectionate and slightly mischievous. It captures that peculiar Indian phenomenon of the past walking arm in arm with the present, of the respectable auntie who forwards risqué jokes, of values that are shifting under the weight of convenience, not ideology. In many ways, this is a book about how India is learning to perform modernity the way it performs tradition: noisily, collectively, and with an instinctive genius for hybridization.

Technology isn't done yet. Not by a long shot. The mobile phone, after all, was just the beginning. AI is around the corner. Virtual influencers, predictive algorithms, deepfake weddings, social credit systems – they are not science fiction. They are early whispers of a future already in motion.

This book is an attempt to decode the present as it morphs into the future. To treat the ordinary as worthy of inquiry. To ask what our screens say about us, and what they are quietly turning us into.

Because while the memes may be fleeting, the mummyji in all of us is here to stay.

CHAPTER 1

Digital Culture

Our Performing Selves

The mobile phone didn't just connect us to the world – it relocated us within it.

Digital technology has restructured everyday life in India, shrinking the distance between desire and fulfilment, inflating the self into a broadcastable brand, and turning the private moment into a public performance.

We are being reprogrammed bit by bit and it is showing up in many different facets of our behaviour.

LADDERS TO ELSEWHERE: OF MOBILE PHONES AND SMALL-TOWN INDIA

THE FADED WALL PAINTING IN Raipur is for an event management company called Crazy Chaps. Only one part has been repainted, the only bit that matters – the mobile phone number. In a small but telling way, it speaks of the centrality of the mobile phone in India; it is as if almost every aspect of one's identity can somehow be encapsulated in this tiny device.

Everywhere one travels in small-town India, one finds the powerful influence of this sliver of technology. Indeed, there are times when, if one were to freeze-frame on a random scene, every single person in it would be doing something with a phone. Mobile phone usage has settled over small-town India like a coating of access, creating intricate new networks of communication while also serving as part rabbit hole into the self and part ejection hatch into an outside world full of nameless opportunity. The small town reaches beyond itself, and suddenly everything is within grasp.

For many, perhaps the most profound way in which it has changed them begins with the act of owning a mobile phone itself. To get a unique number, and with it the ability to reach anyone with a phone and, in turn, be reached by anyone, gives one an address in the new world. The mobile phone is a giant act of inclusion and an assertion of the significance of the individual as she becomes part of a network of possibilities, a citizen of a new collective.

The conferment of identity in a way that could be tangibly experienced has perhaps been the most important contribution made by this increasingly versatile device. Across the country, in so many different ways, the mobile phone is making the individual experience herself as a brighter dot on the map of the world. The self is being experienced both as being connected to the larger collective as well as separate from it. The ability to stay connected deepens ties between loved ones even as it allows for greater physical separation. The mobile phone is altering the constraints imposed by geography and migration and making it possible for many more people to imagine distance as a variable that can be managed.

The difference is most significant in the case of young women, many of whom report that their desire to move to another town to study is easier to convert into reality thanks to the mobile phone. The ability to access someone and, in turn, be accessed in private is something that creates both personal possibility as well as a kind of social anxiety. For old power structures don't get dismantled that easily.

The ability of the mobile phone to unleash a new set of desires among women is the reason why it comes under the greatest scrutiny. It is common to hear laments about the changing values that get attributed to the use of mobile phones by women, and in some parts of India, there is an active policing of its use. Worse, it enables old patriarchal attitudes to find new instruments of abuse, with multiple examples of exploitative MMSes, deepfakes, instances of revenge porn and the circulation of rape videos becoming commonplace.

The ability to stay connected is also making for some interesting new kinds of codes in relationships. For a lot of young people, the idea of a private channel of communication that is invisible and continuous enables a new meaning of romance. In many small towns across India, including the north, where the intermingling of the sexes is actively managed, the mobile phone becomes a vehicle of building and breaking relationships. For boys, the phone encourages risk-taking – *try maar lo, kya jaata hai*, as one young man put it. The idea of couples is becoming more commonplace, but interestingly, very often this does not necessarily culminate in marriage, nor is it intended to. It is conceived of as a device to intensify the enjoyment of youth, before submitting to the responsibilities of adulthood.

For people in relationships, the mobile phone allows for privacy but also creates a new set of expectations. Continuous contact is expected and its absence can create difficulties in some relationships. Being in love now comes with a currency of attention, and unless a steady stream of calls and messages flows, one isn't proving one's affections enough.

The mobile phone, by its nature, allows for the existence of a parallel script to life. The ability to be somewhere else also translates into being able to be someone else simultaneously. People manage multiple lives more easily with the mobile phone. Like the temple-sevak-cum-dancer-cum-event- manager-cum-TV-actor in Konark, who uses the mobile phone to juggle parallel careers as well as play doting husband and father. Or the wrestling-champion-turned-bouncer in Gurugram, who navigates two completely different cultural universes. On one hand, he lives and abides by the strict code of behaviour imposed on him by his guru, and on the other, poses shirtless for his Facebook profile. Or yet another very enterprising young boy from Rajkot, who claims that he needs a phone with multiple SIM cards – multiple SIMs for multiple girlfriends, as he put it. In a world where opportunities are several but mostly fragmented, the mobile phone allows for these to be reconciled and availed of.

The awareness of the self, aided by the camera in the mobile phone, has generated a striking familiarity with being represented in media. Wherever one goes, we find an ease with being photographed, particularly among the young; it is as if they have been waiting to be shot and know exactly how to pose for a picture. The consumption of one's image in all possible contexts is generating a self-awareness of a kind that is unique to this generation. The mobile phone enables a creation of a story about one's life that is today accessible to everyone; each individual is potentially the heroine in her own movie. In some ways, the self is rehearsed and then staged as a performance for the outside world.

A crucial function of the mobile phone is to consume fallow time. It helps inject apparent purpose in situations where it doesn't exist and individuals feel attached and significant more continuously. It also serves as an entertainment box which stores things that are of interest and into which one can lose oneself for a while. A new phone is often 'loaded' with entertainment, that allonws it to serve as a multimedia jukebox of sorts.

The technology itself has been customized both at the supply and demand ends, and this helps. The idea of the prepaid card has been an energizing one – it has set the category free, for it allows for calibrated and controlled consumption. In combination with very low pricing of both the phone and the service, it allows for participation by all, beginning with the lowest unit of consumption. Mobile telephony is an open system that is used in a number of different ways – increasingly, the smartphone is allowing for access to the internet and everything that comes along with it even as it helps project the individual to the world. Some use it with diffidence, trusting an intermediary to 'fill up' the device with ready-to-use software, particularly music, which is then accessed by learning which button to press when.

As a device, the mobile phone is a compact convergence of many senses into a site outside the self. It allows for an intensified experience of one's self as it allows for both the inward and the outward projection of the individual and her desires. In smaller Indian towns, the impact of this technology is understandably profound and can only be understood in a limited way at this point in time. But it is clear that a greater awareness of one's own self as a unit of identity as well as a combination of desires has been set in motion. The mobile phone creates this awareness as well as helps satisfy the needs that this creates. It is akin to an additional sense that people carry around to find themselves and lose themselves in. Glued to a mobile phone, a whole nation lives elsewhere.

THE MAKING OF THE INDIVIDUAL IN INDIA

Historically, the idea of being an individual in India could, generally speaking, only be expressed in the plural. The 'I' was never quite alone, coming accompanied as it did with the overhang of the 'we'. Our sense of identity was akin to that of a grain of sticky khichdi – potentially separate but always clinging on to a clump of the collective. It would seem that now, finally, the idea of being an individual is beginning to take clearer shape, aided by the insistent but implicit nudge provided by technology.

The thing about technology is that it makes change invisible; it moves faster and deeper than our awareness of it. We realize that we are being reshaped by the gadgets that we use, but even as we become aware of some aspects of this change, it is difficult for us to fully fathom how our behaviour changes our thinking. We are used to thinking of the world the other way around. Thought shapes action; forethought and intention are key drivers of the change that we desire to see. In the case of technology, we act with one kind of intention (to take advantage of the benefits of technology) but get changed by the manner in which we access technology.

The mobile phone makes us experience ourselves as individuals without explicitly setting out to do so. The mobile phone, whose reason for being is its ability to communicate with the outside world, has in time become our primary instrument of being wrapped up in our own selves.

We become a unique number and get an individual and distinct address in the world. We process the outside world through a device that has become an appendage to our senses; we cannot bear even momentary separation from this potent personal facility. We make thousands of choices in a day –

clicking, swiping, pinching, dragging, typing, issuing voice commands. We are the dictators of this world, making many more micro-decisions than we ever did, for after all, this is our own personal realm. Our wish, which needs a mere touch to manifest itself, is a command – this is a world that leaps to our touch, the slightest indication of our desire. We can leap from one world to another, hyperlinking our way across domains. Search engines operate on the basis of what we want, and not on what they have in store. The GPS makes us a dot in the world, giving us an eerie out-of-body experience of watching ourselves as we wind our way through the streets. Social media platforms narrativize our life by making videos of the year that went by. Never before have we had such an acute and continuous sense of our own selves as we do today.

Usually, when we talk of burgeoning individualism, the causal variables we work with are things like the influence of the West, the deeper penetration of markets, the power of media, and so on. These are content variables – here, what we hear, see and absorb changes the way we see ourselves in relation with the world. This process of cultural change, too, has an implicit structural element – we are not fully cognizant of how markets and media alter our priorities. For instance, markets legitimize the popular and make very different things comparable by attaching a price to them. But as compared to technology, we do offer a more considered form of resistance when faced with such influences. We worry about changing values, we ask ourselves if we are becoming too materialistic, and we often modify our behaviour in order to preserve our sense of who we are.

But technology works more noiselessly. Coming from a background where we were rarely faced with the prospect of making choices, we now make any number of micro-choices on a minute-by-minute basis. We are continuously, relentlessly, experiencing the world as individuals without consciously meaning to do so. We are developing a sense of who we are, what we like, what we outrage against and suchlike. We fill in little quizzes that promise us new, and somewhat improbable, ways of defining ourselves (What your favourite *Friends* character says about your dream home). We keep indicating our likes and dislikes by tagging a lot of what we see with our opinion. With time, we begin to crystallize a shape and form of ourselves, one that we walk around with in the real world, like a dog on a leash.

The downstream effects of this change are beginning to become visible in India. It is now a common sight for families to be together physically while being lost in their own individual worlds. We see this in the increasing assertiveness of opinions on social media as in the casual narcissism of the way we constantly present ourselves to the world through our words and images. We can see this in the intense involvement young people across the country have with their bodies. We see it in the way people talk about a personal sense of fashion, as they go about finding 'looks' that work for them. We see it in the efforts that are made to invest in oneself and develop skills that mark one out in a crowd. We see signs of this in the highly individualistic acts of creativity that are available for view on the internet. The awareness of one's individuality and the need to flesh out one's uniqueness is a theme that is beginning to find expression in several ways across the country.

The mobile phone as a private screen and as a tool for public self-representation has quietly enabled a new architecture of individual selfhood. The cascading impact of experiencing the world from an intensely individual lens is difficult to predict. In the Indian context, where the codes of the collective held sway, what happens when the young, in particular, start removing themselves from the mainstream and find their own customized worlds? The rise of a fragmented sense of individualism that responds to a personal set of values creates room for a new kind of uncertainty about the future shape of societies.

THE OVERDOCUMENTED SELF?

AFTER A LONG TIME, I had the experience of visiting someone's office and going through a very modern ritual. It involved getting photographed, sharing a mobile phone number, receiving an OTP on it, submitting it at reception, showing some government-approved proof of identity, getting an admission slip, which needed to be duly countersigned by the person being visited for submission on the way out. It is unclear as to what nuclear secrets were being protected at this particular apparel company, but it is reassuring to know that whatever they are, they continue to lie there unmolested thanks to the stringent security.

Growing up, one cannot remember ever being asked to produce any proof of identity, except perhaps occasionally in college. Indeed, one did not have any documents that could establish who one was. Bureaucracy existed even then; the fondness for entering things in registers and issuing passes that needed to be stamped is not a modern affliction. But most of this was an exercise in pure tokenism – one could write whatever one felt like and most of what was written was illegible and unusable anyway. And we certainly had very little interest in documenting our own selves. A few people kept diaries and journals, but for most, life was lived in utter unselfconsciousness, with little need felt to present oneself to the world. Also, those who did have that need were seen as egomaniacal narcissists who had an unhealthy involvement with their own selves.

Today, it almost seems as if the recording of every action of every individual is an end in itself. If official surveillance is one side of the story, then intense self-documentation is the other. As a consequence, both out of choice and out of compulsion, there is very little that we do that does not leave behind an imprint of some kind. In a digital world, every click is on record for eternity. We call it data, but it is a living testament to our existence and what we do with it. What we say, what we like, who we diss, what our vices are, our guilty pleasures, our vanities, all of it being logged into a ledger that has near-divine omniscience.

We are surveilled everywhere, even in the physical world. CCTV cameras that now have increasingly sophisticated facial recognition systems, GPS which tracks our movements, location histories on our phones which tell where we have been at any time, biometric-based instruments like Aadhar that are needed to navigate many public spaces, algorithms that follow us through our meanderings in the digital world – the sphere of the private has shrunk immeasurably.

We are being goaded to surrender privacy, even of the mind. Social media sites subtly encourage us to unburden ourselves to others. Our lives, or at least Instagram-filtered versions of it, are public documents. Even our attempts to shun social media become fodder for our self-promotion. The abandonment of privacy is a project that we carry out with gusto. We vie to be more 'social', to put more of ourselves out there for the edification of others. If Twitter (now known as X) wants to excise us of our opinions, Facebook creates a new grammar of relationships, Instagram makes our lives a visual treat for our audience, WhatsApp helps us broadcast every passing thought to a closed community, while with reels, we turn our lives cinematic.

The selfie allows us, for the first time, to convert mirrors into cameras. We rapid-prototype ourselves as we shoot a flurry of self-portraits. A camera like GoPro shows us what the world would look like if our bodies were cameras. Wearables are on the way that will make our bodies sentient. Already, Fitbit and our regular smartphones record our physical activity – how many steps we walked, how many calories we burned. Sleep apps tell us about our sleeping patterns, including the duration of the period we snored or the number of times we coughed.

Tomorrow, sensors will pick up key health parameters and feed them to a medical facility in real time so as to keep track and intervene when necessary. We now outsource not just the camera, but the editing – we present only a version of ourselves – an even-complexioned, well-lit, streamlined upgrade of the real thing.

What will remain are our thoughts. The unexpressed ones, that is. And even that may not be forever. Technologies that are able to decipher our thoughts are on their way. Then, truly, nothing will be ours alone anymore.

What are the social consequences of such a dramatic inversion of the self? Will we need to develop layers of personae to allow us to stash away a small part of ourselves? Will we never only be ourselves, but a version?

The paradox is that technology ostensibly strives to ensure that an individual gets whatever she desires and needs whenever it is needed and with the least possible effort. But in doing so, it ends up compromising the very things that make one an individual. As algorithms, keyed up to anticipate our needs, ply us with more of what we like, we find ourselves surrounded by mirror images of our desires, unable to break free.

We are moving towards a world where we can all effectively become part of a single organism. The idea of data converts all our actions and thoughts into a single fluid currency that flows constantly. One way of thinking about social media is that we are the extensions of the medium, the nodes that act according to an implicit master script instead of being users in charge of our own destiny. The social media system is a commercial engine, which is harvesting our attention for use by advertisers.

This is a world we have no previous templates of. What might be useful is for us to practise a form of self-aware commentary, one that characterizes the changes that we are undergoing, thanks to an unstoppable torrent called technology. To step outside the immersive grasp of new technologies so as to make sense of what is happening. Till such time as we can.

THE OVERACHIEVING VERB

IF, EARLIER, WE LIKED SOMEONE or something, it usually stayed within us. It gave us a nice warm feeling, it was a little fund of goodwill, a splashy puddle of well-being. Sometimes we communicated our appreciation, most often we did not. That has changed decisively.

The words we used to describe our way of being have now been hijacked to describe our ways of doing. Now, on social media, 'liking' something is an act. It involves pushing a button and displaying our appreciation. This is then aggregated and displayed and becomes a measure of sorts. We seek 'likes', we negotiate them – why should I like so-and-so's admittedly excellent post when she didn't like mine? As with anything that is measured, our likes are solicited, we are specifically invited to like something, and quite often we comply, not because we like it, but because, after all, it takes only the click of a button. As gluttons of appreciation, our need for it is boundless, and the satisfaction derived from it diminishes dramatically.

The verbification of our lives is all around us. Like has become 'liking', games have become 'gaming', what was work earlier has now been substituted with 'working out'. We 'post' frequently, 'share' without giving anything up. We follow, we mute, we swipe, we stream, we unmute, we block. Each of these words takes on a new life when used in today's context. Language is coaxed to perform additional tasks as old concepts take on new connotations.

In an increasingly automated world, leisure gets reframed as a form of work and begins to take on the shape of an occupation. We don't just eat, we are 'foodies'. We don't just speak, we podcast. We don't just think, we prompt.

To be a foodie, we have to fetishize the act of surviving by putting organic fuel into our stomachs. Food has never been a prosaic act of survival, but a life devoted to eating and talking or writing about it is now considered normal. Similarly, one is a fashionista, doggedly pursuing the cause of fashion against all odds. Or one is a fitness freak, mastering the murky art of running a lot without going anywhere.

The holiday is another example of how pleasure has turned into work. Holidaying is hard work. Chatting is an action. Parenting a terrifying new science that needs to be learnt. Partying an occupation. Chilling is what we do, rather than not do. Detoxing is a thing, an active pursuit of not pursuing something actively.

An unexpressed thought is such a waste. The distance between thought and its utterance has shrunk, making blurting the most common mode of self-expression. The loss of interiority is a consequence – every emotion or thought needs to have an external manifestation. Like a traditional Hindi film, where every emotion must be displayed using the eyebrow, we must ripple outwards onto the surface of our lives. Surrounded by screens, we must find things to project. To stop is to vanish. In the market of visibility, shyness is erasure; constant presence is the modern-day proof of life.

The sociality of digital media is of visibility without touchability. We erect transparent glass chambers, and post updates about what remains unseen. It is an act of turning ourselves inside out, converting the withins into withouts. Reportage has a way of crystallizing intention into some form of action.

The news is increasingly about things that can be shown happening, rather than things that are important. On television, the act of talking is not the opposite of the act of doing; talking has taken a dynamic outwardly dimension. War is waged through the voice, and the fate of the nation routinely decided. The anchor is able to imagine himself in the most active way possible, instead of seeing himself, more plausibly, as a deranged windbag.

The noun gives things a name. The adjective qualifies them, giving them texture and lending direction. The verb bustles with its own importance, revelling in its brusqueness. In a world where verbs rule, things keep happening. More accurately, everything gets imagined and presented as an event. Things need to materialize, become manifest. The urge to do things makes us convert thought quickly into some action. The illusion of action has become like a fix we need all the time.

The urge to do things all the time makes us react to everything with a view to improve it. We become the missing magic ingredient in a flawed world; it becomes our responsibility to confer words of wisdom on anything that is transpiring. We insert ourselves as subjects in every conversation, however incidental we might be to it. The world is a problem to be solved and our opinion holds the key to all answers.

Not long ago, we lived in a world with a startling paucity of verbs. We sat near windows, stood in balconies, spent hours drifting in boredom, without having anything to do. We lived off other people's routine activities; we were voyeurs of the uninteresting, dreamers of things unheroic. We can still catch a glimpse of this world in a few parts of the country, although the mobile phone has all but changed that. Perhaps government offices, which often give the impression of its denizens living comfortably without feeling the slightest need for a verb, are the last outposts of this world. Action, when it occurs, seems to happen as a geological stirring in cosmic time. Things move at the speed of file, which is the slowest unit of time known to us. The physical file has a life and mind of its own, and traverses space decorously, unlike its digital counterpart, which travels with unbecoming haste.

The overachieving verb makes us a more active and enthusiastic participant in our own lifescapes. As protagonists with the responsibility to keep the world going, there is an added edge of purpose that is felt among more people than ever before. But keeping one's thoughts to oneself is a luxury worth enjoying. The time has come to revisit the pleasures of not sharing, of not reacting and of not enacting our feelings as they occur.

THE WHATSAPP GROUP – INDIA'S EMOTIONAL PIPELINE?

Every morning, all over India, people are waking up to roses, inspirational quotes in pink, and pious sentiments trimmed to fit in verse. Through the day, we receive a barrage of opinions, memes, 'shairis', regurgitated stories, outrageous conspiracy theories, libel-seeking gossip missiles, nostalgia-laden pictures featuring moustaches, and really long jokes. An instant-messaging app that allows us to connect across different operating platforms, WhatsApp is fast-moving eternity, belonging without end. Belonging to a WhatsApp group is like a lifetime membership of a particularly loquacious and persistent cult.

Unlike other social media platforms, though, WhatsApp builds a sense of community of an intimate kind, even if the group is a large one. We become a circle huddling together, wondering aloud, musing, chortling together, groaning inwardly often, but finding some common thread that we find value in. Every WhatsApp group becomes a kind of family and, like all families, feels warm and dysfunctional at the same time.

It is astonishing how much people who have had little contact for decades suddenly find so much to say to each other on an hourly basis once connected. Reminiscences and old inside jokes are the staple to begin with, but soon every WhatsApp group tends towards sameness, and it is not unusual to find the same joke, video or outrageous lie appearing within minutes on all one's various groups. Everyone drinks from the same stream of consciousness, it would appear.

Unlike other social media platforms, on WhatsApp, escape is not easy. Membership is watched closely, and deserters identified swiftly. Every person who leaves a group does so with an audible gasp rising like a stink bomb among those left behind. 'You are too good for us, is it?', is the often articulated accusation. So one stays on, in mute acquiescence to a shared connection, renewed too energetically for one to be comfortable, but too valuable to be snapped.

The codes of response are more stringent than on other social media applications. On Facebook, thanks to its algorithm, which is God-like in its apparent randomness, one can always miss a message. Also, it takes nothing to click 'like', or type in an emoji or mumble LOL. On WhatsApp, that does not do. Every breathless announcement from an obscure aunt has to be acknowledged in aunt-appropriate language. One has to be alert to the speed of one's response – being a laggard raises digital eyebrows, and abstaining from commenting is not really an option in many cases.

If, on Facebook, one shares lofty articles and cute videos, on WhatsApp, one can share pretty much anything. No quality standards apply. WhatsApp is the headquarters of the desultory, of the thought-mumble that is a lazy stirring at the back of the mind which then becomes a gift that we instantly decant on the world. The closed nature of the community reduces barriers to entry and participation. At one level, everyone who matters is watching, and at another, everything that is being said is in private. It helps that in the fast-moving stream of posts, little is retained as a permanent document. Thoughts on WhatsApp perish quickly, which is something to be fervently grateful about.

Think of it as cultural plumbing; of pipelines set in real time between closed groups that share something in common. WhatsApp is a not merely an app that sits on our phones, but an intricate network that, like its other social media counterparts, has its own structural logic. It enables certain kinds of ideas and actions and discourages others. It connects, encloses, reconnects, reinforces, sucks in participants towards a conceptual centre, among other things.

WhatsApp is our bubble, a digital representation of our comfort zone. Sealed off from light, whispers resound, conversations arc towards the centre, where comfort lies, the consensus of emotions converging in a warm flush. Here, the logic of the group lies in finding sameness and locating convergences. Those dissenting are pushed outwards as they find their comments ignored or petulantly reacted to. After a while, it is simply not worth the effort to disagree. Ideas not fitting into the dominant ethos of a group cannot survive.

If media is air, WhatsApp is what lies underground. It validates all existing ideas, strengthens stereotypes, doubles down on a point of connection, operates through the axis of similarity and familiarity. The whisper becomes louder as it gets repeated, and things that cannot be said aloud – even today – begin, through waves of recirculation, to acquire the currency of legitimacy. The tentative whisper becomes an assertive roar.

An instant-messaging platform like WhatsApp renews fading connections and rescues once-meaningful relationships from withering away. We bask in the familiarity of each other, discovering that our often-tenuous connections are still more significant than the ones we have formed more recently, particularly on other social media platforms.

But the very fact that here we deepen the circle of familiarity and form a group that rallies around some dominant values and ideas makes this platform perhaps the most powerful tool of propaganda that exists today. Its comfortable nature invites wide participation, even from those who are otherwise wary of technology. WhatsApp is idle chatter that gets consumed without too many defences, and without having to test it against any form of external reality. Conjecture hardens into certainty, which, in turn, becomes a fact, which effortlessly converts into a form of consensus. And best of all, it is invisible to the outside world until it emerges as rock-hard certainty.

The world is shaped by ideas which, in turn, are shaped by the way human minds are thrown together. New forms of social media are configured in ways that are producing newer patterns of convergence and divergence in the manner we think and the ideas we agree upon. Of all the new media platforms, WhatsApp helps reconnect us to the dominant ideas of a homogenous social group. Politically and culturally, this has profound implications, the contours of which we have not yet fully grasped.

LEARNING TO LEARN?

'If they needed education to use a pen, an angootha chhaap can operate a computer today,' said the animated young man in Kolkata. He was referring to his facility with a mobile phone and the doors that it opened for him by merely twiddling his thumbs. As part of a study examining the social impact of technology in the country, we had run into this school dropout in a small shopping complex where he was selling costume jewellery that he had taught himself to make by watching YouTube videos. He had learnt to navigate the world that the phone gave him access to first by learning English on his own, which allowed him to use the smartphone with lightning speed, and then by teaching himself ways to earn a living. More than anything else, he exuded confidence about being able to learn on his own.

He is not alone. Elsewhere, ten-year-olds are at the forefront of technology, using it as their primary sense organ. A young kid in Nashik attributed his amazing facility with the digital world to the 'surround'. Technology has become a form of oxygen – it is everywhere and gets absorbed without any apparent effort. Across the country, we heard different kinds of voices that indicated that a new kind of learning was beginning to take place. Some housewives spoke of their new-found ability to expand their range of skills, beginning with the culinary, thanks to videos and WhatsApp groups. A section of retired people spoke of how learning to use the internet gave them a new lease of life – the world suddenly opened up. Old interests were revived, new ones discovered.

Once a certain minimum threshold of familiarity is crossed, the phone becomes an instrument of exploratory travel and discovery. The wonderful thing about a search engine like Google is that you need to know nothing in order to use it. To avail of it, all one needs is to confess one's ignorance – one needs no qualifications or any prior knowledge or expertise in a subject to begin educating oneself on it. In the digital world, one can always start at zero and chase one's curiosity thereafter. And now, we no longer just search, we summon. AI does more than help us find answers. It gives us pre-assembled, ready-to-use solutions.

Traditionally, learning in India has been a tedious affair. Learning by rote has been the norm, and the mental model is that of dense knowledge struggling to penetrate our brains. Most of us immediately forget what we have allegedly learnt once the exams are over – ask any 'educated' person a question about basic high-school physics or geography and chances are that no answer will be forthcoming. The onerous formality of education creates a barrier to those outside its ambit. It all looks and feels too difficult; besides, it is far from clear as to what use would one be able to put the things that one learns in school. Its relationship with real life is tenuous at best.

Attempts to promote 'vocational' education have traditionally met with limited success, partly because of the manner in which they were conceived and delivered, and also because in the caste system of education, these courses were regarded as being inferior. Things are changing, however. Across the country, traditional ideas about what constitutes good education are beginning to change; computer training institutes, airhostess academies, media and event management schools, personality development courses – these are the emerging faces of education in the country.

With technology, it is possible to imagine an even more radical redefinition of the idea of learning. The ability to find one's own way through the thickets of knowledge provides an exciting alternative to the engineered formality of education. Instead of a linear, step-by-step process determined by those who allegedly know better, education becomes an exercise in discovery of those bits of knowledge that are of immediate and direct relevance and interest to the seeker.

The intimate universe consisting of an individual and her smartphone has created a new pathway to learning, one where no one else is watching or interfering. Through trial-and-error and with the help of YouTube videos, Coursera modules, friends on social media and the magic of ChatGPT, people across the country are figuring out things for themselves. This is education in its rawest form, directly feeding a thirst for knowledge. Learning happens without embarrassment or self-doubt and is automatically aligned to the individual's ability to absorb it.

Otherwise, today, education is something that gets injected into us without our consent and without any sense of need. It is a socially legitimate form of conscription; we enlist into a system at a stage when we have no idea of what we are doing and why. We learn because we have to, because it is what everyone must do at a certain stage of life.

And yet, there is nothing intrinsically sacred about the process we think of as education. All of us need teachers, we need texts of one kind or another, and we need some repetition and reinforcement in order to learn, and all of these can potentially be made available outside the formal system of education. We also need to be able to learn all of our lives, and not cram education in a fifteen-year period at the beginning.

Education is being liberated from its stifling correctness and is being set free to be stumbled upon. Knowledge will flow in unpredictable, non-linear ways as those outside its ambit will grab whatever they find useful. The demand-led view of education can give it a new sense of energy and purpose. In a larger sense, perhaps it is time to rethink our traditional approach to education and harness this new capacity we have developed to learn on our own, along the axis of our curiosity. What might help is the development of self-learning modules, which are designed to aid the process of discovery using principles of storytelling and gamification. We are learning to learn in a new way, and that is very good news indeed.

GPS AND THE NEW MAPS OF THE WORLD

THE TAXI DRIVER HAD ABSOLUTELY no idea about the city he called his home. It had been two years since he moved to Mumbai, but he was clueless about the most basic destinations – Fountain, Nariman Point, Bandra. His modus operandi was to hand over his phone and ask the passenger to key in the details of the destination and then he would blindly follow whatever the GPS told him. My colleague who had engaged his services spoke to him and discovered that while he continued to be closely connected with his family back in UP, thanks to his mobile phone, the city that was now his home had taken on a virtual character. The GPS was real; it was the roads that had stopped meaning anything to him in a physical sense. He lived in a settlement along with other people from his part of the world, encased in a digital bubble of GPS and YouTube. Mumbai for him was roads and buildings, and geography was a video game.

GPS has not only transformed how we travel, but it has also changed the way in which we think of ourselves in relation to the world. At its heart, the ability to locate oneself in a moving real-time map is a superpower. With several other layers of intelligence being added on it, GPS allows us to make sense of and to manoeuvre, in a variety of very useful ways, a world that is constantly on the move.

In an earlier time, the compass was armed with only one piece of knowledge, and we found a way to navigate the vast uncertainties of our world using the one thing we could know for sure – the direction where North lay. The map gave us a detailed two-dimensional, but fixed, view of the world. Places now had names and locations. Today, GPS has helped insert time into space, allowing us to frame the world from the perspective of the traveller.

As with all new technologies that begin to shape our lives, one wonders how one ever got along without this. In the world before GPS, road maps were an essential part of the glove compartment. I can remember maps spread untidily on the lap as some member of the family tried their hand at navigation. Only a few people seemed to possess the ability to make sense of a map, which were rudimentary in any case in India, and smooth map-based navigation made that a rarity. And, of course, after using the map unsuccessfully, one still had to fold it back into its previous state of impossible neatness.

But while the struggles with roads and destinations might have been more or less laid to rest, GPS also alters how we experience space, time, and even our own selves. The dependence on GPS makes us detach from, and even distrust, our senses. We get pushed back into our vehicles; having already been shielded from the outside thanks to air-conditioning, we are now hemmed in by knowledge, feeling no need to interact with our surroundings. Like the Mumbai taxi driver, we experience the world second hand. In the case of a mismatch between what we see and what GPS tells us, often it feels as if it is reality that is making a mistake.

With GPS, every road journey becomes a test that we need to excel at. The drive becomes a battle against the road as we try and take the faster route, intent on saving those three minutes that the GPS will help us with. Real-time information makes the future part of the present, and we need to juggle both. We see what is about to happen, and we get armed with the means to change the script. Of course, the greater our ability to look ahead, the more frustrated we get when the GPS reacts too late. The blue line turns grey and then a deep red just as we roll in at the tail-end of a massive jam.

Increasingly, the new technologies of the digital kind are relocating us in a world where we can keep track of all the multiple streams of our life simultaneously. Time is experienced horizontally and does not have to wait its turn to register; we can keep track of people who mention us, events that are of interest to us, conversations that we wish to be part of, all the while living our primary lives. The dot on the GPS, the free-flowing nature of timelines on social media, the infinite scroll on an e-commerce website – our lives are now concretely visualized as ceaseless and simultaneous flows. This means that we are distracted eternally, but we operate as command centres, keeping an eye on our multiple lives and retaining a sense of control over these. GPS today does more than help us find the way – it helps others find us. We are the fixed spot in a turning universe – the dot on a location map that Uber drivers, delivery agents and guests strive to reach.

We have descended into the digital realm, abandoning our perch as users of technology, and becoming embedded inside it. The act of experiencing ourselves as technological artifacts, standing outside the self and watching its progress, is a surreal experience. What it helps produce is an overweening sense of awareness about oneself. We are aware of ourselves at all times. Aware of ourselves in relation with our environment, aware of what lies around the corner.

Maps of an earlier era were invitations; GPS is more like an instruction manual. The map was a chronicler of tantalizing possibilities. The map has come to life today and its mysteries are now a little less daunting. GPS makes maps less about exploration and more about actual access; it focuses on what we need from it. With GPS, destinations speak directly to destinations, and places on the way no longer need to have names. And we are always at the centre of our world in the moving corridor of the self.

DECODING THE SELFIE: THE MIRROR REVERSED?

Tʜᴀᴛ ᴛʜᴇ ꜱᴇʟꜰɪᴇ ɪꜱ ꜱᴏᴍᴇ kind of a clue to the times we live in is difficult to argue with. Its ubiquity is everywhere, if one may be allowed to mirror the superfluous abundance of the phenomenon in question. It seems to be an impulse that is difficult to fight, and, multiplied with the popularity of smartphones and social media sites, the world becomes a receptacle for countless images of the self. It is, in the eyes of many, a sign of the narcissism that pervades this age, as our love for the self spills over into the firm conviction that the world needs us on endless rotation, as we go through the excruciatingly trivial moments of our life.

This is both true and a little unfair. For, at one level, the selfie is just an extension of an age-old desire – to somehow pin down the slippery nature of the self. It is a central paradox of our lives that we are unable to grasp our being as others grasp it. We see everything in the world through an intensely experienced entity that we know to be ourselves but we cannot simultaneously turn the gaze inwards in any satisfying way. The mirror produced the earliest selfies, but it showed the self as a tremulous being, which was always dying to escape from itself, with every little movement indicative of subsequent flight. One could watch oneself completely still, but one could only see oneself seeing oneself in the mirror. The mirror owned the person looking into it; it froze the watcher into being a mirror image of herself.

Trying to photograph oneself in the mirror was a fruitless exercise, for we wound up shooting ourselves in the face, so to speak. Obscured by the camera, the attempt mocked us, for it was an existential dead-end, the erasure of the very face that we wanted captured; erased by our effort to capture it. The camera that we used to shoot ourselves became the reason we could not be shot. A satisfyingly neat irony, if one likes that sort of thing.

The selfie is an attempt to escape the confines of the mirror. It uses profusion as a way of grasping the self in motion as it navigates different roles and contexts. It still needs one hand to be used in the capture of the self, but it does allow us to do things we do without being locked up in the mirror. We might be tied to an arm's length of ourselves, but the selfie captures for future consumption many versions of a quicksilver self. The selfie is a photograph without carrying with it the studied formality that accompanies the act of being photographed. Beginning with its name, which suggests that the self is an endearing pet of some kind whose belly one scratches while cooing adorable names to it in a made-up language, the selfie breaks down the apparent solidness attached to the idea of an individual into a gel-like intermediate state, one that avoids concrete definition and easy categorization. The self is imagined as a blur of different intentions, rather than as a settled mode of being.

It is also part of a need to get inside the self a little better, to unravel it in different ways. We look for some understanding and then flaunt it to the world, seeking validation, which is easy to get – some obliging person will 'like' the form in which we present ourselves. Like the signature, the selfie is an affirmation of one's existence from one's own perspective. There is a phase in life when we scribble our signature everywhere; this in spite of the fact that as a carrier of identity, the signature is completely detached from any kind of reality. It does not evoke who we are, except through a scribbled form of a code called language. The selfie is, at some basic level, a similar exercise in multiplying a sensation of the self. We proliferate our presence by stamping ourselves on to places and moments. With the camera in the past, our eye could be everywhere, now it is we who are omnipresent.

But the selfie does much more for it is part of a much more significant shift that is beginning to take place. Given the popularity of Instagram, the selfie has become part of a more visual culture that is starting to take root. On Instagram, the individual does not merely become the subject of the camera; she becomes the camera. What gets presented is a non-textual account of one's life that follows a very different grammar of communication. The world of text is one of logic and sequence where meaning strives to universality, while the narrative that is made up of a series of photographs comes with no prefabricated meaning and it is the viewer who puts it together in her head as she deems fit. The selfie, as the basic unit of a visual vocabulary, becomes the starting point of a fascinating journey in a new kind of narrative. What we call the selfie is today a collaborative co-production with apps that widen eyes, smoothen skin, make jawlines firmer and tint moods. We are no longer posing – we are designing.

That does not mean that the selfie is not narcissistic, but that it is much more. The human need to come to terms with the strangeness of one's physical self, even as one celebrates its familiarity, has found a new mode of expression. The unbundling of the individual is in progress, as is the need to understand the self better and to circulate this new-found knowledge to the world in ever newer ways. The self is being imbued with much greater significance but it is also simultaneously in the process of being grasped in finer detail. The universe is no longer something that resides outside; even the individual is being imagined as one. The selfie looks out at the world but also wants to look in and find something that has so far eluded grasp.

The selfie is a powerful mode of transport, an instrument of mobility. Across the country, young men and women are seeing themselves as the world sees them and then working hard to fashion their own selves. Bit by bit, selfie by selfie.

PEDDLING INFLUENCE FOR A LIVING

Perhaps the fastest-growing career option, certainly insofar as aspiration goes, would have to be that of an influencer. The influencer is not merely a label that those who manage a reasonable number of followers on social media give themselves, it is a legitimate profession that earns some of its more successful practitioners very respectable sums of money. Brands of various kinds are eager to use the influencers' services to help sell their wares or amplify their message.

Unlike the traditional celebrity, however, they are barely known outside their chosen circle. But within their own area of influence, they can command a following as large, and at least as passionate, as a conventional star does.

It is interesting that the label so openly flaunts the effect that these people seek to have. Normally, influence is seen to be the by-product of popularity. But in a market-oriented world, why beat around the bush? Instead of calling themselves connoisseurs or aficionados, they describe themselves in terms of what utility they provide to those who wish to exploit their talents.

The objective of their existence is largely outwardly directed. The distance between being called influential and influencers may be tiny at first glance but the slight shift in emphasis is telling. The purpose of the influential is not to influence, that just happens as a natural consequence of their main talent. For influencers, however, it would seem that influencing others is the whole point.

At one level, like so many other phenomena associated with the digital world, this represents a democratization not only of the idea of celebrity but of what we deem significant in our lives. The traditional celebrity has to excel, or at least feature, in something that naturally attracts our attention – cinema, music, sports, or, at the very least, glamour and spice. They usually are part of an activity that is larger-than-life, and that scale rubs off on them.

The influencer, on the other hand, engages in far more everyday pursuits. What clothes to wear, where to shop, how to choose between two brands of a gadget, how to wear make-up, how to add facets to your personality, how to study for that important exam, what makes for a good interviewee, these are the kind of questions that a lot of influencers provide home-grown answers to. The communication lacks the sophistication of traditional advertising, and that is what gives it a sense of authenticity and makes it relatable. For the followers of these influencers, what they receive is wisdom from one of their kind on things that they find useful in a lived context. In that sense, the influencers exert much more direct influence on how people behave, for unlike the conventional celebrity, the reason for their popularity is their perceived proficiency at the same acts of consumption that they are pushing for others.

The key insight that influencers operate on is that public attention does not necessarily need big spectacles. The smallest action is capable is generating an enormous amount of interest, provided there is something new about it. Which is why the internet is full of the simplest, and sometimes most ridiculous, videos that garner millions of views. The fact that there are so many people willing to follow the unboxing of products or of people studying or simply going about their daily routines, is proof of this.

There is another kind of influencer whose role is to entertain rather than educate. TikTok-turned-Instagram-Reel stars, stand-up comics, singers, accomplished dancers – a whole new stream of talent is flowing through our lives, unmediated by the gatekeepers who have hitherto patrolled these spaces. The ability to bring one's talent directly to the attention of the eventual audience, without the help of an intermediary, is both liberating and challenging. Potentially, anyone can become a huge star, but the market for public attention is as competitive as it is ephemeral. Influencers cater to a generation that is easily excited and even more easily bored.

Influencers also evoke a sense of resentment, for many see them as pretenders. There is a certain ingrained notion of what kind of people have a right to be seen as celebrities. Without the aura that mainstream media confers on even C-grade stars, and which earns them the right to celebrityhood, the influencer is often seen as a puffed-up self-promoter who is trying far too hard. It doesn't help that in some cases, influencers are not shy about flexing their social media muscles in order to extract some advantage for themselves.

There is a fundamental contradiction that sits at the heart of the commercial role that influencers play. They owe much of their popularity to the fact that when they recommend something, they are seen to represent no other interest but that of their audience. When they start pitching brands and products simply because they are paid to do so, they are essentially monetizing the trust that they have earned – by exploiting it. Some influencers are very careful not to represent any interest that they don't genuinely believe in, but this is far from being the general rule.

It is interesting that the ASCI (Advertising Standards Council of India) has introduced new rules that make it mandatory for influencers to publicly declare their commercial interest in anything that they recommend. This is a necessary intervention, for the money that chases influencers today is growing at a galloping speed, and some form of consumer protection was overdue. In the long run, this is likely to be beneficial for the influencer ecosystem, for it helps legitimize the institution of paid influence selling. What we are seeing is the rise of a new profession – that of consumption. Influencers play the role of catalysing consumption by translating its language in the idiom of the ordinary consumer. As the market throws up an increasing number of choices, and as consumption becomes an important part of one's identity and self-image, their role will only grow.

THIRTY SECONDS TO NIRVANA

T HE MOST POPULAR PASTIME FOR Indians across the spectrum is to stare at one's phone and scroll through endless short-form videos. It is the easiest way to soak up time; it fills all gaps even when they don't exist. There is something mesmerizing about this ability to get fleetingly immersed in bite-sized vignettes from someone else's life.

A young woman mimics her disapproving mother's glare. A young couple dances to an old film track. A teenager imitates the moves from the latest viral video. A man enacts his wife's silent disappointment. A teenager captures the peculiar eccentricities of middle-class Indian households. A young bride expresses her bewilderment at the cultural adjustment she needs to make in her in-laws' home. These miniature performances, both comical and poignant, have become a defining feature of our digital landscape.

Unlike centrally generated media content of the past, where a few 'tastemakers' created material for passive audiences and willy-nilly spoke more naturally to some while leaving out others, today every segment of the audience finds its own content well to drink from. Nobody is left out; creators come from the same background as the audience, and the identification with what they see is natural and complete.

The difference we see in this form of entertainment is that it focuses on the micro-moments of our lives. Unlike cinema and TV, where storytelling has an established grammar, here what we see are abrupt glimpses from lives all around us. Most importantly, these all come with clear authorship – there are no nameless scriptwriters behind the scenes – these are all presented by flesh-and-blood individuals whom we can relate to.

There is something deeply revealing about this impulse to play back fragments of our lives. In India, where tradition and modernity engage in a complex dance, these performances take on particular significance. Young women enacting the stern glances of conservative parents or the subtle power dynamics in a joint family aren't merely seeking entertainment – they're engaged in a subtle form of cultural negotiation.

Through the safety valve of humour, these videos allow us to acknowledge societal tensions without necessarily resolving them. Unlike conventional stories, where every tension must necessarily be defused, here we are content to merely record and observe. We acknowledge the fault lines that are present in our lives, and by making them part of our collective pool of experience, we generate comment without actually having to express an opinion.

Yet there's more at play than mere recognition. These performances serve as a form of coded resistance. When young Indians enact scenarios of patriarchal control with exaggerated gestures and comic timing, they are creating a new language of critique – one that uses humour as its Trojan horse to challenge established power structures.

What's particularly fascinating is how we, as viewers, now construct our sense of self by locating ourselves among these fragments of performed experience. We scroll through countless shards of borrowed experiences, finding bits of our life reflected in someone else's performance. This represents a profound shift in identity formation – a kind of 'geolocation of the self', where we triangulate our position through moments of recognition across digital space.

Much like a GPS system requires multiple satellite signals to pinpoint location, we now use these fragmented, performed experiences as reference points to establish our own social and emotional coordinates. Each video that resonates becomes a pin on the map of our identity.

This mode of self-construction differs dramatically from what previous generations experienced. Rather than developing identity primarily through grand narratives, community belonging, or consistent relationships, we now assemble it through dispersed moments of recognition across digital platforms.

At one level, this makes the audience a constantly evolving work in progress. One is forever gathering bits of oneself, trying to create a composite picture that is never quite coherent. In some ways this is a truer reflection of what it means to be individuals – we are a messy mass of consistencies and contradictions. On the other hand, it creates a perpetual sense of instability, particularly among the young, who haven't quite crystallized a sense of who they are.

The boundary between 'my experience' and 'their performance of an experience like mine' becomes increasingly permeable. Our experiences are broken down into recognizable, performable units, then recombined through collective performance and consumption into new patterns of meaning.

Perhaps most profoundly, this digital mode of identity construction disrupts our relationship with embodied experience. The potential dissociation between lived bodily experience and digital self-presentation creates a split that may manifest in various psychological challenges.

Additionally, these platforms also create new possibilities for connection and support, particularly for those whose identities have been marginalized in traditional spaces. Many young people display remarkable resilience in navigating these complex digital environments.

What seems clear is that we're witnessing the emergence of a new relationship with our own experiences – neither fully authentic nor entirely constructed – but existing in a constant state of reciprocal influence between living, representing life and seeing life being represented. This endless feedback loop brings to mind philosopher Krishna Kumar's description of culture as a soap 'which rinses away the impurities resulting from the daily struggle of living; miraculously, this soap is made from the used, dirty rinse-water'.

EXCLAIMING PROFUSELY IN A DIGITAL WORLD!!!

IF TEXTS WERE HUMAN BEINGS, they would be the kind that backslap everyone around them ceaselessly. There is a level of exclamatory enthusiasm that one displays while communicating digitally that has no parallel in the real world. The overuse of the exclamation mark is rampant – and we don't stop at one; we often need as many as three to make our point. It is no longer enough to say thank you; one must, at the very least, say, 'Thank you!' Or, if one really means it, 'Thank you!!!'

The exclamation mark is the added dash of enthusiasm that helps our words leap off the page. Language embraces tone as cymbals crash in the background. We read not squiggly symbols, which is what written language really is, but hear the resounding voices of real-life people emphasize with force what they have to say. Our love for superlatives and the frequency with which we use text messages today has ensured that this is an overused device. It allows us to substitute lengthy and often tedious protocols of social grace with a single character. We compress enthusiasm, packing it into this symbol, the only problem being the tendency to overuse it. Linguist Gretchen McCullough argues that the exclamation mark is increasingly being used to communicate sincerity rather than intensity. As the use of superlatives abounds (wow, awesome, amazing), the exclamation mark becomes a way of communicating, 'I am not just saying it, I really mean it.'

It makes us aware of the symbolic richness that is delivered by the system of grammar that we use. Embedded in these tiny symbols lies a wealth of meaning, which becomes more apparent at a time of transition, like today. As the gap between text, image and speech narrows, our inventory of linguistic devices needs to be expanded and enriched.

Interestingly, there is already provision in our existing linguistic resources to capture nuances of speech in text. A bracket, for instance, allows for the digressive nature of speech – our ability to ramble on and dive into the bylanes of a thought while speaking. It divides our communication into two levels – the surface sentence and the sotto voce digression that we amble through. It imparts to print a facility otherwise available only to oral culture. It is akin to our lowering our voice fractionally in order to add flavour, texture and a little spice to our principal point. It is an aside, a conspiratorial whisper, an interesting sidelight, or just the product of a rambling mind aware of its own drift.

Then there are italics. What a glorious way to underline (yes, there's that too) emphasis. It imparts a finicky specificity to what is being said, as if the sentence is pausing to enunciate an important constituent clearly so that its full import is understood. The oral weight of an important thought is reproduced, somewhat ironically, by the visual device of a thinner font that is slanted rightwards. Using bold text serves the same purpose, if less elegantly. It is not clear why this should be deemed so, unless it is because it is a little vulgar in displaying its impatience. The underline, too, signifies significance in the way that emphasis or inflection does in speech.

A really interesting device that is used is the set of symbols deployed to convey the fact someone is swearing. It is the visual equivalent of the bleeping sound. The @#$%&! sign (called a grawlix) manages to convey inarticulate frustration and annoyance without having any content that is meaningful. It does so by capturing the essence of swearing – the words used are by themselves not important and certainly cannot be read literally. They are used to shock, to cross a line that is otherwise taboo, in an attempt to convey one's emotions. The %##%@ sign does the same. Interestingly, there is no standard notation for this – any combination of symbols suffices to convey the intent.

To add to the resources we already have is the new world of emojis. With emojis we are introducing to written text a layer of emotion that it otherwise wholly lacked. Communication becomes more direct, with the emotional intent of the message being graphically reinforced. The reaction meme is another new, largely visual, way that is increasingly used to respond to what is being said. Here, images from popular culture or animated clips are harnessed to express a wide variety of emotions – admiration, ridicule or disgust being prominent ones.

A lot of linguistic devices are part of what theorists like Walter Ong call 'secondary literacy', the phenomenon when written language begins to take on hues of the spoken word. Otherwise, there is a formality to the written text; we certainly don't write the way we speak – whether it is an article, an exam paper, an academic text, official letter, or even a postcard in the earlier days. Written language brings with it its own implicit rules; the language system we use in both oral and written communication might be the same but the way in which we deploy both is distinctly different. Or it has been till now.

What has changed is that today, we communicate using text as if it were speech. Unlike an earlier time, today text messaging occurs very often in real time. We message someone who instantly messages back – the idea of written two-way dialogue, which was otherwise only possible when we spoke to someone, is now an everyday occurrence. Our language needs to correspondingly adapt to this new situation, resulting in the written word carrying what Ong calls the 'temporal immediacy of oral exchange'.

Language is an alive adaptive instrument that embraces new modes and finds ways to fulfil its essential task. Those who view it as a pure bounded space that needs to be protected, miss its vitality and inventiveness. The sheer vibrance of linguistic innovation that are we seeing today merits an exclamation mark. For once!

A NEW IDEA OF MONEY?

'In six months, our valuation went up from $5 million to $30 million, and in another three months it was $100 million,' a New Age business whiz-kid told an adoring audience at a conference recently. Speaker after speaker told us similar stories of dizzying numbers, both gained and lost, as they narrated accounts of their journeys. In the start-up world of today, it would appear that things happen only suddenly, and most often without adequate explanation.

Something fundamental is changing about money and the culture that surrounds it. For the generation that grew up in the 1970s and 1980s, and called itself the middle class, money was weighty, it moved very slowly, if it moved at all, and needed to be prised out of the unyielding hands of the spender. Bank passbooks told stories of its gradual accretion, and getting one's passbook updated was an act carried out with anxious diligence. As the ECG of our lives, our 'bank balance' was a palpable thing, an anchor that moored us and weighed heavily on our minds. The middle class experienced what could be called the poverty of the full stomach – one could buy almost anything that one really needed but very little of what one desired.

Post economic reform, the idea of money changed. Money started moving – it now no longer had only weight, it also picked up velocity. Money became energy, it generated frisson both in its coming and its going. Spending money was no longer a leakage that evoked dread but was something that brought about a pleasant flush of excitement. The younger generation started making more money – sometimes drawing more as a starting salary than what their parents retired earning. There was bewilderment (an aunt asked me when she found out that my starting pay was Rs 2,000, 'What exactly do you do that they pay you so much?') as the scales changed, but there was still some correlation between what one did and how much money one had – an MBA or an engineer, particularly a software one, got paid that much more. It was strange but over time, it came to be comprehended.

That comprehension is crumbling today. What we are seeing now is that money has become a blur of intention, action and consequence. In this alternative universe, the laws of physics do not seem to apply – money materializes, morphs from one form to another, and moves in an electronic blink of an eyelash, a tepid tap on the enter button of one's phone. The numbers make no sense, people starting out get valuations that cannot be explained using conventional economics; nothing about it follows scripts that we are familiar with.

With cryptocurrency, money has become even more mysterious. Now it exists only in an abstract form and eludes regulation. The notion of value itself becomes much more fluid, as currency becomes an asset class.

The culture around money-making has changed. Traditional businesses imagined money as the distillate of everything they did; it accrued over time and hardened into wealth over generations. It was kept shrouded in mystery, and information about it was eked out only to those who must absolutely know. It was spoken of seriously by serious men, often in cryptic code intelligible only to those in the inner circle.

The next generation of business, the one post liberalization, saw money differently. Money could be used to buy and sell not just things, but businesses themselves. Growth became the imperative and economics became shinier and pointier, streamlining itself to deliver to these new expectations. The market seemed alive with new opportunities, and those who combined risk-taking with a nose for what the market wanted thrived.

In the digital era, the latest generation of entrepreneurs has taken this to another level. The idea of valuations makes the present nothing more than the future in a hurry. The accumulated hypothetical gains of all tomorrows get counted as value today, and one gets rewarded accordingly. People generating this energy are no longer the banks but private equity funds that are nothing but a thin layer of ambition and greed that sits on top of piles of slow money and plays fantastic games with it. Consequently, money now comes without the attendant gravity – it is spoken of airily and imagined as something that can be contrived using very little reality.

What we are seeing today is the beginning of the dematerialization of money itself. It was always easier to spend money using a credit card than cash – the amount spent was only a number, never a painstakingly counted wad of notes. A card is flashed, then swiped, both whooshes of intention, unlike cash, which is meticulously transacted. Now, with newer forms of electronic payment, the materiality of the card, too, is likely to reek of the past. With UPI, money is gas not just for a privileged few, but for everyone.

What kind of a life does money made in a flash live? Could the new lightness of money, along with the new economy based on sharing rather than buying, alter the very meaning of consumption? In an Uberized world, the incentive to buy things is not as strong as it used to be once. In the future, when we could all manufacture things by printing them out thanks to 3D printing, will the idea of the material become less sacred? Will the world of tomorrow value assets as much as the world of today does? Will the role of money be to help us float from experience to experience, and will we consume the skin of things, rather than the things themselves?

New forms of money don't change the truth that for too many Indians, its reality is a fact that they cannot ignore. Money is vapour, not because of its new velocity, but because it disappears so fast.

A WIRELESS EXISTENCE

A concept that occurs frequently in the realm of spirituality is that of detachment. Participate in the whirl and whorl of life around you but with an air of detachment, knowing that excessive attachment to outcomes and relationships is the primary source of human misery.

In that case, one could argue that the world is turning extremely spiritual. We sit together in families, detached from each other, work remotely from home, and shop for whatever we need while scrolling endlessly through the millions of options on our fingertips. We live in a wireless world, communicating constantly with the outside; always there, never here. Increasingly, our primary residence is in the ether. The physical world increasingly serves either a recreational role or is a burden to be carried reluctantly.

Of course, there is nothing spiritual about this detachment, for it is accompanied by an ever-increasing attachment to ourselves. We live in a world that seems to revolve around us; we are the main characters in the story, not only of our own lives but of the world. The mobile phone sucks us in in ever-narrowing circles, catering relentlessly to our likes and dislikes, our whims and prejudices.

And this is just the beginning. With the coming of AI, many of the physical places we need to visit might not need our presence. We can imagine a world where every child has a personalized AI avatar, teaching him or her individually, based on the methodology that suits the child best. We could conjure up eerily realistic travel destinations and experience them through virtual-reality headsets that make travel less attractive. We could consult doctors from the comfort of our home thanks to advanced sensors and AI diagnostics. None of these possibilities is in the realm of science fiction, nor is it located in a distant future. These are capabilities that exist in some form already and will soon be refined to levels that make them viable in a mainstream sense. The human body has already been effectively rendered vestigial; it is now time for the human brain to not have to tax itself too much by carrying the burden of thinking.

Living an untethered existence and having the responsibility for filling up all the empty spaces in our lives ourselves can become a stressful effort. And there are a lot of empty spaces to fill – there is an entire virtual universe where we begin from zero and have to build up a persona, or, for that matter, several personae, from scratch. On the internet, one has to be born consciously – it does not just happen. Unlike the real world, there is nothing really organic about its digital counterpart. Every act that marks our presence on this digital map is a pixel that helps identify who we are. Where we travel, whose video we like, which restaurant we dined last night at, which obscure artist's passing we mourned, and who did we abuse given our political leanings – each of these needs to be broadcast in order for us to become someone.

The strain of making all these efforts shows. Particularly among the young, we find that the burden of figuring out all the new rules that one has to live by is taking a toll. Jonathan Haidt, in his book *The Anxious Generation*, compellingly argues how early exposure to digital devices is limiting the development of young minds and making them prone to mental health issues early on.

We try and cope in other ways. We are not used to being this untethered. Historically, the past has always been part of our identity – our names bear witness to this. Our first name is a bow to the present, our surname a connection with the past, and in different parts of the country, other parts of the name can identify the father, husband, or village one hails from. Our names are a form of social GPS that pinpoints our location on a spatial and temporal map. And the name is just one of several ways in which we live secure in the comforting grasp of the past.

As the past loosens its grip, there is a self-conscious and assertive reclaiming of some dominant symbols of continuity. Caste and religious identities are being affirmed in defiance of the modern discourse that has tended to underplay their significance. Here, identity is actively performed; it is a deliberate act of assertion rather than mere observance. The present in that sense is not an effortless outgrowth of the past, but one that is customizing a past to its liking.

We form other elective groups in order to reduce the sense of wirelessness that we are experiencing. Political ideology is an increasingly important part of our self-definition today. What used to be preferences that changed from time to time have become entrenched positions, fortresses of beliefs that are zealously guarded and fiercely battled over. Ideological labels that do not make much sense in the Indian context are also embraced and fought over.

But politics is not the only arena in which identity games are played. It has become critically important that our identity is determinedly plural – we need to have many interests and belong to many mini-universes. We could be foodies, or old-Hindi-film enthusiasts, word-puzzle enthusiasts, or passionate followers of motocross races; and unlike the past, these affiliations now take on a more formal shape, with groups of people coming together and forming a coherent collective.

In a world where we can operate out of anywhere, be self-sufficient in ways that we could not have imagined earlier, and interact with the outside world much more as individuals, the sense of being alone in an existential sense is often difficult to escape. We are finding new ways to mitigate this, but in the meantime, the future is rushing headlong at us, bristling with new challenges.

MEMES FOR MUMMYJI

IT HAS BEEN GENERALLY ACKNOWLEDGED that, rather than mainstream media, the key source of energy during the 2024 elections was found in alternative digital channels. The national TV media has ceased to be a source of credible information, or opinion, for that matter, except for those supporting the government. For any alternative perspective, therefore, the answer lies elsewhere. The influence of voices like Dhruv Rathee, Ravish, Ajit Anjum, and many others has been enormous, with each of them racking up millions of views with their videos.

Of course, alternative media is available to everyone, and in the past, it was the BJP that was the master of the digital and social media game. In 2024, however, it found itself challenged by voices from the other side. Part of the problem lay in the fact that, because mainstream media throttled the voice of the opposition almost entirely, it helped create a market for other views. Also, given the blanket coverage that Mr Modi and his government receive on TV channels, there was perhaps a sense of overexposure and exhaustion at the by-now-familiar tropes that are repeated.

The democracy of disparate voices creates a wide-ranging menu for people to choose from. The fact that so many voices that were opposing the government found traction suggests that there was a hunger that needed to be satisfied. A democracy of this kind, which comes without any centralized regulation, has room for all kinds of views, including those that are extreme. It spawns many conspiracy theories in the name of 'truth', and creates an entire group of people who make themselves susceptible to highly implausible 'alternative' facts that they are convinced have been kept hidden from them.

YouTube videos and other short-form videos are arguably the most powerful agents of change in India. Whether it is entertainment, fashion, beauty products, technology, self-improvement, or politics, the unfiltered voice of the country finds expression here. Given our addiction to the phone, these formats are ideal for browsing mindlessly through, and their impact is both wide-ranging and deep.

But it is not just alternative media vehicles that are powerful; the form in which information and influence are transmitted is also changing. The meme is arguably the most potent and fastest form in which opinion travels. The meme is a shard of content put together with a combination of text, visuals, and even video, and captures a particular slant on anything of interest in popular culture, be it an event, a person, or a statement made by someone. It is an act of invention and subversion, often using humour to get its point across. As a form of communication, it has exploded in popularity and is now the most basic unit of communication in the digital world.

In the 2024 election, for instance, the 'paw-paw' meme was devastatingly effective. It seized upon a BJP ad that showed a young girl tearfully telling her papa that Mr Modi stopped the war to get them to safety. In that single word, it collapsed a world of meaning – it ridiculed the gullibility of those who believed the claim, it flipped the meaning of Mr Modi's standing as a paternal figure for his followers, and it helped deflate many serious messages from the government's side.

When Rahul Gandhi was given the moniker of Pappu, it did him far more damage than any diatribe about being part of a dynasty. It undercut his legitimacy and made everything he said or did irrelevant. Everything was coloured with the tint of Pappu. It is only in the last couple of years, thanks to his Bharat Jodo Yatra and his new-found confidence as a politician, that he has been able to rise above that characterization.

The power of the meme is that, unlike an argument, it is impossible to counter. One can like it or dislike it, choose to ignore it or share it, but there is no arguing with it. The only option is to produce memes that are effective but carry the opposite message. And like all things in popular culture, there is no saying as to which meme will catch people's fancy and which will die unheralded. The meme also is accessible, much more so than an explanation. It collapses a narrative into an image and allows everyone to participate in the conversation.

The meme is not only an alternative form of expression but also a new mode of persuasion. Traditionally, we think of persuasion as being about changing people's minds, thereby getting them to act in the way we desire. We put forward arguments and use credible authority figures to put forward our message.

The meme works differently. Change here happens through imitation or subversion. Its ability to rapidly recirculate through an organic process, thanks to its shareability, adds to its power. By slipping past the rational defences of the receiver, it delivers its message with greater precision and accuracy.

For example, there was a video by Jyoti Nooran that went viral. It showed a feisty young woman walking out on a feudal husband, leaving his palatial house, and tearing his picture in the process. It spawned thousands of short videos in which various young girls imitated the actions set to the same music track. The motivation to imitate came from wanting to be part of the popular discourse, but in doing so, it made the issue of not taking injustice lying down in a marriage that much more salient. It was a far more effective way of delivering this message than, say, a public service ad tackling the same theme.

As the media landscape around us changes and does so dramatically, the rules of communication, too, reflect this transformation. We will listen to new people and communicate in new ways. We are already seeing the effects of this change in many critical areas of our lives. And more is changing as AI becomes a more integral part of our lives. With AI now able to generate memes on demand, the meme gets automated, making it the default response to any event.

SCAMMED DIGITALLY?

Not a day goes by without one hearing of someone known getting scammed online. The amounts involved vary – but the stories have a similar ring. A voice on the phone asks you for an OTP or for some identity details, and before you know it, your bank account is lighter by a considerable sum. You click on a link unsuspectingly, and your phone is cloned. In so many cases, it is virtually impossible to figure out what one did wrong.

To top it all off, the protection available to ordinary citizens is almost non-existent. Overworked and overwhelmed cybercrime units shrug their shoulders and express their inability to get ahead of the scammers, and the government seems to have no interest in taking any note of the problem.

The older and the digitally unschooled face the brunt of this problem, since they struggle to comprehend a completely new way of being. But even the educated and the digitally adequate are not spared. Calls from the customs department for an alleged drug shipment with your name on it, threats of jail from the ED, a cryptocurrency opportunity that seems too good to pass up – the stories of well-educated people who, in theory, should know better, getting scammed, are legion.

What these scams point to is the fundamental unease we have with having an entirely new universe with a completely different ecology being thrust upon us. On the face of it, we can navigate our way smoothly, marvelling at the convenience available to us at the click of a button; we follow a sequence of steps that we have learned in order to perform in the digital arena. But the moment something goes wrong, our disorientation at having all our foundational concepts – time, space, money, identity – getting redefined spills out in the open.

The problem is that what the digital world has done is to infiltrate the minutiae of our everyday life – paying bills, buying groceries, booking tickets. Unlike hardware-oriented technologies of the past, where the shock of the new was limited to learning how to operate the new gadget, here one has to reinvent one's entire mode of being.

When television arrived in Indian homes, or when landlines became commonplace, the learning curve was gentle, the risks minimal. At worst, a person unfamiliar with the new thingamajig would be unable to use it. Today's digital misstep can empty bank accounts, steal identities, or compromise entire networks of relationships.

The anxiety manifests itself in curious ways. Watch a group of middle-class Indians discuss their latest encounter with digital fraud, and you'll notice how these conversations have become our new ghost stories – cautionary tales, each more elaborate than the last, shared over dinner. Like all good ghost stories, they serve a social purpose, creating a shared vocabulary for our collective fears.

There is a constant sense that we are doing something wrong; there is a small sense of relief when any transaction is successfully concluded, as if we have passed one more test. This provides fertile ground for scammers to exploit our inherent tentativeness. They insert themselves into the cracks of our doubts, shifting shape as their methods evolve. They understand that in this new world, even the most cautious among us are perpetually off-balance, never quite sure if we're following the right protocols or breaking some essential rule we didn't know existed. What makes it easier for them is that a lot of crimes go potentially unreported. There is a sense of shame inherent in getting tricked, particularly for people who think of themselves as being educated and worldly-wise.

It helps that the digital bureaucracy enables this by requiring an endless succession of compliances – we need an Aadhar card for everything, even entering a building, and every few months we are required to update our KYCs, as if in this period we have somehow magically turned into someone else. So when a voice on the phone tells us confidently that we have messed up, we believe them.

In a short period, we have dismantled the trust markers of the physical world – the granite facades of banks, the official letterheads, the face-to-face interactions that allowed us to read intent and character. The digital world offers its own pale versions, all of which can be cloned or stolen. It is not just that we don't know who to trust, but that we don't even understand what distrust means anymore. In a society like India, where so many business transactions have been based on trust and personal relationships, losing these markers can turn out to be devastating disruptions. And now AI has made the scam even harder to detect. It can clone voices, and speak in familiar tones and accents, dismantling whatever remains of the human elements we trust.

In the midst of all this, one must acknowledge the heroism of ordinary people, who have, despite all the challenges, learnt to adopt this new way of life to a substantial degree. The vegetable vendor who masters QR-code payments, the grandmother who learns to video-call her grandchildren, the small-town entrepreneur who builds a digital presence – each is performing a small miracle of adaptation.

The scam is like a glitch in the matrix – when we are able to catch a glimpse of the terrifying disorder that lies hidden beneath the seeming order of a shiny new world. It creates a fleeting experience of cognitive vertigo when we suddenly realize that our money is just data that can be manipulated, that our identity is a thin construct that can be stolen or hijacked, and that our sense of security and well-being is largely illusory.

We live in two worlds that have two different operating systems. On the surface, we are doing the same things that we have always done – connect with people, buy things, store money, look for good deals –, but digital reality is a thin veneer of order that rests on assumptions that are invisible to us. We find this out the hard way. Scams point to that moment when we understand that technology, however advanced, is a poor substitute for society and its institutions.

OTP: ONE-TIME PERSON?

NOTHING IS MORE URGENT THAN an OTP. It can arrive unbidden at any time, and regardless of whether you're in the middle of a presentation explaining why you haven't met your annual target or on a hot date with someone special, you have to stop what you're doing and answer the call of nature, as it were.

For OTPs are the new natural. No door opens without them, and life comes to a standstill if one is not prompt in responding, sometimes within seconds, lest it expire.

There was a time when being oneself was a matter of presence. You showed up, and that was enough. A familiar voice, a shared memory, a face remembered in good faith – these were once sufficient proof of identity. Today, none of that quite suffices. Instead, we await a six-digit code, dispatched by a distant system, valid for 30 seconds.

The OTP is our passport to ourselves. Its great advantage is that it does not depend on memory, already overburdened with passwords that stand in for personhood. It allows us to pay, log in, and access what is already ours. It hovers somewhere between a key and a ritual – without it, nothing moves. Its authority is absolute, its presence fleeting. The irony is poetic: something so temporary now stands as the final arbiter of permanence.

Never before has the act of being oneself required such relentless reaffirmation. Aadhar, PAN card, passport, driver's licence, voter ID – our bureaucratic lives have long been strewn with identity proofs. But these were used occasionally, ceremonially. They also connoted a kind of stability. Your Aadhar number was yours to hold and to cherish. The OTP, however, inserts itself into the everyday. It is the heartbeat of a system that no longer trusts memory, continuity, or human judgement.

Technology has altered the nature of identity. It has made it transactional, procedural, and external. The self is no longer a given; it must be retrieved. The simple declaration – I am me – no longer holds weight. It must be accompanied by a ping and a password, a fingerprint or a face scan – a code that proves you are not an impostor in your own skin.

The only way we can exist today is by encrypting the self, converting it into electronic gobbledegook. Our identity must be locked in a vault, accessed only through codes, passwords, and biometric tokens. We cannot remain in our natural state; we must be reborn in digital terms – a version that bears no resemblance to who we are, only to what we can be verified as. This is safety, yes – but it is also a kind of exile.

The real power of the OTP lies in its elegant refusal to rely on memory – human or machine. It bypasses both recall and storage, offering instead a live sliver of certainty, generated in the now. It doesn't ask us to remember or depend on the cloud to recall who we are. Instead, it creates a brief moment of clarity – valid only once, seen only by us, and then gone.

There is a strange intimacy in this transaction, however impersonal the mechanism. The OTP arrives unannounced, asks nothing but recognition, and disappears without a trace. In a world obsessed with permanence and tracking, its vanishing act feels oddly personal.

In this sense, the OTP is more than a tool – it is a philosophy of control. It belongs to a world that cannot tolerate ambiguity, that sees every access point as a potential breach. The idea of identity theft adds emotional weight to what is essentially administrative. We no longer fear being misrepresented – we fear being locked out. Not of our devices, but of ourselves.

We are moving towards a world where even memory isn't enough. Our pasts live not in recollection but in databases. Facial recognition systems remember us better than we do. Our location history knows our path more reliably than our own minds. The self is increasingly outsourced – stored in the cloud, backed up by tokens and timestamps.

And yet, for all its precision, the OTP is fragile. It expires. It mistimes. It fails to arrive. It inserts a pause between intent and execution. In that fleeting moment of waiting, something peculiar happens: a modern form of vulnerability. We are locked out, not because we've forgotten who we are, but because the system doesn't remember. At the end of the day, the OTP is not a way of identifying us, but the device that has become our surrogate self.

Perhaps the story of the OTP is only beginning. As every other marker of identity – face, voice, fingerprint, behaviour – becomes replicable, as deepfakes and the relentless march of AI blur the idea of the authentic, the OTP may emerge as the last bastion of truth. Ironically, its power lies in the fact that it cannot be stored, reused, or faked. It is a ghost that proves you're alive – just for a moment.

In the end, it may not be the permanence of data but the evanescence of a code that secures us. A fleeting flicker that says: this is me, now. Not always. Just now. And that may be the only kind of truth we can trust.

THE MARKET(PLACE) VIEW OF
THE WORLD

THE COMING OF MARKETPLACES HAS changed our lives in
significant new ways. Amazon, Facebook, Twitter (now called
X), Instagram, WhatsApp, Zomato, TripAdvisor and their ilk
have dramatically democratized access at both the supply and
demand sides. These platforms are open to anyone who wishes
to use them and hence are inherently inclusive. The e-commerce
marketplaces, for instance, have enabled small producers to reach
consumers they had no previous access to, putting them at par
with strong legacy brands. They have also given people residing
in remote places the same kind of access to quality products that
their counterparts in larger cities have historically been privy to.

The same is true when it comes to the marketplace for
opinion, although here the democratization has produced
mixed results. While it has allowed the hitherto-silent majority
to express itself at par with those previously privileged with
the microphone, it has at the same time allowed for the free
circulation of conspiracy theories, innuendo, vicious personal
attacks, particularly aimed at women, and all manner of trumped
up news.

In a marketplace of opinions, all views get equal space. And
there is no authority that sifts these on the basis of quality or
authenticity. It takes no responsibility for the views that populate
it. Unlike traditional publishers, its reputation and commercial
viability is independent of the quality of content found on it.
Its business model rests on how engaged its users are – after
all, it has no content of its own and is entirely dependent on
how much it can excite its users into contributing their views.
The more provocative and extreme the views, the greater the
response, both by those in support and those who are opposed.

This happens in part because the marketplace accommodates different kinds of views on the same platform and accords equal importance to every strand of opinion. Unlike the past, where different streams of thought had to fight for their own significance and where fringe ideas remained at the fringe, today there is no concept of the fringe. If an opinion finds enough takers and there are no barriers to it getting that chance, then it becomes a legitimate mainstream view. The idea that Joe Biden stole the 2020 elections was an irrefutable fact for 40 per cent of those living in what is touted as the world's most advanced democracy.

In the pre-marketplace days, the market, too, gave room for all kinds of views. It drove all content towards the popular mainstream. As it played a more active role in media, we saw a shift in journalistic values towards a greater focus on what the audience sought, rather than on what was deemed to be intrinsic newsworthiness.

However, the market did not put all views on the same pedestal. Each stream of opinion came weighted with its history and reputation. There was no dearth of conspiracy theories in the past, but in the hierarchy of opinion that was then followed, it received a relatively peripheral place in the media ecosystem. Unless one sought those views out, it was not easy to get access to them.

Today, the flood of opinion comes unweighted – opinion with any and every ideological slant meets with the same lack of any pre-configured hierarchy. If a nutty opinion has enough followers, no matter how outrageous, it will be given the same prominence as any other. The rise of the anti-vaxxing movement has a lot to do with the rise of the marketplace.

Twitter and Facebook can throw up their hands and plead that it is they who are, in fact, being democratic because they do not discriminate between opinions. And, at one level, this is true. The effects that we are seeing today are not so much an outcome of intent, but of inherent structure. In other words, corporations do not need to be evil for a change of this magnitude to occur (although that is a bonus).

What this has enabled is a shift in the process by which opinion is generated. Unlike the past, where the opinion originated among those deemed to be specialists, the expert commentators, and then circulated among the rest, today opinion is formed on these marketplace platforms and strongly influences media outlets in how they understand and present news and opinion.

One of the results of this influence is the lack of discrimination in what constitutes news, a decline in the standards used in determining whether a particular news item meets the minimum standards needed to qualify as a fact. Indeed, the desire to report facts itself is no longer the engine that animates many news outlets. In the marketplace for opinion, there is no cost, social or economic, for circulating half-truths or outright lies. With time, as these false narratives gain currency through repetition and circulation, they become as valid as the truth. No material difference remains between the two.

The incentive is to mirror escalating passions – an organically evolving upward spiral of hate is built into this structure. The angry crusader, more extreme conspiracy theorist, the believer who feels unheard – these voices are more engaged, and generate greater responses, both for and against. The mainstream gets drowned out by the noise generated by the extreme flanks of opinion. And it escalates on its own as part of an organic, inevitable process.

As a result, the epistemic pool – the combined body of knowledge that we find ourselves amidst – is now of a completely different character than in the past. Today, the accretion of knowledge is unregulated, unmediated and indiscriminate. If, earlier, we learnt of the world from books, newspapers, journals, magazines, the odd pamphlet, and advertising, today a bulk of our education is being carried out by tweets, blogs and social media posts generated not by experts but by any person who might have a view and an audience. The pool may be more democratically organized, but it is undeniably shallower. And it stinks.

THE DIFFICULTY OF STAYING STILL

THE LATEST DARLINGS OF THE financial world are the new players who deliver groceries within ten minutes. This is as close to magic as one can imagine, one which dramatically collapses the interval between desire and its fulfilment. It also underlines a key feature of our digital lives – an inexorable bias for speed and constant movement, even if, as in this case, no one has asked for it.

The world is being cast in the mould of our mind, which knows no constraints and can move with dizzying speed and inexplicable contrariness between subjects, idle fantasies and desires. The need to be the centre of the world, to get what one wants when one wants it, the ability to move erratically from one subject to another – these are all being catered to by the technologies of the day. The fickleness of the mind, its 'chanchal' character, is at the heart of the design of today's digital world.

Hypermobility is its defining feature – everything around us is moving all the time. On the mobile phone, nothing stays in a state of rest. Timelines move all the time, WhatsApp messages arrive in a steady torrent, and if we post something, comments and likes begin to trickle, sometimes flood, in. Modern life has always been thought of as fast-moving, but in the digital world, motion is the default setting.

Earlier, when we read, it was we who did the moving. The book or newspaper was immobile and disconnected from any other object in the world. Our eyes scanned a page, sometimes running a mental finger down the text, we flipped the page when we wanted to move on, and when we finished reading we had the option of sitting back and absorbing what we had just read.

Today, both the text and our attention are in a state of constant motion. Digital text is fluid as it updates itself constantly. Text comes booby-trapped with active links intent on torpedoing the linearity of our attention. Hypertext encourages us to travel at the speed of curiosity. Even as we locate ourselves in a flowing streaming timeline, the implicit mental model of a river or a stream is misleading. For it suggests a certain linearity, a trajectory of certainty. A river has a set course, and defined banks. Our digital journeys, on the other hand, leap around from one river to another, they combine more than one stream as we multitask our way through the day.

The prefix 'hyper' gets pressed into action to describe the multitude effects that follow. In a hyperreal world, we are hyperaware, hyperactive and hypersensitive to any stimulus. In today's world, attention is the scarcest resource that exists, and we try and minimize the opportunity lost by focusing on one thing by instantly drifting to another. The need to react, to insert ourselves into the fast-moving narratives that are rushing by, produces an anxiety and a state of permanent dissatisfaction, something that is part of the design of social media. As writer Jia Tolentino puts it, 'It is *essential* that social media is mostly unsatisfying. That is what keeps us scrolling, scrolling, pressing our lever over and over again in the hopes of getting some fleeting sensation – some momentary rush of recognition, flattery or rage.'

On the surface, of course, we are very very still. Hunched over our phones, glazed eyes attached to our screens, fingertips moving lightly over touchpads, we appear to be locked in still solitude. We see the same behaviour in our bedrooms, in bus stops, in conference rooms while pretending to listen to someone drone on about the difference between goals and objectives – everywhere we perform the charade of stillness while everything is leaping around frenetically on our screens and in our minds.

We do much less, and yet live in a world of ceaseless motion. The world today is run by eyeballs and fingertips. We have reduced our bodies to their lowest possible unit of functionality.

The thumb is the most used part of the body as it relentlessly scrolls through the many worlds we occupy simultaneously.

The simultaneity of production and consumption is one of the reasons why we no longer can separate the two actions. In an earlier time, the act of production was carried by one set of people at a different point in time, which then was consumed later by another set of people. On the internet, production and consumption are so closely interwoven that one is constantly switching modes. Read a text, send a post, receive likes, react with an emoji – this kind of interaction is ceaseless.

The ability to fill up all gaps in time, to never let our attention go hungry, always having some activity to lose oneself in, makes life feel unrelentingly continuous. The absence of fallowness, of time to soak in all that we have been exposed to, produces a state of hyper-attentiveness to elsewhere, a state of perpetually divided attention.

No wonder that our interest in notions of mindfulness and slow living is on the rise. The desire to opt out, to make things stop moving, to let our attention settle rather than scatter is an impulse that will only grow. Implicit in the idea of a digital detox is a mental model of the existing overload of stimulation as a form of poison which needs some form of countering. Interestingly, stillness is being repackaged and sold to us digitally – complete with reminders, sonorous voices, white noise and AI-powered breathing guides customized for us.

Well before the advent of the internet, Jacques Ellul argued, 'Modern man does not think about current problems; he feels them. He reacts, but be does not understand them any more than he takes responsibility for them. He is even less capable of spotting any inconsistency between successive facts; man's capacity to forget is unlimited.' If this were true over sixty years ago when this was written, it is terrifyingly true today. In the world of the infinite scroll, there is no memory, only movement.

THE LURE OF PASSIVITY?

The younger generation today faces the challenges of finding its way in a world where all the rules are new and options are aplenty, but there is little clarity available in determining which path to take. How does this generation cope with all the pressures that it has to deal with?

Ironically, part of the cure they seek is to go back to the problem. Mindless scrolling through reels, taking hours to decide on what to order from food-delivery apps, doomscrolling endlessly on X, browsing through shopping sites, creating wish lists and filling up carts, browsing Pinterest, asking ChatGPT to solve their life's problems, and going through the thousands of selfies they have taken to admire themselves, there is an entire virtual universe to get lost in. Consumption, or the idea of consumption, is a powerful drug that numbs more than it excites today.

The act of browsing – flipping through infinite options without any real interest in finding anything – is seen as highly relaxing. There is no pressure to perform; no one is judging how you look or act; there is nothing to prove or demonstrate. It seems like we are consuming time, but it might well be that it is time that is consuming us as we surrender to it without imposing ourselves in any way on it. Taking inordinately long to make small decisions is a form of rebellion against the presumed importance of life's big decisions.

Opting out of the high-pressure context we are surrounded by holds a special charm. It can take the form of sleep, which has become an increasingly coveted commodity today. A slew of product categories are presenting themselves as sleep panaceas, whether they are mattresses, special-sleep apps, or melatonin-based gummies that promise sleep without you getting addicted.

Just slacking or chilling and watching some cringe-worthy content on an OTT channel or YouTube while munching on something can produce a state of narcotic bliss. Even the act of responding to people on social media is, more often than not, a way of providing cheap validation. Liking someone's post or sending an emoji in response to a selfie is the kind of low-stakes endorsement that requires virtually no effort and comes at no cost.

The endless scroll is the invention of our time. Combined with the touchscreen, it maximizes dopamine reward per unit of effort. Just a flick of the fingertips produces a world without end, a world to get lost in, one that occupies the mind without leaving any residue behind. The empty fullness of time is best experienced when scrolling through options without any underlying need for them.

Procrastination is the other device that is useful. Postponing being defined or making choices that feel irrevocable both give the young some additional room that is craved. Switching jobs easily, often for reasons that feel flimsy to older generations, is part of this quest to escape early definition. The desire to keep one's options open, whether at work or in romance, is a driving motivation that is on display. This is not indecisiveness but a new mode of living – one where withdrawal is not a failure, but camouflage.

The other way of easing things for oneself is to cut out as many things as possible that are deemed toxic. This is a word that pops up often in conversations and is applied equally to people as well as content. This cuts across generations, of course, as evidenced by the popularity of cat, dog, and baby videos on social media. The desire to shut out noise and escape the poison that is being spewed from so many directions acts as an escape valve in these times.

Rebellion is exhausting; passive involvement in trivial things is far more rewarding. It is not that rebellion does not exist, but more often than not, it takes symbolic forms. Being a desktop warrior comes without the costs that would otherwise need to be paid in real life.

Curiously, nostalgia is another form of escape. There are a large number of short-form videos and stand-up comic acts that reference the behaviour of earlier generations and recall simpler times. It is understandable when sixty-year-olds hark back to their growing-up years, but for a generation that is inundated by the present, it is unusual to have such an interest in the past.

Passivity, of course, is not the exclusive domain of the young. Technology is trying its hardest to turn us into high-functioning vegetables. Bit by bit, everything that once required effort is now getting automated. It is not easy to get lost because GPS takes all the effort out of finding a new address. No maps spread out awkwardly on the lap; no asking random strangers for directions; no arguments about the route to be taken. Similarly, there is no need to go shopping or visit a theatre to catch a film. No need to even pop across to the video library to pick up a film. No need to queue up to pay bills or book railway tickets. Everything that was considered a chore in earlier times can now be carried out with the greatest ease.

To top it all, algorithms hunt down our preferences in algebra and spew out options before being asked to. Our bodies were already useless; now it is the turn of our minds. ChatGPT makes even mental effort an option. And this is merely the beginning of the AI revolution to come.

This is, at one level, an enormous convenience, but it comes at a price. Not everyone thinks of this induced passivity as a curse, however; for the younger generation, it is a mode of release. It is a way of dealing with the relentless flow of the digital world; since there is no way to stop it, the only option is to go along with it while simultaneously detaching oneself from it. That is the magic of technology. The answer we seek to escape the problem only serves to make the problem that much more acute.

CHAPTER 2

Culture

Between Samaj and Samay

Tradition no longer stands still. It scrolls, swipes, and hashtags its way into the present.

Technology is the medium that shapes how we think of ourselves and behave with others.

Here, we look at the changing codes of gender, love, family, and aspiration in a culture that is improvising its way through modernity – stretching old structures without quite snapping them.

BETWEEN SAMAJ AND SAMAY

Modernity is, at its heart, a sense of todayness, a feeling of being one with what is happening around the world. Among the many changes that can be attributed to the coming of the smartphone, one that is often not acknowledged is how it has made the idea of today a tangible and living presence in the lives of people in mainstream India. The phone, with its endless streams of information and interaction, is an embodiment of a throbbing, pulsating, ever-refreshing present. As an agent of today, it has found an irreplaceable place in the hands of millions who are otherwise located in a slow-moving cultural milieu, where traditions and customs have dug deep roots and change is adopted gradually.

The interaction between these two forces is revealing. The popularity of Karwa Chauth as a festival over the last few years is emblematic of this interplay – not only is it a celebration that, in its original intent, underlines the wife's sacrifice for the husband's long life, an idea one might have imagined would slowly lose currency as the power balance between the genders begins to shift, it has also moved beyond its cultural origins and been embraced by a large number of women who come from parts of India where this was never part of traditional custom. It is clear that this popularity has much to do with representations in popular culture, with films like *Dilwale Dulhaniya Le Jayenge* downwards playing a big role in promoting this festival. Of course, today's Karwa Chauth is a far cry from the festival as it was celebrated in earlier times, with accent being much more on the celebrations that follow the fast, rather than the fast itself.

The new version of the festival underlines an important change that we are seeing today – the renegotiation between the two primary axes that influence the make-up of our society and determine the rate at which it changes. The idea of 'samaj' is the notion of society-in-practice, the intricate network of kinship ties, hierarchy, customs, rules, both explicit and implicit, that govern our everyday behaviour and guide us in what we can and cannot do, while 'samay' is the idea of time-out-there, a sense of what the world as a collective is permitting nowadays. The interaction between these two axes – between who we are, where we come from and what continues to give us a sense of identity and belonging, and what the world outside is moving to, what is being found acceptable and what is no longer in vogue – helps define what we end up doing, and how much change we can absorb without feeling disoriented.

These axes are by themselves not new, for they are ways in which the past negotiates with the present. What is new is that the sense of the present is now far more accessible and immediate than it has ever been, thanks to the technology that is available in virtually every hand.

In earlier days, samaj called the shots and samay was the weak voice of the modern, invoked often but largely in order for it to be reviled; sentences beginning with 'aaj-kal-ke' (today's breed of) were almost always deprecatory in nature, whether one was speaking of the youth, language, fashion styles, haircuts or daughters-in-law. Samaj was our anchor; it gave us the certainty of knowing who we were and marked our actions with a self-assurance that was validated not by external sources but by internal foreknowledge – we simply knew what was right and wrong and how things were meant to work. This certainty produced both comfort and frustration, as at one level, social adjustment was made easy, while at another, those with individual desires that were deemed to be at odds with the wishes of samaj, were dealt with summarily.

Over the last few years, we are seeing an accelerated change in the relationship between these two forces. The idea of samay, that intangible sense of todayness, is becoming increasingly more influential than samaj, certainly in urban India. With digital media as the new sky that we all live under, the sense of samay has become a tangible and powerful presence in our daily lives. We are exposed to many ideas and influences simultaneously; tradition is no longer vertically arrayed in time but is found increasingly horizontally stretched across space. We embrace the traditions of others – be it in terms of food, attire, festivals and icons – as ours more readily than ever before. We legitimize practices alien to our own cultural background because we get licence to do so from the world around us, which has now taken up permanent residence in our homes, thanks to media.

The signs of the power of these new sources of influence are everywhere. Increasingly, change in India is no longer a step-by-step linear process, but one which is both simultaneous and asymmetrical. New technologies have made progress accessible to everyone and, as a result, we can see pockets of dramatic change coexist with its more gradual forms. It is not unusual to come across, without any warning, a street youth in old Bhopal proudly showing off an 'emo' haircut or a young girl in Karjan, Gujarat, talking knowledgeably about the kind of beauticians required in Australia. We see new ambitions, new benchmarks to measure oneself against and new mirrors to strut in front of. OTT series, talent shows, social media and mobile telephony are combining to create a new sense of possibilities and legitimizing new modes of behaviour.

Of course, samay is not independent of samaj; it works to modify it rather than bypass it completely. Like the Karwa Chauth example, where a sense of samay has given new meaning to an old custom, the idea of today does not negate the past, but breathes into it new imperatives and shapes it in a way that is more productive in today's context. Samay is not the opposite of samaj, and while on the face of it, it appears to be an adversarial force, in practice it often works as its ally by helping tradition stay relevant, albeit in a more sanitized form.

And this is only the beginning. As the influence of the internet increases, it will affect both the speed and nature of change we will see. The digital world knits us together in a community of today; it multiplies the idea of now, converting it from a dot in time to a canvas of simultaneous possibilities, a network of people, events, ideas and connections. The timeline of our lives gets broken up into smaller moments and each moment begins to seem more pronounced in its existence. The digiscape connects fragments of now into a more integrated sense of today and locates us within its ambit. We are, more than ever, children of today, and are therefore recycling the present into the present, using samay as a reason for justifying what we do nowadays. The modern becomes its own justification.

What is interesting is how samaj has hit back, through the instrument of politics. The unselfconscious, unbroken sense of continuity with the past might have begun to loosen its grip, but it is being bolstered by a more deliberate effort to construct a past that is deemed desirable by today's standards. The veneration of the cow, the inexorable pressure put on non-vegetarian diets, the annual attacks on Valentine's Day celebrations, the projection of the Ram Mandir as a collective source of pride – these are but a few ways in which culture is being repackaged and resold as a bulwark against the forces of samay. In some ways, the idea of samay itself is being reframed in a way that it becomes an adjunct to samaj. The interaction between the two, the attempts of each to co-opt the other, for each to become a version of the other, are likely to continue. In ever newer ways.

MORE FREEDOM, LESS INDEPENDENCE?

Social change in urban india is a complex process. It is easy to think of change under the broad head of gradual modernization, but at a more atomic level, this label is not a particularly useful one, as it gives us the illusion of a linear movement from one point to another. Some of the changes that are being seen around the country throw up new patterns that deepen our understanding of how things are changing.

On a research project that involved extensive travel through small-town India, an interesting phenomenon was observed by some colleagues. They had gone to a family that had two daughters, and when a request was made to meet some relatives that lived in a nearby village, the parents volunteered that their daughters accompany the team, along with their 'bhai-friends', who would take them on their bikes. The 'bhai-friends' turned out to be a couple of boys who were friends of the girls and were trusted by the parents not to be up to any 'hanky-panky' with the daughters.

The idea of rakhi brothers is an old one. The device allowed boys and girls to mingle without attracting unwanted social attention, but with time and misuse, the institution has fallen out of favour. Although very similar in form, the bhai-friend is based on the new understanding that some form of friendship is possible between a boy and a girl, but just to be sure, the protective covering of 'bhai' is added to the mix. If, in earlier times, the emphasis was on the 'bhai', today being a friend is the operative part of the concept. The device of the bhai-friend is an enabler of good times, a pseudo-boyfriend who does everything the original article would, without the romantic bits added. Bhai-friends are, to use today's language, friends without benefits. The girl gets freedom to do things that were otherwise denied to her, the boy gets to be in proximity to a girl, which might otherwise have been a pipe dream, and the parents of the girl feel comforted that their daughter has a chaperone who comes with an assurance (no guarantee, of course) of no hanky-panky.

As a device, the bhai-friend is as yet a sporadic local phenomenon, but echoes of this spirit are found even elsewhere where young people pair up as boyfriend/girlfriend. Often, this relationship is treated as a casual and decidedly transient phase in the lives of the boy and girl, which allows them to enjoy their youth before settling down into matrimony, which will be conducted very much in line with the wishes of the parents, both in terms of timing and choice of partner. In most cases, the people in question think of these relationships as a passing lifestyle choice rather than a serious life decision. What makes it interesting in a subversive way is the phonetic play at work here. The fact that the phrase sounds like a boyfriend gives a frisson to a relationship that is otherwise explicitly marked out as platonic.

Another interesting observation came from a new kind of family institution that was discovered – that of the family disco. A young recently married girl, who lived in a joint family, while extolling the many freedoms that she enjoyed, pointed to the fact that the entire family would occasionally hire a discotheque in the afternoon and go dancing together. Beginning with the grandfather, down to the youngest child, everyone would troop down to a discotheque and groove to the latest Bollywood songs. Again, this kind of 'the-family-that-boogies-together-stays-together' spirit can be seen in ceremonies like the wedding sangeet, which has, over time, become an elaborately choreographed production, involving the entire family.

Both these observations, local as they are, tie in with some larger patterns that can be discerned about the changes we are seeing unfold in India. One is an ability and a desire to separate the notions of freedom and independence, of azaadi and swaraj, if you like. Freedom is defined in terms of being able to do what one was barred from doing earlier, and this is actively sought.

Independence, on the other hand, is about being able to make decisions about one's own life and is a much more contentious space. Increasingly, people are enjoying many more freedoms in terms of being able to go out more often, consume what they like, mingle with people of other sexes and express themselves physically and emotionally with less restraint. Do what you like, but do it with the family or with its blessings, is the motto, and it works for most, if not all, of the young person's desires. The idea of independence is sought, but with greater diffidence. In some cases, like that of young girls awaiting a match, the need is a strong one, and it simmers fiercely, while in others, it surfaces only on occasion.

The nature of change in India seems to be infinitely intermediate in nature. Like in the case of the bhai-friends, the desire is to escape the double bind presented by tradition as well as modernity. Finding one's own mate independently is culturally undesirable, while not having a boyfriend in today's times is socially unacceptable, and having a bhai-friend allows for an intermediate solution that accommodates both sides while creating more room for the individual. Societally, the granting of more freedoms is traded for the continued denial of personal independence, and this intermediate solution represents progress but keeps definitive change at bay. The construction of the idea of freedom thus comes with its own boundaries, some of which can be negotiated and others not.

What it also underlines is that there is a need to move beyond simple binaries to understand how people across the country are responding to change. Social mechanisms are being reimagined to take greater note of the individual, but they stop short of ceding control to the individual. What is certain is that people are trying to find newer and more innovative mechanisms to align social institutions with the reality of their own lives. New social customs are being manufactured, and as a sign that society can be made flexible and more adaptable, this is good news.

THE FEAR OF MARRIAGE

In the mythology of the Hollywood romantic comedy, men and women view marriage very differently. If about a few hundred films are to be believed, men loathe commitment and run away from the idea of marriage while women dream wistfully about the big day since they are five. The idea underlying this stereotype being that men fear being tied down while women seek it. The whole Mars, Venus thing.

In India, things look a bit different. Given the nature of the social customs that surround marriage, for men in India, marriage is an institutionalized assertion of continuity, while for women, it represents, more often than not, an acceptance of change that they cannot control nor fully comprehend at the time of the marriage. While this divergence in the meaning of marriage is quite apparent in an arranged marriage, even in a 'love' marriage, it is the woman's life that changes more significantly, and in a manner that is often outside her control.

This is why for many young women in India today, nothing is feared more than the prospect of getting married, or, as the case might be, 'married off'. The anxiety is heightened by the fact that young women across our cities and smaller towns do enjoy relatively greater freedom than they did in the past, which deepens the divide between the life they live before marriage and the prospect of a completely different kind of life afterwards. This has always been the case, and inherently the institution of marriage obviously comes without any guarantees, but what is happening today is the opening out of the gap between individual desires and social institutions, resulting in an inability to accommodate the changing nature of expectations that individuals have from their own lives.

In a study that I was a part of across the country, we found a striking pattern that was common to a large number of young women in small-town India – a greater sense of freedom coexisting with a dread of marriage and the consequences that would unfold as a result. Interestingly, while it was acknowledged by some that they would prefer a love marriage, for most the issue was not about how the match was to be made, but about the transformation that would follow the act of getting married. Conceptually, there is no problem with the idea of getting married; the problem lies in the reality that accompanies it. Marriage converts a young individual into a social artefact; a shroud of expectations, explicit and implicit, surrounds the young woman as she crosses that decisive threshold. Increasingly, women chafe at the idea of ceding control over their lives, without knowing exactly what they can expect to get in return.

In the past, elaborate social and cultural mechanisms prepared a young woman for this transformation. While the overall level of personal freedom was clearly much lower, it existed in a cultural ecosystem that made this seem effortlessly natural; it was seen as being part of the world as it was meant to be. More fundamentally, individuals, both men and women, were described primarily through their roles. Marriage thus was not a relationship forged between two individuals but an alliance that fused two families together in a particular way. The variables were generic – by not emphasizing in individuals a sense of self, marriage as an institution did not have to try too hard to accommodate individual peculiarities.

Things have changed, more so for women. But the nature of the arranged marriage process, which has otherwise shown remarkable elasticity, has been unable to accommodate this new variable – that of a cultural fit between the individuals and the families based not on the usual yardsticks at all but on the compatibility between the individual units in question. A 'good marriage' is seen as one where the girl continues to retain some control over her life and actions, and there are enough instances where marriage does become the most liberating and empowering event in a woman's life. It is precisely this possibility, as well its relative rarity, that imbues the prospect of marriage with poignancy for so many young girls. Many find excuses to postpone marriage, studying longer and insisting on working a while before agreeing to submit to marriage. Many have a 'bucket list' of things to do, as they enjoy what they see as their last fling with freedom as much as they can.

For men, the change has not been that marked. Although the rise of women in many spheres does produce anxiety in men, for they have not been equipped with the means to deal with the changed equation, when it comes to marriage, they have a vast cultural apparatus that works invisibly in their favour, one that implicitly reinforces entrenched roles and re-establishes traditional power structures. For the man, marriage is more of the same, an institution that leads them waddling off in well-fed security towards settled middle age. Women are made ready for marriage all the time, but men walk into it without any training, even in today's times when gender equations are changing. Even in love marriages, traditional roles sneak in insidiously, and even the vocally progressive woman often finds herself reverting to a gendered role, seemingly of her own volition. One only has to look at the vast number of reels on social media where young women are enacting, often with cutting humour, their fears of life after marriage.

As long as being a woman in India is primarily about playing a useful role, things will not change rapidly. Till the individuality of women gets fuller acknowledgement, till every woman is seen to be unique, a full person with depth and many layers, the change we will see will stay at a superficial level. In today's times, marriage does not complete a woman; it is the woman, fully realized, who completes it. Till this is recognized, many young women across the country will think of marriage with anxiety, hoping to take flight, but waiting to be extinguished.

THE LEAGUE OF DISAPPOINTED WOMEN

Over the years, through the course of many research projects, one has come across many kinds of stories. Some of the most striking ones involve women across age, income and social class. While most of these changes are of an exceedingly positive kind, a few give one pause.

One pattern that is unmistakable, because it appears so frequently and across virtually every social group, is that of a deep disappointment that many women are beginning to express with the men in their lives. For the most part, this is a quiet kind of disappointment, rather than active unhappiness, one that lives deep and burns long, and years of having lived with it has turned it into a cloak that women wear, one that protects them from further hurt. A sense of compromise, reeking of failed expectations, laces their utterances. Some expectations were belied, others stillborn, rendered irrelevant in the light of their futility.

A large part of the problem lies in the way marriages got fixed, and still get fixed, in a large part of India, with the girl having limited room to exercise choice, and hence getting into a lifelong relationship with only a vague sense of what lay in store. Unspecific hope that exists without a map, that shrinks bit by bit, till it shrivels up into a thin point of disappointment, which she manages by continuously lowering her expectations. On the surface, life goes on, in some cases with the appearance of external contentment, but the nagging sense of compromise lies dormant, emerging only briefly, and that too, once in a while.

The biggest issues tend to be the most mundane. The boy's family has a 'bahu'-shaped hole that is waiting to be filled, but the 'bahu' in question is an individual too. The individuality of the woman is troublesome, and often, in the first years, the project of 'rounding off her edges' is carried out with precision and dedication. Motherhood comes in and acts as a form of rescue, as the woman's time is whisked away from under her nose, lost in the welter of chores and responsibilities. Being a mother often becomes both a source of joy and an escape. Roles wrap themselves around her, without leaving too much free surface area for her to feel anything much. But the disappointment does not go away, it merely hides deep, and surfaces occasionally, in an argument, a conversation with friends, or just in the freedom of solitude.

A large part of it has to do with the feeling that men do not 'get' their wives, even in 'love' marriages. They simply cannot see beyond her body and her role. It is not that there always is an absence of affection or care for the spouse, but what is missing is an interest in and understanding of what drives her as a person. It is assumed that the woman and her life are inseparable – there is no room that is left for her, the individual, within this space. This feeling of being invisible while ostensibly being at the heart of the family is a frequent experience and one for which many women struggle to find an outlet. There is an inherent asymmetry in the evaluating gaze; the woman sees the man as a person and has more reason to be disappointed. The man sees her as a role and as long as she does her bit, her happiness is taken as given.

There are disappointed men, too, but except in rare cases, they have little need to mask their feelings. The disappointment is advertised loudly and frequently. Culturally, the ability to complain about the wife is enshrined as a fundamental right. The 'wife jokes', upon which so many WhatsApp groups depend to provide their regular dose of humour, is a time-honoured device which allows men to complain about their wives in an apparently affectionate way. Portraying the wife as a martinet whose word is law, and whom the man shows an exaggerated fear of, the 'wife joke' is a culturally sanctioned way in which men can show their resentment for whatever balance that might exist in a relationship.

There are more aggressive responses to the change in the gender power equation, too, but the dominant reaction is one of incomprehension, as something foundational is in the process of being redefined. Centuries of slow change in the relationship between the genders does not make it easy for such rapid shifts to be absorbed easily. There is a small but growing sense of victimhood that is brewing among men, as they rail against what they see as the overcompensation that is taking place in the public discourse about gender.

There is another pattern that appears, more frequently nowadays. The pallid presence of a man who has given up. He himself has given up on the quest for self-respect and now resides at the periphery of the family's consciousness. Across the country, we came across quite a few families where the man has stopped mattering, either because of his failings, or because of his inability to provide value to the emerging aspirations of the family. Women, who were disappointed quickly but acted fast, showing a brisk and brusque disregard for the spouse. They channel their disappointment into something productive and take charge of their own and their family's destiny.

On the positive side, one can also witness the rise of coupledom in a much more fully realized way in marriages that are enjoyed, where the pleasure of partnership gives rise to feelings never experienced before. But not everyone is as fortunate, and, in a society where marriage is for keeps, both as compulsion and culturally encouraged choice, the league of disappointed women just finds a way to get on with their lives, one day at a time.

THE RISE OF FEMALE ENTREPRENEURSHIP?

Everywhere one travels in the country, one comes across a new breed of female entrepreneurs. They don't give themselves that label, but in a variety of small ways, entrepreneurship is blossoming at the smallest unit of change. The efforts are varied; not all ventures are full-time, some are carried out quietly, others with full family support, but there is a common spirit that runs through all these efforts.

A chain of beauty parlours in Gaya. Chit funds in Warangal. An online portal for women in Jalgaon. A dress rental business in Aurangabad. A catering service in Coimbatore. Cooking classes in Rajkot. Jewellery made out of technology waste in Gurugram. A skilling centre in Rajahmundry. A hostel in Bikaner. What was common to all these businesses that I encountered was that they all had been set up and were being run by first-time female entrepreneurs.

Some activities are an outgrowth of jobs traditionally considered to be 'suitable for women'. Adding on tuition to a formal teaching job, gradually moving into it full-time and turning it into a business, is one kind of pattern. In some cases, a hobby or a skill gets converted into a business. Beauty parlours can today be found in every galli-mohalla in the country. Small boutiques, sometimes run out of a spare room in the house, too are easy to spot. Some women have catering units that supply home-cooked food, or cooking classes that turn culinary skill into an organized enterprise.

In other instances, women convert their social networks into a money-making enterprise. Chit funds are extensions of kitty parties, and often get combined with multi-level marketing of products. Becoming entrepreneurs gives women much greater flexibility than employment in a regular job. The hours are not fixed, there is greater control over one's time, and it is possible to operate from home. Technology is helping. Setting up online businesses is much easier, and needs little by way of physical infrastructure. The mobile phone is a godsend, for it simplifies access and substantially reduces physical travel. It serves as the new storefront, allows for products to be sold over WhatsApp and for customer service to be carried out while lulling one's child to sleep. Plus, being able to stand outside the hierarchy that every formal job comes accompanied with, represents a kind of freedom that is highly valued. One does not work under anyone else, one is not answerable to others. Socially, too, as some women pointed out, this makes things easier, for some of the traditional hesitation that exists about having to mingle with and follow the instructions of other men do not apply. Of course, in the course of conducting one's business, such considerations do not count for much, but a veneer of social respectability is useful for women in smaller towns as they emerge into being protagonists of their own venture.

At a deeper level, the urge to do something more, to squeeze out greater opportunities from the cards one is dealt, is an underlying feature of a lot of these efforts. One can see a restless urge, an itch that must be scratched, a sense that deep inside the self lies untold potential that must somehow get harnessed. A very common sentiment that we encountered was that 'I am not just a housewife.' This surplus ambition that powers entrepreneurialism is a vital palpable force that can be seen among women of all ages and classes across the country today.

Interestingly, female entrepreneurship does not unsettle men in quite the same way as a woman working in a formal job often does. The fact that there is no designation, no rank that can serve as a relative measure of success and no fixed salary that becomes a benchmark to compete against, turns out to be an advantage, for it sidesteps issues to do with the bruising of male egos. The money made in business has a fluid quality; in general, in India, small businesses have little idea of how much exactly they make, and this, too, is useful.

This is why a lot of entrepreneurial activity is conducted in the name of 'doing something on the side' or by way of 'keeping busy'. Part of this characterization comes from the woman's pragmatic understanding of the need to downplay ambition and even success, so as not to threaten the existing power hierarchy with the men around her. Even in instances where the woman was making more money than her husband, one often saw a low-key description of her work. Of course, this is not always the case; there are examples of women doing really well and men learning to live with it. In these cases, traditional roles are overturned and a new power dynamic is established, but this happens infrequently.

This is part of a long-standing pattern that we have seen where the work contribution of women has been consistently undervalued and inadequately acknowledged. The housewife is widely seen to be 'not working'; a description that completely ignores the contribution that the woman makes to the household. It is most stark in the case of women working on farms, where, in spite of doing the bulk of the work, almost all of it manual, there is virtually no acknowledgment of her role. There is no such thing as a woman farmer, no word in our languages that describes this; only men can get this label in spite of often doing very little actual work on their farms.

Increasingly, the capabilities and imaginations of women across the country can no longer be contained by constraining circumstances. An ability to find a way from amongst one's crowded life is propelled by a fierce desire to impose oneself on one's environment. Entrepreneurship becomes an uncontrollable leakage of intent, an overflow of imagination into reality. Running one's own business gives a sense of agency and freedom that few other activities can match. Female entrepreneurship is a form of untethering, a release of desires and aspirations that render the idea of boundaries a little less relevant. The change may as yet be small, but it is unmistakable; the ability to lead life on one's own terms and to create something of enduring value is a profoundly significant shift that we are seeing today.

THE GREAT GENDER PUSHBACK?

Is the tide turning? The last few decades have seen a consistent growth in gender rights. There has been an implicit agreement about the direction of change in the areas of women's education, career opportunities, legal rights, and reproductive freedom. Attitudes towards different expressions of gender and sexuality have also liberalized. The change has not been even, not always to the satisfaction of those affected, but the overall thrust of the change has been unmistakably positive.

But things seem poised to change. A noticeable feature of the 2024 US elections was the explicit nostalgia expressed for an older time when gender roles were more sharply delineated. Vice President J.D. Vance's repeated barbs aimed at 'childless cat ladies' were a pointer to the expectation that the primary role of women was to reproduce and confine their ambitions to the family and the home.

And this is by no means an isolated event. The world over, we are seeing signs of a masculine backlash against the change in the power equation between the genders. Figures like Andrew Tate have risen to prominence on the back of an unabashedly hypermasculine world view. They explicitly argue for a society that is dominated by male impulses and locate women very much at the other end of the power spectrum. The belief that male strength and female submission are part of the natural order of things is one that animates this kind of thinking. Some of the tenets of this stream of thought are that female sexuality needs to be controlled, that aggressive materialistic acquisition and the flaunting of consumption are the sources of social and sexual capital, and that vulnerability, empathy, and emotional complexity are all signs of weakness.

Social media tends to amplify extreme views, and, as a result, this kind of perspective has received disproportionate attention, which, in turn, has attracted many more to the fold. The glorification of 'alpha men' and the explicit disavowal of women's autonomy has created a movement of sorts globally. In India, too, we have seen the rise of hypermasculine films like *Animal*, which clearly touch a chord.

In India, gender disparities have been a foundational part of its social organization, and a change in that hierarchical order, which has been underway for many years now, is an obvious source of anxiety and discomfort for men. Unused to dealing with women's agency and the fact that women have begun to subject male behaviour to scrutiny, the reaction to the emerging gender has been one of anger, and, in more than a few cases, violence. Groups supporting male rights have also sprung up, trying to redress what they see as an imbalance.

More worrying is the fact that fertility rates are dropping worldwide. What we are seeing is a significant drop in population growth levels in countries across the world, with the birth rates below the replacement rates in ninety to hundred countries. While, in the short term, this might be good news, since it will ease the burden that the human race puts on the planet and its resources, in the long run, this is likely to create pressure on women to reproduce. The idea of what some sociologists have called 'reproductive nationalism' is a narrative that is already in the making.

The other source of anxiety comes from the economic pressures we are likely to face as a result of the replacement of many jobs thanks to AI. And while many argue that the loss of jobs will be transient as the world transitions from one technological age to another, this period is likely to further erode women's role in the workplace. We have seen this at work recently when Covid happened; women's participation in the workforce dropped dramatically as jobs became scarce.

An enabling factor in this countermovement is the overall rightward shift we are seeing in the political sphere. It is being argued that what we are seeing is, in part, a reaction to the woke overreach of the last many years. This has meant that the political mainstream is leaning towards a much harder line on issues of race, gender, and sexuality. In developed nations, falling fertility rates along with rising pressure of immigration help create an environment where the pressure on women to reproduce is likely to grow. We are yet to fully comprehend the extent of change that Trump's America is likely to bring about in the world. In India, too, there is a strong strand in our political thought that is much more comfortable with a more traditional equation between the genders. The current political stage is dominated by a decidedly masculine discourse based on strength.

It could be argued that worrying as these trends are, change is too far underway to be reversed that easily. Women have adjusted to a new mental model of themselves, and there is little chance that they will want to go back. And even families are today dependent on women's participation in the workforce. Scaling back consumption needs is not going to be easy; if anything, these are only likely to grow.

It is also possible that instead of going back to the old order, we might arrive at new models of social organization that are based on gender parity rather than difference. An AI-dominated world could unleash changes of a kind that might seem far-fetched today. Radical new forms of reproductive and social technologies that reduce biological constraints, create models of collective child-rearing, and new parenting models could reshape the landscape. Marriages and families could look very different a few decades from now.

However, for now, it looks like what will play out will be a period of tense negotiation between two powerful forces: the seemingly inexorable drive towards more freedom and personal agency on the gender and sexuality front, and the strong counterforce that looks to go back to a time with a more traditional division of roles between the genders.

A NEW VOCABULARY FOR NEW TIMES?

FROM A TIME WHEN WE tiptoed around the subject of race, religion, sexual orientation, and caste, now we are surrounded by these labels, which are being used freely by people of all political persuasions. The modern vocabulary teems with notions of whiteness, Islamophobia, Hindutva, Savarna, homophobia, transphobia and the like. Far from escaping identity labels, there is a growing recognition of their centrality.

At its core, what we are seeing is a shift in our mental model of inequality. Implicit in our earlier narrative, the marginalized one was considered the aberration and the rest were deemed to be normal. Even the word 'marginalized' suggests this – that there is a mainstream, consisting of good, concerned people like us and then there are the others – less fortunate, as we like to call them, who need help.

Inequality needs two sides and yet our vocabulary has place only for one. We talked extensively about the underprivileged, but never acknowledged that on the other side of the same equation, there must be people who were overprivileged. In our minds, the latter represented reality as it was meant to be, something that was so obvious that it need not be noticed, let alone acknowledged.

What the new vocabulary does is to recognize the imbalance in its complete form. Being 'upper' caste is part of the same problem as being 'lower' caste. Without explicitly acknowledging this, any attempt to challenge the caste system is flawed. Similarly, when we talk of racism, without recognizing that privilege of any kind was as much an aberration as discrimination, any conversation, no matter how well-intentioned, is incomplete.

So far, in fact, the presence of a positive intention has been something that has been sufficient as a starting point. The desire for greater equality equalled nobility that was reinforced socially in several ways. The two modes by which the question was addressed operated within two different frameworks – philanthropy, which accepted inequality but tried to alleviate its effects, or activism, which challenged the idea of inequality itself. When it came to economics, there was relative clarity that inequality as a problem had two sides that needed to be addressed simultaneously – those that didn't have enough as against those who had too much.

However, when it came to social inequality, this clarity was largely missing. What we are seeing now is a correction of this imbalance. It also helps that the hitherto-marginalized voices, which needed to be spoken on behalf of by the more privileged, are now more assertively seeking to speak for themselves. The white saviour phenomenon, which defined much of the liberal discourse in earlier decades, is being exposed and challenged. The idea of do-gooding, without an acknowledgment of the structural inequality that animates the act of helping the 'less fortunate', was never as innocent as it was claimed to be. Today, questions are being asked and responsibilities being fixed. The reason why reservations are so widely resented by the so-called 'general' class is precisely because of this default mental model. The historically privileged class is deemed to be 'general'.

While it is difficult to mount an argument against the need to explicitly acknowledge the fact that any imbalance must necessarily involve two sides, there is a new set of issues that arises once this recognition takes place. The trouble with bringing structural inequalities to the fore is that by itself that changes nothing. The problem identified is so wide-ranging and deep that no individual action can sufficiently change things. When the critique is this fundamental, the only way to solve any one problem is to first solve all problems. One cannot change being born white or upper caste; recognizing one's privilege might make one a more sensitive human being, but that has no real value insofar as changing things is concerned.

What it can lead to, and we see ample evidence of this today, is a plunge into competitive virtue-signalling, where we cleanse our language and symbols retrospectively of a taint that by definition cannot be cleansed. Recognizing one's privilege in no way lessens it; the smarter people have figured out that one way to obscure this fact is by being aggressive in calling out others.

Globally, we see the rise of this excessively 'woke' brigade that fights structural disparities by blaming others, and by doing so they implicitly absolve themselves of any real culpability, not that it would help in any case. Accompanying this is the rise of the hitherto marginalized, who are today far more active participants in the conversation. They are keen to speak for themselves, and quite legitimately believe that the injustices of the past that they have endured have to be made up for. There is little patience for the developed world BS that has kept hierarchies constant.

The privilege warriors speak too much and change too little and those opposing them have too much to lose to even contemplate any change. The battle becomes one of words and symbols, what can be said and what cannot, who has a right to speak for whom and who does not, than about more substantive underlying arguments. And this suits the opponents of change just fine.

Sometimes, the truth is not enough. Knowing what is wrong is useful but only up to a point. Some change necessarily requires time, for it depends on the gradual change in an entire mode of thinking. And no one can argue that the world has not changed. Attitudes towards gender equality, alternative sexualities, race, caste have changed significantly over the twentieth century. Importantly, these changes have not come without someone agitating for them. That is the dilemma. Pushing for change is critically important, the trick is to know how hard.

THE PARADOX OF MODERN MASCULINITY

IT IS NOT EASY BEING a man in today's world. That is certainly what a lot of men believe. The rules are new, the landscape is full of invisible potholes, and nothing that they do seems to be good enough. There is a sense of emerging victimhood, felt strongly by a section of men, resulting in a complex set of often contradictory behaviours, from alpha-male strutting to anxious self-doubt.

Beyond today's gender reckonings lies a historical context – men grew up torn between the unconditional love without accountability they received from mothers while simultaneously facing limited affirmation but consistent judgement from fathers. This fostered a combination of emotional dependency and chronic inadequacy, resulting in what psychoanalyst Sudhir Kakar called 'the maternal paradise and paternal tribunal dynamic'. At one level, the man could do no wrong, such was the unquestioning affirmation he received, and on the other, nothing he did was good enough. The mother forgave everything, and the father approved of nothing, leaving the man forever dangling in an emotional no-man's land.

The lethal mix of entitled narcissism and crippling self-doubt created a fractured sense of self, which the man tried to overcome all his life. As long as masculinity was expressed through external roles – provider, protector, wielder of authority – this inner inadequacy could be masked, but in today's time, the demands from masculinity are more complex and the old codes aren't sufficient.

There exists a paradox at the heart of this masculinity. The patriarchal order, which is frequently held responsible for trapping women in its structural folds, does the same to men. While they are the beneficiaries wielding asymmetrical power, they, too, are trapped within its rigid confines. This puts them in a peculiar bind – they can hardly complain that being assigned vastly greater power is unfair even though that power comes with strings attached in terms of the roles they are expected to play.

As women become more expressive and exercise greater agency, for men it seems as if the world is moving in the opposite direction. They continue to feel the burden of traditional expectations while having a whole lot of new ones to navigate.

It doesn't help that for the first time in our cultural history, men find themselves being actively judged by women and often found wanting. This represents a seismic shift in the power dynamic, one for which most Indian men possess neither emotional tools nor vocabulary to deal with. Having never had to consider women's assessment as consequential, they now face the destabilizing reality of external judgement from those who were expected to obey.

As women claim greater freedom in articulating their needs, desires, and identities, men frequently misread these signals through a distorted lens. They interpret signs of female autonomy as sexual availability, something that popular culture encourages, and find it frustrating when the apparent promise does not materialize. The resulting frustration can curdle into resentment or violence.

The emerging decoupling of marriage from sex creates a new set of anxieties. The traditional arranged marriage system virtually ensured that every man had access to companionship regardless of their individual attributes. Today, as women exercise more choice, men with lower social capital feel relegated to the fringes. This produces genuine anxiety, particularly among men who recognize they may not possess the attributes that women freely choose.

Because there is a historic correction taking place in gender power relations, many men feel that the world is arrayed unfairly against them. They perceive institutional structures tilting towards female advantage, their concerns dismissed while women's complaints receive immediate legitimacy.

This sense of injury breeds a new set of reactions – the rise of men's rights activism and anti-feminist rhetoric offering both community and explanatory frameworks for men who feel displaced by changing norms. A term such as 'feminazis' reflects this perspective, equating efforts towards equality with oppression because any reduction in historical privilege feels like discrimination to those men accustomed to advantage. The structural advantages they enjoy are invisible to them; what seems real is the incremental privilege they see women enjoying. Individual instances of women taking undue advantage of this new gender narrative help legitimize this sense of grievance.

Even the communication between genders has become a minefield. The male defensive refrain of 'not all men' collides with female frustration at having systemic critique derailed by individual exceptions. From a woman's perspective, continually acknowledging exceptions feels like being asked to comfort those with more power rather than addressing urgent concerns. From men's view, the refusal to make this concession appears as unreasonable rigidity.

We find ourselves at an impasse of understanding. Men experience genuine disorientation as traditional certainties evaporate, yet their interpretation often fails to recognize both historical context and the continuing advantages they hold. Women pursue necessary freedoms while sometimes underestimating the identity crisis this creates for men raised with different expectations.

The path forward requires a delicate balance – acknowledging men's genuine confusion without legitimizing harmful reactions and recognizing women's rightful autonomy without dismissing the disruptive social consequences of rapid change. Until we develop frameworks that allow both genders to navigate this evolving landscape with greater understanding, we remain caught in a dialogue of bewilderment – two worlds in transition, speaking different languages, each struggling to comprehend the other's reality amidst the ruins of an old order and the uncertain foundations of a new one.

OF YOUNG LOVE IN SMALL-TOWN INDIA

WHILE WORKING ON A RESEARCH project in small-town north India, one found, not surprisingly, that while, like most other parts of India, it was seeing some signs of change, gender certainly wasn't one of those areas. Attitudes continue to be fixed, and the space granted to young girls, in particular, continues to be extremely limited. Co-ed colleges are often formally segregated on the lines of gender; in some cases, common canteens are also not allowed. A boy found talking to a girl is liable to be reported to his parents. Amidst this overall picture of stasis, however, lay a small but unexpected sign of change.

While the young women that we spoke to were quite clear that they had no control over whom they would get married to (indeed, as were the young men), they were not averse to talking about their crushes. They showed a certain amount of freedom in confessing to having crushes. The crushes that were admitted to comprised both the fantasy figures that lay safely tucked away in the recesses of their social media pages as well as some in their immediate neighbourhood. Names were not mentioned, but the subject was discussed freely and with discernible excitement.

The crush allowed these young girls to experience the headiness of falling in love without any of the cumbersome consequences that would inevitably follow in the social milieu that they were part of. While the crush – this idea of a one-sided innocent yearning that need not have an address – is a universally experienced emotion, in these parts of India, there is a certain additional poignancy brought about by the fact that the graduation to the real thing will, in almost all cases, never happen. The crush is not a prelude to the real thing, it is the only thing that can possibly exist. The acceptance of this reality is so complete, the consequences that would follow are considered to be so dire, that even wistfulness is rarely expressed.

Indeed, what is a big mark of change is that the crush can be so freely admitted to in such cloistered conditions. It allows the mind to explore possibilities that the body cannot, and in doing so, it opens up pathways in the imagination that might otherwise have been stifled completely. The presence of a crush, or several crushes, has almost become an institution, in the sense that it has come to be accepted that everyone will have their own crushes. But it is equally true that these fantasies can be admitted to only because they are considered to be explicitly out of bounds of possibility.

The crush lives in an intermediate space between fantasy and experience, the commonplace and the taboo, the inconceivable and the impossible. The crush is preordained to be crushed, which is why it is allowed to live briefly – the implicit cultural legitimacy enjoyed by the crush has a lot to do with the self-denying nature of the idea. The digital world is part of the package, for it enables feelings from afar. It permits several intermediate degrees of familiarity, and in doing so vastly multiplies the range of possibilities that can be imagined without being acted upon. On the flip side, it also opens up young girls to the possibility of harassment and stalking, but in the main, it is seen as a solitary window in their otherwise airtight lives.

That does not mean that young romances do not exist at all in these parts of the country. Some of these romances go the distance, while others have less happy endings, as newspaper headlines show. Most small towns have a few designated spots where young couples hang out. Even in the college romance, new notes of a more contemporary kind can be detected. In some cases, the college couple go around with the explicit understanding on both sides that nothing more permanent is on the table. The college romance is, in these cases, seen as a lifestyle choice, one that multiplies one's capacity to squeeze more freedom out of the few years where life comes without the constraining responsibilities of settled adulthood. For young women, in particular, this period evokes nostalgia even as it happens, so deep is their sense of its briefness and transience. The nature of the relationship between the boy and the girl, too, has newer elements. There is a matter-of-factness about it all – old gender codes are changing. Presents need to be reciprocated equally, and it is not unusual to see the girl paying for their outings far more than was the case earlier.

Of course, there are many parts of the country where the young enjoy considerably greater freedoms, and the crush here is a way of entering the world of romance on tiptoe. This is the classical idea of the crush – the unripe phase where the intensity of feelings does not quite translate into anything material in real life.

There is an India where for a girl to admit to any romantic feelings outside the institution of marriage is considered dangerous. The frequent anger that seems to erupt against young couples across several parts of the country is a sign that as a society, the idea that the young have the freedom to make life choices based on their feelings as individuals, rather than as social beings, is one that produces resentment and fear. Like many other things in India, change comes slowly, and in a covert and muted form. The radical comes hidden within the apparently mundane. Changing a system that is intricately organized so as to keep things in place requires stealth and time. In doing so, both sides find their own victories – things change while they remain the same. The sight of young girls speaking about their crushes with shiny eyes and singing hearts, without any expectation that their desires could come true, represents this kind of change, which is simultaneously heart-warming and heartbreaking.

LIBERALIZING FAMILIES?

IN THESE DIVIDED AND ANGRY times, striking any note of optimism that everyone can share in is not easy. But perhaps we overemphasize the things that divide us, and there do exist common strands of experience that we can take hope from.

There is a puzzling gap that one encounters between the headlines and the trend lines in India. Reading the newspapers, watching electronic media or browsing through one's social media feed, a certain kind of picture emerges. Of an India riven by divisions, driven by anger, and deeply unhappy with the way things are. However, a different kind of reality is also on display when one travels across the country and interacts with the same cross-section of people that populates social media, which, in my professional life as a consumer analyst, one is called upon to do regularly and on a fairly large scale. Here, the mood is much more even and has been for several years – there is a sense of continuity and hope; looked at from the vantage point of urban middle-class everyday life, the world seems to be a more stable and contented space. Of course, there are pockets of unhappiness and anger, sections where everyday life is hard and the future feels bleak, but, for many others, the sentiment is more positive.

One of the primary reasons why the sentiment that drives urban middle-class India is more positive than what we can discern from media representations has to do with the family as an institution and how it has evolved with time. There is a new kind of a template that is emerging for families today that is rooted in the codes of progress rather than scarcity. The rise of the Collaborative Family, where the family acts as a back-up band for the individual rather than seeking to contain her, can be seen in large parts of the country. The family here becomes a common resource, which uses its collective abilities to nudge each individual towards their own personal goals. This allows it to deal with change positively, by balancing the needs of stability and growth.

The family has always been a cornerstone in our lives; it has been a binding force designed for resilience in difficult times. But in an earlier time, belonging to a family was a given, and came along with duties and responsibilities. The family had a code, a way of doing things, and submitting to these rules was an important part of the act of belonging. It offered great support and comfort, but it also asked individuals to sacrifice key aspects of who they were in order to belong. People had assigned roles that they needed to play and there were expectations that they needed to fulfil. Stepping out of line came with costs; families could be warm and inclusive but they could turn cold and hurtful. The exercise of authority, most often paternalistic in character, was an important part of how families functioned.

The collaborative family of today has a different character. The stories one encounters across towns large and small have similar elements. Of families rallying around an individual, surrounding her with belief and support, and encouraging her to do more. More room for the individual, more space for women to express themselves and pursue their own goals, looser exercise of authority, greater role played by children in decision-making, the family acting as a cheerleader for each member – these are characteristics that are part of this emerging template of collaborative families.

The many escape hatches that technology provides serve currently not to sever ties, but to make them a little more discretionary. Everyone potentially has more room to breathe, more places to go and more places to curl up and hide out as an individual for a while. It becomes possible to calibrate the connection one maintains with other members of the family, and several simultaneous intensities in relationships can be managed thanks to different kinds of social media channels.

In this kind of family, the nudge is felt across generations. Parents find themselves more alone, having been separated from the kind of support that large joint families unquestioningly provided. They are somewhat lost; they are cognizant of their role as guardians of tradition but do not quite know what that translates into. They lean on each other more regularly and include children in key areas of decision making. The younger generation finds the overhang of parental authority to be less stifling, and there is a greater sense of being on a common journey, as each member of the family navigates a new reality along with others. People are no longer locked in their roles – individuals breathe far more easily in families today than they did in the past. The goals of each individual get more attention and active support; the family imposes less of itself and its ways.

That is not to argue that all is well with families in India. There are dysfunctional families, even families that behave horribly with their own, as we have seen in many highly visible instances. The treatment of the elderly in India is getting shabbier, and parental pressure on children is seriously undermining childhoods. Women might have won some freedoms, but even in this emerging template for families, they haven't quite won their independence when it comes to making decisions about themselves. The collaborative family is an emerging reality but is by no means the only one.

There might be a long way to go, but the evolution of the role of the family unit is a significant development. At a time when politics is so much about culture, it is important to note that in a lived sense, the evolution of a more modern sensibility continues organically. For now, at least, the implicit momentum of modernity runs deeper than the political climate of the country seems to suggest. Regardless of their political leanings, families are quietly liberalizing.

INSIDE THE GREAT INDIAN WEDDING

IF THE NEW INDIAN WEDDING with all its excesses feels daunting from the outside, from inside it is terrifying. Having been involved in the organization of a wedding over the last few months, one has developed a new understanding from within the belly of the beast. Having visited many weddings slack-jawed and bug-eyed at the sheer amount of preparation that went into these Bollywood-fuelled mega-productions, the prospect of organizing something even mildly passable was a daunting one.

A friend had warned us that the most difficult thing about wedding preparations would be the clothes. One heard him but felt that in our case that was unlikely to be much of a big deal. After all, we were all sensible people with only a passing interest in things like wedding finery. As it turns out, that understanding was not quite accurate. We took months agonizing over the process. Each function had its own grammar in terms of what kind of clothes to wear – lehenga, sari or gown. There were colours to worry about – apparently, they had to align with the décor, about which we had no clue. Every item of clothing cost as much as a liver transplant and the entire effort created more drama in terms of emotional turmoil than seven saas-bahu serials put together.

Not only were we so involved with clothes, but so were all the guests. There is apparently this new convention that decrees that all functions come accompanied with a dress code. Indeed, in some of the recent weddings that one was invited to, it became necessary to shop for the outfits – so specific were the demands. We had mandated no dress code, something that one thought would please the guests. On the contrary, barring a few, it seemed to be a source of great confusion and uncertainty. It was as if we had deprived people of a familiar crutch without which they had forgotten how to dress up. Apparently, the whole point of being invited to weddings is to have an excuse to buy more clothes of a kind that one will almost never have reason to wear again.

The menu was another task that took weeks to complete. Serving regular dishes with names one can decipher is an act of risible naivete. There must be an abundance of exotica, while ensuring that familiar palates are also taken care of, because after all, what Indian celebration can do without some version of 'chaat'? The list of options had to be large so as to make it impossible for a guest to try everything.

The other, more vexing part of organizing weddings is that one is forced into making decisions based on hierarchy. This is not a new dimension – in fact, Indian weddings have always had an acute sense of the relative importance of guests. Who needs to be taken extra care of, which 'foofaji' is prone to tantrums, how much cash should be given by whom (after all, this is zealously recorded in a little diary by some relative). But now there are other, more modern aspects to this hierarchy. If the wedding is an outstation one, as it was in this case, the first question that arises is who to invite and who to leave out. Only so many people can be accommodated (and afforded). If one is using more than one hotel to put up guests, then comes the tricky question of who to locate where. This becomes even stickier if the hotels are discernibly of a different grade. Even within a hotel, the questions arise as to who should get which room. Intricate Excel sheets, endless iterations, and many mix-ups later, the problem was solved by figuring that nobody really cared as long as there was enough alcohol.

Decoration in an earlier time was largely a question of erecting a shamiana and putting up some flowers, with a preponderance of marigold. The most heavily decorated object in the wedding was the bridegroom, who wore a floral purdah through which he tried to occasionally mark his presence at the event. Now, of course, décor is a whole new science at par with advanced quantum biology. Themes are brainstormed and then storyboarded, every event has its own aesthetic signature, and is its own construction project. Without a designer and a wedding planner, even thinking about décor is a hopeless enterprise.

The other significant change that has taken place over a generation is the decisive shifting of the power equation. In an earlier era, the role of the bride and groom was to take up the space allocated to them and to follow instructions, the more arcane the better. They had an ornamental role – the marriage was a ritual between families, and the bride and the groom were the mute instruments through which this relationship was consummated. Their principal role was to look dazed and coy, and, occasionally, the other way around. All decisions big and small were taken by the parents. Today it is the couple that takes all the decisions. Unlike the past, there is a great sense of clarity about what they want the wedding to be, and the role of the parents is to be supportive, rather than lead. And to sign the cheques.

But eventually none of this matters. When things come together it is always because of the people. All the ridiculous over-the-top arrangements help, but the fact that the wedding today is genuinely designed for enjoyment is what really makes it special. I have no nostalgia for weddings of yore – they were tedious, dreary affairs that never seemed to end. And the less said about the 'bidaai', the better.

For all the absurd extravagance that goes into a modern wedding, it is a whole lot of fun. And even for the hosts, thanks to the many professionals who have sprung up as part of an organized industry, it is possible to have a great time even while worrying about all the moving parts.

THE TROUBLE WITH MODERN LOVE?

I**T'S COMPLICATED. IN A NUTSHELL,** that is the status of young love in India today. Over the last decade or so, we have seen dramatic changes in the romantic landscape of the country. The vocabulary, grammar, and modes of enactment of romance have changed beyond recognition.

Growing up, falling in love was something that happened largely in movies. To be sure, there was much pining in the name of love, many lingering looks, and deep sighs, but almost all of it was one-sided. Relationships were largely imaginary, and while there was no dearth of claims made on one's chosen one – 'meri waali' – no actual contact was made with the object of one's affections. People in films fell in love only to encounter much drama; even there it was seen as something inherently alien. It was almost seen as an affliction – 'prem rog'– as if it were a form of typhoid.

Change took its own time, but it got there in the end. Market institutions like Valentine's Day did much to bring the idea of romance into the open. It directed commercial intent towards a pent-up need among the young. It made the idea of coupledom a desirable lifestyle choice. It gave an avenue for expression, something that, earlier, was possible only in the repressed form of the film song.

The mobile phone changed everything. It gave a direct pipeline, hidden from the outside world, to the young and opened up possibilities undreamt of before. The hesitation to initiate a conversation, that was the hallmark of awkward and abortive romantic desires, was replaced by what-does-one-have-to-lose braggadocio in messaging someone on a social media app.

Romance has entered the mainstream of young lives. Even in small towns, fourteen-year-old girls speak nonchalantly about their crushes. The idea of dating has become far more commonplace, as has the word 'relationship' in its plural form. Couples get together and break up; people get dumped or ghosted.

The idea of choices, particularly in this arena, is a new one. In older Hindi films, the only way to resolve a love triangle was by bumping one of the people off. The idea that a choice could be made of one over the other was unthinkable. Today, choice exists in every sphere of life, and its presence in the area of romance has changed in fundamental ways.

For one, love is today a marketplace. Not metaphorically, as bemoaned by Hindi film songs in the past, but literally. Dating apps allow the young to choose potential partners like they would a pair of jeans. Scroll, swipe right or left to approve or reject. The hunt could be for marriage, a stable relationship, a quick fling, or just a random hook-up.

For an older generation, gawking at the amount of freedom available today, the truth is that the new ease of finding romantic relationships is as enabling as it is confounding. In an earlier time, romance, if it at all existed before marriage, was a singular event – you fell in love; it either ended in marriage or it did not. Today, it is not that simple. Getting into a relationship is easier, but knowing whether that is 'the one' is far more difficult.

There is an array of choices; there could always be a better partner if you scrolled enough on dating apps. The list of demands from the partner has also grown; it isn't that easy to get satisfied with what one has. And temptation is everywhere, so staying attached is not that easy.

Which is why there is a range of relationship modes to choose from, particularly in the metros. There are situationships, which refer to relationships without labels, where the two people are just going with the flow and seeing where it takes them. There are 'friends with benefits', partners who enjoy a sexual relationship without any emotional involvement. There is a small set of people who describe themselves as polyamorous and who do not believe in monogamy. The gradual legitimization of alternative sexuality has further accelerated and widened the nature of this exploration.

More importantly, the search for commitment is itself not a given. In a digitally driven world, the young have to figure out so many things from scratch that the idea of stopping somewhere and anchoring one's life is difficult. The self is always a beta-version of itself, a project in the making. In the search for romance lies embedded a search for oneself. The relationship becomes a laboratory in which one tries out different versions of oneself.

We see a lot of therapy talk in today's relationships. Partners are giving each other advice and helping each other figure out their place in the world even as they are navigating their own relationship. Phrases like setting 'boundaries', 'red flags', 'triggers' and 'being triggered', 'gaslighting', and 'toxic patterns' abound. This is enabled by the profusion of content on social media, which delves into the minutiae of relationships.

In many ways, romance has become work. From finding a partner, designing a marketable bio, enacting the romance for the consumption of the outside world on social media on a day-by-day basis, 'checking in' periodically to keep the relationship going, navigating the relationship with the partner's friends and family, to figuring out whether the relationship has run its course and an exit has to be managed, it is all hard work. Love was always a complex affair, but today, the complexity has advanced to relationships before marriage. In an earlier time, even in the case of 'love marriages', the real discovery of one's partner happened after marriage. Not so in today's information-saturated times.

While this is most true in the larger towns, a version of this reality applies in the smaller towns too. Structurally, romance has moved from residing in a dream state to finding itself located in hard reality. There is a certain cynicism, a level of hard-headedness that has become part of its grammar. And while it is much more accessible, it is complicated.

DRIVEN BY IMPULSE

THE INTERNET IS FULL OF caste videos. Expressions of caste pride are rife; we see influencers with huge following plugging their own castes, be they Jat, Yadav, or Gujjar, in videos and songs. Now one can understand a similar phenomenon occurring for castes that have historically been marginalized, and while that is also happening, it does not seem to match the scale and aggression of the more powerful intermediate castes. Casteism has gone nowhere despite all efforts, but such overt affirmation of caste roots is something new.

As is the case with masculinity. There is a strong pushback against the gender-equality narrative that was the default ideal in previous decades, with a figure like Andrew Tate at the forefront. In India, too, on social media, we see the rise of many voices that make a strong case for retaining the status quo when it comes to the role of women. Women who stand for feminist ideals are targeted specifically, with no holds barred.

Across the world, what we are seeing is the return of impulse. The story of progress over the last few centuries has been that of separating human action from impulse. Education and technology worked together to achieve this. As we began to understand the world, we developed a 'learned view' against a primal instinctive one. The education we receive when we are very young is a good example of how this training is imparted at an early stage. We stood in straight lines; we were addressed by our surnames or roll numbers; the importance of discipline was drilled into us. The impulsive needed to become socially responsible and compliant adults.

Technology, too, played a similar role. The Industrial Revolution separated our means of livelihood from our lives. We lived in cities rather than traditional communities; we consumed not what was immediately around us but what was manufactured and packaged. Mobility gave us exposure to the world, and we learned more about cultures far removed from ours. The prevailing ideologies of the time emphasized a desire to move towards a society of lower discrimination on the axes of gender, class, sexuality and caste. We were acutely aware of how we should act, and we consciously suppressed our instincts when they told us otherwise. After all, that was what being civilized and modern meant.

Social order was achieved by subordinating the needs of the individual to the needs of the larger collective. Our evolutionary impulses were overlaid with a more deliberate set of reactions that we learned to adopt as our own. Avenues of public expression were limited, and these were largely controlled by the educated elite, which had learned its order-making lesson well.

The change started with television, which, by its very nature, is set in relentless and continuous time, leaving little room for reflection. It accelerated the forces of consumption, which make us more impulsive in character, thanks to the barrage of advertising that we were subjected to.

The internet brings a change of another order of magnitude. At one level, it speaks to our learned selves and offers us more room for expression. We are connected to diverse cultures; we can delve into any subject with great depth; indeed, it has made knowledge more accessible than it has ever been in the past. It has also accelerated the process of individualizing us. Each one of us has a personal relationship with the outside world, thanks to digital devices.

But its deeper impact is that it speaks effortlessly to our instinctive side. Because it is instant, offers interaction, is networked, and provides anonymity, it allows us to express what is on the outermost surface of our minds. We react impulsively, confident in the knowledge that we are at the centre of our own personal universe. Unlike most technologies of the past, it makes us revert to who we are at our most impulsive. All the learning that had gradually accumulated and guided us towards a certain world view and a set of actions is being overrun by something far more powerful and primal. Those in power, in particular, have been emboldened to become unapologetic about staying in power. Caucasians, men, people from the upper caste, the wealthy, the autocratic, and those from majority religions are all asserting their right to keep the world as it is.

The Trump phenomenon is a classic case in point. It is almost a testament to how far the strong can go to protect their fiefdoms. Here we have a person who lies, cheats, has been convicted of sexually assaulting a woman, incited a revolt against the state, and is, in every way, in the most visible way possible, a revolting human being. And yet, he has regained the presidency despite all this. All of this simply doesn't matter because he speaks what his constituency sees as a certain truth that connects with them at the instinctive, reptilian level.

What this has meant is that a large proportion of people seem to care less about more abstract ideals like the fairness of democracy, the integrity of institutions, and the upholding of basic social courtesies, even whether something is factual or not. On an everyday level, everything is available to us at our fingertips, quite literally. In a touchscreen-navigating world, every whim is indeed a command.

And this is just the beginning. The idea of the factual has already collapsed, and rapidly improving deepfake technology will further erase the distinction between what is real and what is not. AI, which presents itself as an omnipotent force, will lead us in ways we will have little control over. Already, the algorithm is able to discern what impulse really drives us, and it is designed to further exploit that. Paradoxically, it is technology that is taking to us to a more primitive version of society, and we are being swept along.

NO FORMALITY, PLEASE?

As a well-known advertising tagline reminds us, '*Har ghar kuchh kehta hai.*' Every home speaks volumes about its residents. But the carefully curated home, with every piece chosen to bring alive the spirit that animates the dwellers of the home, is a relatively recent phenomenon. In large parts of India even now, and certainly in the past, the home was a place where the self sagged, the body flopped, into something worn and comfortable, where rooms came without territorial claims, and space had a fluid quality that could miraculously accommodate many more than what physics would decree.

Travelling across the country, it is common to come across homes that do not believe in dividing space up by function. Barring the showcase, that little space in the drawing room devoted to the perfunctory performance of formality, made up of curios collected from here and there. The home is an imprint of one's lived life shorn of any pretensions. You can see refrigerators in the bedroom, have scooters parked in the living room, find large rooms that are nothing more than dumping grounds for accumulated stuff. In this mental model of the home, everything is functional and tells a story about the people living there without trying to.

Today's formal home is built on a sense of self that is acutely self-aware. We are constantly conscious of how we appear to others, and our actions are imbued with a relentless need to come through to others as we like to imagine ourselves. Equally, the sense of individuality of each member of the household has grown to a point where the erstwhile fluidity of the home is insufficient to manage the expectations that individuals have of themselves. Individuals need their personal space, room they call their own.

The formality extends to many other aspects of our social life. We no longer drop in unannounced on friends and family. The earlier ability to accommodate anyone at the dining table, where impromptu visits always somehow turned into mealtimes, is no longer present, even though many more households have help at home. The shape of our life has become more rigid, its outer boundaries have become more sharply defined. Convenience is now of paramount importance, and we are mindful first of our own, and then of others on whose hospitality we are careful not to impose.

Visiting friends now has an elaborate air of ceremony about it, when viewed from the lens of an earlier time. We need to fix up the visit well in advance, and in many sections of society, we cannot go empty-handed, so flowers, a bottle of wine, some gift for the house, a cooked dish, is now seen as de rigueur. And then, of course, there is the mandatory thank-you text that is sent the day after.

The marriage invitation is now an Eastmancolor production, with invitations from the more affluent becoming minor tourist attractions in the neighbourhood. Even the more functional WhatsApp invitation is now an elaborate affair; an audio-visual presentation set to background music. The marriage itself, of course, is a series of discrete events, each with its own theme, menu and dress code. The idea of a dress code for a wedding would seem ridiculous given that we wear costumes and not clothes to weddings – there already was a well-established dress code in place. But that is apparently not enough.

At one level, it is a loss when we can no longer take each other for granted. Should daughters have to tell parents how they feel about them? Should parents constantly feel the need to reassure their kids that they love them? Should there be a need to celebrate events like Father's Day and Mother's Day? Should friends not be able to land up at each other's places simply because they feel like doing so?

There is a reason why formality exists in the world. There are occasions where we feel the need to stand outside our raw unfinished selves and don an appearance – one that acknowledges the importance of the context. We dress consciously for an important office meeting, a wedding, we write in an unnaturally officious way when communicating with our superiors, we speak in a language far removed from the everyday when we make a presentation. The formal is a way of affirming the power of the institution, whether it is the workplace, marriage, or a social event.

The modern rituals that have evolved around relationships have, at their heart, a deep understanding of how important these relationships are. As the way in which we lead our lives changes, and as work, technology, distances, a growing sense of individuality combine to put pressure on once unselfconscious relationships, the new rituals try and ensure that we continue to communicate more overtly and with greater frequency how we really feel. Like many rituals, often the gesture is an act of tokenism, we do not always feel what we communicate, but this has always been true even otherwise. Relationships of all kinds are built on the bedrock of small hypocrisies.

We express things more formally today because we are anxious that unless we do so, we will lose what it is that we are trying to preserve. Unless friendship is underlined with formal gestures of closeness and gratitude, it is feared that it will not have the strength to sustain itself.

It is interesting that we think of the modern as a time that does away with the meaningless rituals of the past. But what we have done is to replace one set of rituals with another. The marriage ceremony may have been shortened, but in the name of celebration the rituals of marriage have multiplied. It is common, in north India, for people to say, 'No formality, please,' as a way of demonstrating the closeness of a relationship. It is interesting that we try and communicate the same sense of closeness through acts of formality.

FRISKY AT SIXTY

IT IS PROBABLY NOT WIDESPREAD enough to be called a trend, but one has noticed, in one's immediate circle, the rising tendency of sixty-plus women to refer to themselves as 'girls'. Along with this, there is a rise in all-women groups who travel together, go out for boisterous evenings, hold kitty parties with loud enthusiasm, and generally behave in a way unimaginable for an earlier generation.

Historically, in India, girls became women far too quickly (while men stayed boys all their lives), and therefore the reclaiming of this label at an age where one probably has grandchildren who are girls is interesting. In earlier times, too, all-women gatherings were not uncommon, with 'ladies clubs' (populated by many Mrs So-and-Sos) being the staple form in which these took place. But there was an air of studied propriety about these, a determined effort to play the role of responsible, mature women. The kitty party signalled the loosening of this restraint, but it is only recently that even these have become more relaxed, with the odd group deciding that alcohol is a necessary ingredient for such get-togethers.

Of course, this shift is not limited to women alone. It is no secret that the senior citizen today does not take their seniority too seriously. There is a stubborn refusal to fade gracefully away into the background and an airy dismissal of the idea that they take to pursuits suitable to their age (religion, tending to grandkids, joining laughter clubs, providing guidance on rituals).

It is true that men have always had the cultural licence to be boys and have always managed to find some outlets for this part of themselves. Whether it was making their workplace a boys' club, where they could shed their donned personae, or in the nudge-nudge-wink-wink trip to Bangkok under the pretence of an offsite, they could, in addition to fulfilling their responsibilities as householders, express their more uninhibited sides. But once they retired, even they were expected to turn appropriately geriatric.

The reasons for the changes we are seeing are many. This is the first generation that has a reasonable number of retirees with an economic surplus, and it shows in the way they imagine and live their lives. For many, their children are settled and self-sufficient, which means that financially, their responsibilities have been reduced.

In an earlier time, retirement was an anxiety-inducing event. For those in service who derived so much of their sense of self from their designation, retiring was like a steep fall into ordinariness. For those in business, handing over the baton to the next generation created feelings of insecurity and irrelevance. One's youth and middle age are noisy times, full of the cacophony of work and family responsibilities. Even holidays that are taken are desperate attempts to escape into a short-lived sanctuary, and even these are often tainted by the sound of the mobile phone ringing at inopportune times. Financially, too, there was a dread of being dependent on one's children, and the prospect of facing neglect at the hands of the next generation was all too real.

And while these concerns continue for a large part of India, there is a section that has managed to free itself from the onerous responsibility towards others and is able to focus on themselves. There is a strong recognition that after sixty, the overhang of mortality feels more palpable, and while medical science has prolonged lifespans, it offers no certainties about who wins the longevity lottery. In any case, the real need that is felt is not necessarily longevity, but rather a kind of agelessness. So, for many people, their sixties and seventies turn out to be the best periods of their lives.

An enabling factor is the better levels of fitness that we see in the older generation today. There is much greater consciousness about health, exercise, and diet that allows older people to remain active until a much later age. It is not uncommon to see retirees take to physical activities with enthusiasm. There are friends who have started running marathons and going on treks after crossing fifty.

Which is why travel is the biggest pursuit of this cohort. The effort here is not just to visit distant places but to put distance between their previous lives and their new ones, to explore not just new lands but new sides of themselves. Bucket lists are made and ticked off, and, depending on one's pocket, trips, both domestic and international, are eagerly availed of.

The biggest difference, however, comes from the mindset. Earlier, notions of age-appropriate behaviour were consonant with the inevitable decline of one's physical and mental faculties with time. A lifespan was seen to have a rhythm, a rise and fall that was embraced rather than denied. As one aged, one's looks became less important, and one's concerns turned inward, first towards the family and then towards more spiritual activities. Ageing was a process by which we gradually extracted ourselves from our lives, fading into the collective label of the elderly, until we were ready to go.

One could argue that there was wisdom in this and that it represented a more mature outlook towards death. The current obsession with longevity often succeeds in prolonging death rather than life, as we use medical science to keep ourselves alive without really having a life to live.

The change that has happened is unlikely to be rolled back because almost all the reasons why we embraced the older mental model of ageing are being dismantled. Several youth-extending technologies have come to the aid of this group, Viagra not being the least of them. With the world revolving around the individual, it has become increasingly legitimate to focus on extracting every bit of pleasure and meaning from one's life. Mortality, of course, lies waiting. But the sixty-somethings of today are not just alive; they are kicking.

TRADITION AS HABIT?

WHEN A MEMBER OF OUR staff lost his ninety-year-old mother, then as per tradition, he shaved off his hair and undertook to stay off milk or any dairy product for a year. This was a truncated observance of the original rituals, which involved, among other things, walking barefoot for a year. The change in the tradition happened organically as it became impossible to follow its rigours, so a practical accommodation was made, as is the case with several traditions.

When we regard traditions in today's day and age with a contemporary lens, it is usually with some suspicion. This is understandable, for in the name of the past, we can justify many practices that are impractical and, more importantly, regressive. The operating assumptions governing society have changed, and to fight against the organic evolution of norms in the name of tradition can be stifling and constraining. This is true of many traditions, but particularly those that involve the role of women. Social customs of an era tend to support the dominant power structures of that time, and a mindless insistence on continuing these in the name of tradition can mean the perpetuation of these power imbalances.

That being said, the truth is that human beings need tradition. We need to be reminded that we are part of a continuous chain of life, that our overinvestment in the idea of being individuals does not blind us to the fact that we are small links in a large, interconnected chain. We are born out of life, not just into it, and life will go on well after we are gone. We need to mark extraordinary events like birth, death, and marriage with a special kind of awareness that everyday life does not provide us with. We need to acknowledge their significance and remind ourselves that we are part of something much larger, something that gives our lives shape and meaning.

Tradition is the temporal representation of continuous time. It translates this abstract idea into lived reality. It is only by practising something that visibly does not belong to the present and which has been practised by generations before ours, that we are able to experience some sense of being connected with the past. To be modern and to be only modern is to be suspended terrifyingly in an unmarked landscape with no familiar features.

And yet, it is common to think of tradition as something vestigial that holds us back from moving ahead. We value the new and the ever changing, we breathlessly ask what the future might bring. The past is seen either as a chain or cast in an idealized mythic form to support a political project. Our relationship with tradition is becoming more self-conscious, either by way of becoming more contentious or more performative.

There is a modern tendency to overvalue other people's traditions and undervalue one's own. The traditions of an exotic other define their uniqueness and must be preserved while one's own traditions are regarded as being less defining of who we are.

But we can never really escape tradition. We might trade one kind for another but the idea of following a routine that we invest with meaning above the ordinary is a deeply ingrained one. We make traditions as easily as we disregard them. Every family constructs its own little traditions, be it a made-for-Facebook Diwali puja or an annual family reunion at an exotic location. The traditions we make may not survive time, but they serve the same function as those we confer with cultural value.

The difference between routine, ritual and tradition is a matter of time and meaning. Routines provide comfort but are a trifle shy on meaning, whereas rituals have meaning embedded in them even if that is not always apparent. Rituals are often followed without full or even partial awareness of their origins and meaning, but the sense of continuity that they provide does not depend on that.

There is an inert part of tradition that allows us to follow it without really knowing what it is that one is following. Take the example of weddings. Unlike the Western world, where marriage vows are increasingly deliberately crafted and consciously taken, in India, few have any idea what the wedding mantras that are invoked mean. The vows are implicit in our understanding of the institution of marriage. While modern priests do give a little sermon on the meaning of marriage, this is usually lost in the cacophony that surrounds a modern Indian wedding.

Everything about the wedding today is a modern retelling of tradition, but importantly, there is little desire to move from tradition as an anchor. The ceremony might be compressed into an attention-span-friendly duration, the bride might wear Aviator glasses and have her own 'baraat', but the ritual of the 'baraat' isn't going anywhere. We need the familiar flagstones of the past to travel in the present in our own way. The comfort of being cocooned in some version of tradition is a source of great comfort.

Is this a kind of hypocrisy, this playing tradition-tradition even as we hollow out its intent? Or is this what tradition is meant to be, an ever-evolving part of our lives that anchors us without limiting our choices? However much it may have changed, the wedding today is essentially a celebration of tradition, no matter how progressive the people who participate in it may regard themselves to be.

The larger issue is that we think of the modern not as the outer skin of time, but as time itself. Implicitly, by locating ourselves in the now, the only connection we have with time is our possible future rather than our already lived past. The fact that we will, in the fullness of time, be nothing but tradition is lost on a world that is obsessed with enacting modernity. We are constructing tradition every single day even as we believe that we are dismantling it.

CHAPTER 3

Modes of Living

The Recreational Body

The body is our primary asset, and it is being imagined and used in ever-newer ways. What was once done because it was necessary is now curated as lifestyle.

India has a new, more layered relationship with food, health, holidays, and the body – where khichdi becomes a comfort statement and the gym selfie acts as a calling card. Consumption becomes self-expression; leisure becomes labour.

AN ENEMY CALLED FOOD?

W HEN DID FOOD BECOME AN enemy? As a generation that grew up in times of constraints, in childhood we did not get to eat all the indulgent things we lusted after because we couldn't afford the good stuff. Today, we can afford to eat what we want, but are no longer allowed to do so, most often by an annoying voice in our head that seems to know more than what is good for it. If we do give in and indulge, we are extremely hard on ourselves and feel pangs of guilt that rob us of whatever little pleasure we had eked out.

We now think of food as a perpetual suspect, and every morsel that we put into our mouths needs to have its Aadhar card verified. In a single generation, food has gone from unconditional friend to malevolent foe, always out to thicken our arteries, weaken our immune system and contaminate our bodies in general.

In an earlier time, food was thought of in aggregate terms. A full meal needed all elements, and fresh home-cooked food was, by definition, good. We ate what was in season, because that was all that was available, we ate when we were hungry, and ate as much as our stomachs could hold (not always true). Measurement was frowned upon, recipes were not precise, the idea of calories was unheard of, let alone notions like glycaemic index, and the relentlessly cruel body mass index. In our home, counting how many chapatis we ate was not permitted. Health was an ideal, but one that was at ease with the approximate. All of us were broadly healthy; occasionally, the balance between the elements got disturbed, which needed to get realigned again. Disease was the exception, but it was part of life.

The idea of food today has become atomized into a never-ending array of labels. The idea of breaking food into its component parts and then finding a variety of ways to describe these parts has created a new vocabulary of anxiety. As food has become detached from its origins, and as every meal becomes a question to be answered anew, we are losing our instincts about food, the stuff that we are made up of, and regard it with the air of a sceptic.

Even in its pleasurable form, food must deliver on several fronts. For one, it must be *presented* in order to stimulate the taste buds. This is surely a First World view of food – for people who eat without ever getting hungry, food has to advertise itself and coax the salivary glands to perform. When one does not trust food in its natural form or does not need it viscerally enough, only then can the aesthetics of presentation assume such importance. Even otherwise, the pleasure in eating is increasingly getting located in the idea of food rather than in food itself. Where was it grown, under what circumstances, how authentic is it, how experimental, who cooked it, how is it served, what is the ambience of the place where one eats, what is the service experience like – these factors assume ever greater importance.

The mental model of food has shifted dramatically. At its core, food is effectively a way of redistributing the energy of the sun in order to keep life going. Plants draw sustenance from it, which, in turn, gets passed on to the animals who feed on them, and then to other animals who feed on their animal prey. Into this cycle what gets added is culture, as every group defines its own energy vehicles in its own terms. Food is local, just as the need it satisfies is a universal truth shared by all forms of life. No other animal interrogates the food it consumes.

From being where we come from and who we essentially are, food is now an external agent that infiltrates our body, to do good and bad. What is forgotten is that food is an intrinsic part of who we are. The human body produces food; mothers feed their babies with the produce of their own bodies. The externalizing of food is a part of the process by which we alienate our bodies from the world in which they reside. It is an act of withdrawal;

a refusal to allow the body to exist in an unselfconscious way within the ecosystem in which it belongs.

Where does this come from? Part of the problem comes from the surfeit of processed food that is now part of our lives. Industrially produced food walks away from the interdependent ecosystem that produced food. The combination of human labour, traditional knowledge fine-tuned over millennia, a sense of time and place, and the emotional embrace of the nurturer is lost. What replaces it is a concentrated amplification of pleasure notes in food. What we get is an enactment of food, a simulated spectacle mounted to drive us into consuming more. Food no longer comes with presumed good intentions, and that destabilizes our view of it.

But other factors seem to be at work too, which make us regard food, even what we cook at home, with greater suspicion. Is it a form of consumption guilt, the price that we extract from ourselves for living a life devoted to pleasure? Is it a heightened form of narcissism, one in which we believe so much in our own preciousness that the food we eat, and which gives us sustenance, needs to pass an entrance exam before being consumed?

We are also seeing a pushback on this dominant view of food. Newer sets of doctors and nutritionists are arguing for a more commonsensical view of food – the idea that we should trust tradition and time, and that we should think of food not as a foreign object but as the building block of our physical, emotional and cultural selves. We think far too much about food, and far too little of it.

THE FAMILY HOLIDAY THEN AND NOW

COME SUMMER VACATION TIME, AND social media is full of people wearing Bermudas grinning at us as they sip something lurid in some place exotic. Vacation snaps are to social media what showcases are to middle-class drawing rooms – pictorial windows that give others a glimpse of the best parts of their lives, spent lolling about on the beaches of Bali or the sidewalks of Rome.

Competitive holidaying is a bruising contact sport, and nothing makes us happier than making other people miserable about our happiness. Of course, holiday photographs make all happiness generic – it is impossible to distinguish one family or location from another. Everyone becomes the same person on holiday, or so it would seem.

In some cases, this particular property of holiday photographs can be quite revealing. Many traditional families on holiday present a completely different picture from what they do in normal everyday life. Traditional roles get relaxed, the clothes get way more daring, and sometimes, altogether different people emerge from under their everyday selves. People travel not merely to reach somewhere else, but to also become someone else. It is difficult to tell what is being enacted – the holiday persona or the person one pretends to be in regular life.

The idea of the holiday has begun to take on dimensions of a giant project. Every year needs to feel different, not just from previous years but from the holidays other people might be planning. The idea of a week- or ten-day-long period packed with superlatives makes the holiday less like a pause and more like an accelerated and anxious affirmation of enjoyment. We must have so much fun, and it must look like we are having so much fun, especially on social media. From the free welcome drink to a free day at the spa, every element in the holiday counts.

The holiday has evolved considerably over time. Growing up, holidays had a rudimentary quality – they were meant to plug us back to our roots, and recharge the connections that made us who we were. Every year, one headed to one's hometown, after having reserved the train months in advance. Nothing much happened in one's hometown; indeed, most hometowns were designed to be that way, but it was still a wonderful time spent in the bosom of a bewilderingly large family. The holiday month (or even two) started slowly, droned by for a while and then galloped alarmingly as it was time to go back to one's primary life.

There were other kinds of holidays that were permitted; the pilgrimage being the most legitimate. Families travelled together, carrying bundles of many kinds, and a lot of shouting in the name of organizing took place. Pilgrimage travel made the idea of budget holidays feel lavish, and between dharamshalas, dormitories and cramped houses of really obscure acquaintances, there was little scope to spend money. Occasionally, one could also go to a hill station to walk up and down mall road and get one's photograph taken while wearing a 'traditional hill costume', which someone from Garhwal would have killed themselves before wearing.

Then there were the package tours, with an impossibly large number of destinations being crammed together to deliver a feeling of value for money. The south Indian temple tour was a staple, and as a child, the idea of being lugged across from town to town to wade through enormous crowds to visit what at the time seemed like the exact same temple was hardly a treat. In retrospect, the worst tours were the ones where large families were packed into the Matador, a vehicle designed as an orientation programme for hell. A virtually windowless metal box that disdained the idea of suspension, the Matador could take in an infinite number of people, simply by always being able to accommodate one extra person. Breathing was optional.

The Maruti changed holidays for good. This was a new luxury, this ability to jump into a car, which, in turn, darted on to the road and took us where we wished to go, led by the merest whisper of an intention. Our life began to have a radius; in our case up to ten hours in a day. The freedom that the Maruti brought was unparalleled; the idea of a zippy, reliable, affordable car made travel feel like an imperative.

It is only post liberalization and the relaxing of the foreign-exchange norms that international travel began in any real sense. It began with a somewhat narrow focus on shopping and a particular kind of sub-culture popular in some specific streets of Bangkok. Flying to Thailand was cheaper than flying between Delhi and Chennai, and full use was made of this startling anomaly.

For those born after the 1980s, it might be difficult to explain the lure of the foreign to the Indian mind. In Gujarat, for instance, newspaper ads were routinely taken out to welcome back someone from an international sojourn, or to bid them farewell. Massive groups would travel to Mumbai to see a departing relative off or to receive them. Among the three things that one asked astrologers, 'the chance of foreign travel' was bound to be one. Getting phoren Wrangler's jeans, even ones that did not fit, was as exciting as 'fir meri ungli uski ungli se chhu gayi'. The idea of being able to settle abroad was, and continues to be, a fantasy even today in many parts of the country. The ability to go abroad for a holiday, just like that, thus strikes a very resonant chord.

The holiday serves many purposes. It detaches us from a life that seems to consume us with its rhythm. It allows families, separated by goals and technology, to come together for a while. It allows us to live out our fantasies in a concentrated manner. It helps us find aspects to ourselves that we didn't know existed. It also helps us show the world how splendid our life is. It stints on its most basic ingredient, time, and fills up what little is retained by an overriding compulsion to have fun. The holiday of today makes us work at having fun, and we have the pictures to prove it.

NEW TALES OF THE KITCHEN

THERE IS A NEW KIND of kitchen in town. It has no doors. It blends seamlessly into the living room and looks as if it is an integral part of the decor of the house. All the surfaces gleam, cupboards are flawlessly choreographed in matte unison, and taps gleam with manic pride. The ingredients are all tucked in, and a modern electric chimney tries valiantly to gobble up the smoke that cooking regrettably throws up. The process of cooking looks painless, fun even – young couples toss salad into a bowl while blending smoothies and chatting with trendy friends who drape themselves all over the living-room furniture.

Or so it would seem, given the rapid emergence of the concept of the open kitchen that a lot of homes seem to be embracing. At one level, it feels violently impractical given the unholy mess that putting up a delicious Indian meal inevitably leaves in its wake. There is also the sneaking suspicion that this trend is fuelled more by the real estate developer's desire to save space than any demand from the consumer. In any case, the idea of assailing guests with the sights and smells of the entrails of the cooking process is not a pleasant one.

In an earlier time, the kitchen was the emotional centre of the home, the place where all the action took place. The women gravitated towards the kitchen, the beating heart of the home. The sense of home came from the kitchen and its products – the proverbial 'ma ke haath ka khana' being made here. Gender roles were absolutely clear: it was the role of women to mount all household meals, no matter what the size of the family.

In an essay exploring the need for imagining theatre differently in India as against the West, Girish Karnad argued that while the living room was the setting in a lot of Western plays, in India that made no sense, for here it was an empty space, mounted for public display. The real action, he averred, was in the kitchen, where emotions were on the boil.

The open kitchen may have its disadvantages, but it is an important sign of change. While it is easy to dismiss this trend as one borrowed from images stolen from Western popular culture, the fact that so many people find it desirable says something. At a symbolic level, it indicates a desire to extricate oneself from the consuming cocoon that was the kitchen. It points to the fact that cooking at home has lost some of the sanctity associated with it. Home-cooked food, 'ghar ka khana', is now only one of the options available in a home.

This change has been some years in coming. First, food moved from the floor to the table, which was significant in many ways. It was accompanied by a general distancing of food from its natural origins. The 'standing kitchen' was the counterpart to the dining table, both testifying to the adoption of a culturally alien idea of eating.

Turning the raw into the cooked is an act of culture, of the application of a specific set of technologies and protocols to raw ingredients, and the kitchen has always been the home's little culture factory. In an earlier era, the kitchen was awash with the sights and smells of what went into cooking. Smoke was a defining part of the kitchen, and there was no mistaking the fact that it was a site where active manufacturing was taking place.

The other shift has been from the past to the present, from food being part of our inner lives to being both a product and an expression of our outer selves. I grew up at a time when food was tradition, where recipes were handed down from generations, with each generation adapting it marginally to keep up with the times. Learning to cook was about journeying inward in an organic, almost effortless way. Today, cooking is more about being connected to the outside world, way beyond the cultural imprint of the familiar. Cooking shows, recipe books, blogs, and YouTube instructions have made it much easier for cooking to venture outward. If, yesterday, food was home, today, it is travel.

And the kitchen today is proof of that. In its new, almost antiseptic order, we see an attempt to erase signs of the effort that goes into cooking. The very fact that a modular kitchen can be 'installed' in the home is a remarkable development. The idea that something that otherwise came into being in a gradual organic manner, gathering bits of many pasts into its present, can be summarily replaced by a brand-new installation with no trace of history is truly a sign of dramatically changed times.

Food habits have transformed, too. The family is far more receptive to shorter, snack-like meals, and the availability and growing social legitimacy of the option of ordering in has eased the burden that daily cooking could impose on the homemaker. For some, cooking has become a source of pleasure and discovery and is seen as a worthwhile way to expand one's horizons. Many more cuisines are being tried at home, exotic new ingredients are becoming far more commonplace, and new formats of food are being eagerly embraced.

The responsibility for cooking is also beginning to broaden. As more women work outside the home and as more men begin to take an interest in cooking, there is some change in the stereotypical roles assigned to the genders. It would be unwise to overstate the extent to which this change is occurring, but there is undeniably some movement on this front.

There are parts of the world where the kitchen is no longer a part of the design of new homes, as young couples live off food deliveries, but there is no danger of that happening any time soon in India. With all its changes, home in India continues to be where the hearth is.

EATING OUT AT HOME?

Could there be homes in the future without a kitchen? It is already happening in some parts of the world. In particular, young couples who lead busy and often asynchronous lives feel no need to use precious space for a full-blown kitchen, making do instead with a small pantry. They eat out very often and order in the rest of the time. The idea of buying all the paraphernalia that goes into a kitchen and then devoting a significant amount of time and attention to the task of dreaming up menus every day and cooking the meal and cleaning up thereafter feels like too much work.

Even for those who are not contemplating such a drastic move, thanks to the ease of ordering food in, the centrality of cooking at home has receded just a little bit. Food delivery apps today allow us to order in from a vast variety of culinary options, and it takes less time to get a gourmet meal delivered than cooking even a simple one at home. In times of lockdowns, of course, the utility of being able to order in became even more valuable.

The loosening of the grip that the idea of home-cooked food – 'ghar ka khana' – has on the Indian imagination is a seminal shift that needs to be fully understood. Home-cooked food enjoys a strong cultural cachet, being attributed with qualities of freshness, nutritional value, and, above all, with the transference of love from the homemaker to the family. Traditionally, the lines between home-cooked food and the food available outside were sharply etched. The latter could only be an occasional indulgence and was never viewed with anything less than suspicion. Besides, eating a meal together was an affirmation of the idea of home itself – home was where the hearth was. The idea of a mother cooking and serving hot food to the rest of the family became, for many, an emotional signature that captured the essence of being home. Mothers believed that all problems could be solved with food, and, for the most part, we were happy to go along with that notion. To be fair, schizophrenic emotions are associated with 'ghar ka khana' – yearned for when unavailable and spurned whilst living at home. With food delivery apps, at least for those at home, there is always an option to get in something from outside. If not an entire meal, then at least an item number that adds pizzazz to an otherwise predictable meal. A new intermediate category has now been introduced between 'ghar ka khana' and 'bahar ka khana'; we now have 'bahar ka khana' ordered in at home. Interestingly, for those living away from home, we have also started seeing the reverse – 'ghar-type khana' available for ordering in.

The sanctity of families eating together has, in any case, been rudely disturbed by screens of all description. More and more families find themselves eating separately in front of their own chosen devices. Air-conditioners have driven people into the comfort of their rooms, further hastening the dismantling of the idea of a common shared meal where the family comes together and discusses matters small and big. Even when the family gets together for a meal, most often individuals continue to dwell in their private mobile universe, marking their perfunctory presence with occasional grunts.

Food delivery also changes our relationship with food. The idea of every meal as a distinct entity that needs to be curated, creates a higher level of expectation from food. A meal does not merely provide sustenance, it must excite us in more ways. Being able to order in widens the range of choices, increases exposure to newer forms of food from the comfort and cultural safety of home, making everyday meals an elective choice. The cloud kitchen has created a standardized range of options to order, no matter where you might live.

Geography has become less important, transforming the idea of going out. Places with food signatures continue to maintain their attractiveness, but over time the very idea of place can get diffused. If one can order a Chandni Chowk specialty sitting at home, sometimes even if that happens to be in Bangalore, then what sustains the magic and mystique of a food destination? In a more fundamental way, given the highly diverse dietary habits in the country, where the cuisine famously changes every 100 kilometres, this comfort of ordering 'outside' food in can, over time, change food habits. Restaurants in many parts of the country lean towards offering exotic non-local fare and are thus likely to nudge behaviour away from dishes cooked at home. But is food really ever only about eating? For many, the experience of eating in is nowhere near that of eating out even if it is the same food from the same restaurant. Similarly, the joy of eating home-cooked food has less to do with the taste of the food and more to do with the need for a stable rhythm in one's life.

The idea of the hearth, the 'chulha', is central to our imagination of a home and this is unlikely to change in a hurry. Just as important is the idea of going out. We need to have an inside and an outside in our lives, and we need these to be coded differently. We need to wear different clothes for different occasions, and mark both time and place with particular kind of foods. In that sense, however easy it might have become to order whatever one fancies from home, the emotional needs served by both ideas do not disappear.

The idea of 'ghar ka khana' remains, even if we eat less often at home. 'Ghar ka khana' gives us the emotional reassurance that the world continues to be round and that we are smack in the middle of it and that however far we might have strayed, a return to the origin is a mouthful of 'ghar ka khana' away. That being said, what are we ordering for dinner today? And from where?

THE QUIET CHARMS OF KHICHDI

Some time ago, there was a proposal that khichdi be named the national dish of India. That did not come to pass, but regardless of whether khichdi deserves that title or not, and glossing over the question of whether, in a country like ours, any one dish can or should be classified as such, it certainly gives us an occasion to talk about something that has been a significant part of most of our lives.

The sniffy comments about this simple dish made by assorted food snobs tell one part of the story. The experts on health and culinary tradition have other stories to tell. But as someone who has grown up relishing khichdi, what follows is a very personal tribute to this humble dish.

The simplest possible combination of the two major food groups, khichdi is food at its comforting best. A hot meal of khichdi shushes the senses, evens out temperamental stomachs, and satiates without leaving any residue behind; khichdi burps taste of nothing.

My memories of khichdi are many. In our Gujarati household – and we lived outside the state most of the time – khichdi was most commonly our Sunday lunch. It was a meal that was looked forward to with quiet pleasure; it had a wholesome quality that made for hearty satisfaction.

The consistency that was most preferred was wet without it becoming runny, with grains just a little bit squished up. Ghee was poured in generous quantities; as children it was fun to make a mound of the khichdi, dig a little hole in the centre, and fill it up with ghee. Into this mixture went some spiced potatoes, a special jeera-clad onion salad, chaas, papad, and some mango pickle. Or, as the Hindi saying goes, khichdi ke chaar yaar – dahi, ghee, papad aur achaar. Together, this unfussy confluence of simple tastes came together week after week in a very precise way.

The masterful simplicity of each ingredient in the meal bears reflection. Rice, dal with almost no spices, cooked without ceremony. Unlike the idea of khichdi as mishmash (*'kya khichdi paka rahe ho?'*), an ungainly dumping together of disparate ingredients, the reality of it was the wordless harmony that existed between the two major food sects.

Khichdi blended rice and dal together as if they belonged. Ghee, which makes the world feel plumper, adding a rich emulsion of pleasure to anything it is poured on, accentuated the bland fullness of the taste. Potatoes, that staple filler of blank spaces with several kinds of awesomeness, cooked with mustard seeds and left dry. Papad, the provider of crunchy service on demand, the attendant always ready to confer its crackle on a meal. Pickle, the little bite-sized compression of a universe of very expressive flavours, seething naughtily in its own juices. Onion, the simple slice of a food that served as spice, an ingredient that turned any dish slightly sideways, a dash of knowing worldly wisdom added to things bland.

In our house, with khichdi, and only with it, the onion was slathered in oil with jeera and salt sprinkled on it, and it set off the potatoes particularly well. And to top it off, chaas, gentle and kind, making one's stomach, and by extension the world, a calmer place.

In some parts of the country, khichdi is looked down upon as a diet for those convalescing. This makes it the poor cousin of food; the stuff we make do with when our bodies are not quite ready for the real thing. I have never quite understood this view of khichdi, for it passes up on the pleasures of simplicity and confuses it with ordinariness.

The idea that food must always perform, that it must necessarily transport us somewhere else, is a rigid view of its role in our lives. There is a time and place for that, indeed there must be for food is travel, and food is music, but food is also home.

And the thing is, getting simple meals right is not easy. A cup of tea, scrambled eggs, 'nimbu-paani', coconut chutney – these everyday foods are very elusive when it comes to getting proportions just right. Khichdi is no exception, and getting the balance of the ingredients right was both very easy and extremely rare.

With some people, notably mothers, getting khichdi right was effortless, while in other cases, something always seemed a little off. With simple foods, it all comes down to proportion, timing, touch, restraint, love – there is no particular technique or skill involved, nothing dramatic by way of ingredients or presentation. The person cooking works with very little, and does so with instinct, as a habit. Perhaps simple staple foods are nothing but an organic overflow of the person cooking.

Khichdi derives its power from what it is not. It chooses to sidestep the flashy culinary razzle-dazzle, choosing instead to let the taste come to the food, rather than the other way around. There might well be other ways of defending this noble food, perhaps from the perspective of health, perhaps even from the standpoint of culinary heritage, but personally, the truth that khichdi spoke had nothing to do with these. It held things together, it sat in the middle of everything, right at the centre, with no interest in anything that lies at the edges. Khichdi is home, comfort without any reason, taste without any credentials.

The stomach full with a hot meal sleeps easy. We regain an alignment with the world, things slip back into place, afternoon heat settles on us, and our eyes find it no longer useful to stay open. Slipping into khichdi-induced sleep on a hot summer Sunday, under a reluctant fan, to the distant buzz of some insect, life takes on a timeless drone of inevitability. The complex, the layered and the textured can be great, but only the simple can be perfect. For all the excitement that food offers today, a retreat into khichdi-land is an essential antidote to the rigours of the day.

IN CASH WE TRUST

Demonetization came and went, and India's UPI experiment has been a huge success, with even small transactions being paid for digitally, but our fascination with cash is still alive and well.

That demonetization was traumatic is an understatement. When 86 per cent of the currency in circulation becomes illegal virtually overnight, pain is inevitable. Given the cause that was at stake, there were many who looked upon the inconvenience as a necessary price to pay, while others took a less generous view. For the poor, in particular, who had little access to alternative mechanisms of payment, the problem became a particularly difficult one. Even so, the official expectation was that the transitional problems would abate in a while. The government also believed that this would hasten the shift to a cashless economy, making life both easier and more transparent.

We now know that it didn't turn out that way. In the short run, it certainly did make a big difference, largely because there was no option, but with time, the overall cash in circulation has come back to original levels. While the adoption of digital modes of payment has gone up, cash still is king.

And for good reason. Cash in India is not merely a symbolic representation of value. Cash is the idea of value captured and owned. Sitting on a pile of cash gives pleasure both metaphorical and real. Cash is preferred not only by those who have avoided paying taxes; it is the instrument of choice for the country at large.

But there is some value that is placed on the device of currency notes over and above the value that it signifies. With cash, value has a permanent residence; it 'settles down' with its owner, even if its role is to be in a state of constant circulation.

Cash is not merely money in physical form, it changes the way we regard and spend it. It is easier, for instance, to spend money using a credit card, for the outflow seems more theoretical than it does when paying in cash. The difference between Rs 2,000 and 20,000 is a slip of the pen in one case and a complex exercise involving withdrawing money from the bank, carrying it in one's wallet and counting it (twice) before handing it over. The tangibleness of cash is mirrored by the continuing need felt by many for one's passbook to be updated, not on some screen but in the book by pen and ink.

Earning money needs to be signified concretely. Those whose life's earnings are in the form of a few high-value currency notes do not decode demonetization in quite the same way as those used to money in its conceptual form. The idea that it is possible to delegitimize one's life's labour is to shake the foundations on which one's life is constructed. What if some money is not exchanged? What if some paperwork, that bane of those living on the margins, is incomplete? And then, of course, there is the reality of how business works in India. Digital transactions are regrettably traceable while cash roams free. Cash is the lifeblood of vast sections of the economy, including politics. Real estate transactions in India would come to a standstill without cash. The system is so deeply ingrained that nothing can truly work without cash.

India will move away from cash, but the move will be gradual. The talk of 'cashless' is easy, but it ignores that there is a cultural dimension to the physicality of cash. Digital wallets operate on a transfer of intention, where a promise to pay gets converted into an intention to buy. For this to work at scale, one needs to have become comfortable with the idea of surplus and develop the confidence that money will come without having to struggle or think about it all the time. One needs to develop trust in institutions, in a context where the evidence around is overwhelmingly to the contrary. Even in e-commerce, the innovation that unlocked the market was Cash On Delivery, for there still exists great anxiety about thinking of money in terms of a flicker of intention. Cash gives the individual control over value, it allows a transaction to sigh with satisfaction as it gets completed.

To convert one's worth into worthlessness, even if for a small period, is to make everyone nervous. Psychologically, money works on a convention of mutual deception. We agree to call something money, and that is good enough. But to have the thinness of this convention exposed in such a way is to cause great anxiety.

To cut off 86 per cent of one's currency even for a few days is akin to cutting off water or petrol. And unlike water and petrol, the reintroduction of currency cannot happen overnight. Apart from all the other arguments in favour of and against this move, what needs to be acknowledged is that it caused an undercurrent of tentativeness, one that burrows itself deep in the cultural marrow of this country. Since there is little palpable sign of how much black money exists, the success of this move would always have been invisible. The uncertainty, however, might linger. Nobody wants to fight for what is already theirs. It is almost like having to re-earn what one has already laboured to earn.

Actions of this kind can never be neat. Transient untidiness can be forgotten, but the unease that it potentially creates is deeper than mere inconvenience. Demand may not automatically go back to normal levels. The idea of economic progress is not statistical but experiential, and in that sense creating uncertainty about money might produce the unintended effect of unsettling people – in a way that alters their sense of economic well-being. In a market economy, money is the measure of everything, and once the measure itself becomes wobbly, one's entire world shivers.

THOSE IN AIR-CONDITIONED CABINS

OVER THE COURSE OF A single generation, a huge swathe of the Indian middle class has embraced air-conditioning. We find ACs in our offices, cars and bedrooms. It has become a regular, fairly commonplace part of the lives of this segment of society. Even so, when one is criticized for being removed from ground realities, one is somehow always believed to be 'sitting in an air-conditioned cabin'. Access to air-conditioning appears to make any opinion fluffy; a product of the ivory-tower la-la land that one clearly resides in.

Air-conditioning is often used as the primary descriptor of elite detachedness and of a form of ignorance that is, in the main, ignorant about itself.

At one level, air-conditioning is potentially a sign of civilization – of rising above the biological, of cultivating the ability to not react immediately to one's physical surroundings. It brings alive the idea of being cool, detached from one's life – not getting caught up in the heat of the moment. But equally, the express purpose of air-conditioning is to render a person oblivious to a primary experience of reality.

In a country like India, it is, in many ways, the most articulate symbol of the class divide that exists in the country. Social divisions take many, often complex, forms but class and the mindset that it engenders is quite accurately captured by access to the ability to regulate the temperature for one's comfort.

Historically, air-conditioning was truly an elitist idea. Growing up, it felt a little bit like magic, available only to the truly well-heeled, and visible largely in films, where men in dressing gowns had heart attacks. I had an uncle who worked in a multinational company at that time, and although not given to wearing dressing gowns (and having heart attacks at the top of a spiral staircase), he did live in a bungalow whose bedroom featured an air-conditioner. Sneaking up to that room and feeling the divine luxury of a cool white bedsheet was as close to the idea of heaven as was possible to imagine. Or, for that matter, walking into an air-conditioned movie theatre (not to be confused with the deceitfully titled air-cooled one, which featured fans that were mounted on side walls so high up that any effect that was produced had more to do with sound than air). The 3 pm show in the middle of summer meant that one could transit from peak heat to an absolutely delicious chill in an instant.

The specialness of the air-conditioner in our cultural imagination is very much a part of our life today, albeit in other forms. Although the AC is now much more widely prevalent in households that think of themselves as middle class, and given that its cost is not that dissimilar to that of a reasonably expensive phone, it is still regarded with a degree of reverence.

The older generation still uses air-conditioning with the utmost restraint, switching it on only for a few hours when truly required. There is still some talk of not giving the children an AC in their room lest 'they get used to it'. Quite clearly, cheating the heat in such a spectacular fashion counts as luxury, whereas the facility provided by other gadgets is valued, but not quite in the same way.

Heat is a sign of life and direct contact with too much life is intimidating. The sun saps the will, sweat melts the resolve and shrivels up all good intentions. It underlines the experience of scarcity, sharpens the sense of deprivation, and makes poverty that much more graphic. In India, there is no larger truth than the sun. The idea of the presumptive desirability of the sun, an idea so prevalent in the West, is meaningless in India. The sun is what one escapes from; it is what shade is for. The ability to render the sun irrelevant is a primal power invested in human hands. This is the work of the gods and is so much more than mere technology.

The greater access to air-conditioning has begun to change our landscape in different ways. Families have become a little more insular with the arrival of air-conditioning. The bedroom door is now shut, the television moves to where the AC is, and as against an earlier time, when the notion of privacy within a home was virtually non-existent, today, rooms have become more closed spaces. Every room becomes a mini ecosystem of its own, with its own ambience and taste. Air-conditioning divides the home into zones with temperature boundaries, and family interactions have become more formally structured.

The idea that air-conditioning has a civilizing effect is not easy to observe in the Indian context. If the driving on the roads is anything to go by, then greater personal comfort has not translated into calmer behaviour. If anything, personal comfort seems to deepen the divide between the self and the other, by instilling a sense of entitlement and privilege. The car AC is the father of road rage. The actions of the other seem incomprehensible as one zips about in cool comfort, the outside seeming even more intolerable. The impatience with the slightest inconvenience seems to be growing; the anger that entitlement unleashes seems paradoxically to be greater than the one that is the product of deprivation.

Lee Kuan Yew once called the air-conditioner the greatest invention of the twentieth century. To the surprise of many, he had identified it as one of the key variables that would help Singapore become a developed nation. One could argue that in Singapore's case, an early emphasis on air-conditioning helped shape its work ethic as well as its 'temperature-controlled' political culture. Technologies can bring about profound changes in the way society and human life are organized. The light bulb erased the difference between night and day and changed the world in more ways than we can imagine. The watch redefined the idea of time and made it a collective imperative. Air-conditioning potentially changes the world in equally fundamental ways. We can see some of these changes begin to unfold in India, but it is early days yet. For now, the criticism that 'sitting in air-conditioned cabins confers on one an insularity' still holds some merit.

THE NEW QUALITY OF WAITING

IT IS TELLING THAT DOCTORS have something called a waiting room. It underlines the fact that when we are made to wait for what feels like hours every time we catch a cold, it is not an accident, but part of a well-designed plan. Time becomes blank in a doctor's waiting room. It starts out with a shape and a sound but as minutes tick on, and the scene around one stabilizes into a form of permanence, time begins to lose definition. It is no longer something we are inside, but something we can observe with a degree of detachment. In the old days, when doctors had clinics that tried to conjure up an image of homeliness, there were a desultory set of magazines that lay around, headlined by a Russian publication called *Sputnik*, daring us to read them. Reading those magazines made time feel even more wretched. Now, of course, as medicine has become corporatized, the cozy sitting rooms of yore have given way to large halls, which have television sets that are almost always tuned to some obscure news channel that is determined to make us unhappy about something.

In some government hospitals, waiting is never idle. In places that do not have a formal system of queues (and even in places that do), one is always at war with other patients, either trying to break the queue through acts of artifice and even bribery, or to prevent others from doing so. Waiting here is a stressful event, for one can never let one's guard down. In India, this kind of waiting is quite normal, given that there are always ways of cutting the queue, whether at an airport, ration shop or railway reservation counter, and one toggles freely between trying to do so oneself and hating anyone else who tries to do the same.

Waiting, which would seem to be a state of blankness, bland and empty, is far from being so. Every different form of waiting comes with its own timbre, firing its own set of neurons in our brains. Desultory waiting, anxious waiting, hopeless waiting, excited waiting. Waiting for a flight. Waiting in a flight. Waiting in a traffic jam. Waiting at a level crossing. Waiting for the flight to land. Waiting to cross immigration. Waiting for a class to end. Waiting for food to get delivered. Waiting in a queue. For a film ticket that might at any time become unavailable. For a computer to boot. For the phone to ring. For the result to appear on the website.

When we wait, time has a way of losing its apparent objectivity. Subjective time is full of caprice, behaving differently at different times. It drips. It sits still. It stretches. It yawns in slow motion. It stutters. It curves. It expands. It vanishes, rolling up into a ball. The clock hand resigns. Time ceases to matter. One lives in a time-free zone.

Waiting becomes easier when time is accompanied by activity. When there are markers of time, then time breaks down into manageable bits as it counts down. Queues that are long but moving feel infinitely better than those that show no inclination to move. A longer route where traffic is moving is preferable to a shorter one where it is stuck.

The mobile phone has made waiting easier. In a larger sense, too, the digital world has taken a big bite out of the need to wait. We can pay bills online, complete banking transactions, buy things while twiddling our thumbs, or, more precisely, by twiddling them.

Now one is forever occupied, lost in the screen. There are messages to read and send, reels to scroll through, games to play and cat videos to watch. But it has also made waiting a permanent condition. As it has the state of being alone. One is always waiting for something to happen even when something is happening. And we are always alone even when we are with people. We are now perpetually in a doctor's waiting room twiddling our thumbs, impatiently waiting for the next screen to load. Every time we do something, Something Else is knocking impatiently on our windowpane.

Time certainly had a different quality earlier. Speeches lasted for a few hours. Trains were always delayed by an indeterminate amount of time. We waited eight years to buy a scooter. As a rule, things refused to happen. When anything happened, anything at all, it engaged us. We sat on porches and at windows feeding off other people's activities. Time had no exchange value. So what if you waited? Boredom was an arena, a large barren space into which imagination had no choice but to bloom. When we found devices that held time at bay, we juiced them for everything that they were worth. Newspaper read word for word. Every book by one's favourite authors read over and over again.

Interestingly, in the early days of the digital, waiting for a connection to materialize as we dialled up our modems, was a defining element of our experience. Nothing was more frustrating than the sound of the device straining almost physically to break through the static and deliver a connection, and nothing sweeter when success was finally achieved.

All around us, technology is conspiring to eliminate the very idea of waiting. Today, one of its central quests is to completely demolish the gap that exists between desire and its fulfilment. The digital world is focused on finding ways to understand us well through the data trail that we leave behind and then delivering to our needs with ever greater speed. The world is being served up to us, and the universe is rearranging itself around the individual. Whenever we want something, wherever we might be, the idea is that thought must not be separated from action for an instant longer than necessary. But this might turn out to be elusive. No matter how much we try, we will always find a way for our reach to exceed our grasp. We will still find some reason to wait.

THE SLIM-FIT CONSPIRACY?

That organized fashion is a tyranny is well known. In the name of what is currently in vogue, many abominations have been inflicted upon men and women down the ages. On the whole, one must say, when looking at period films or serials, we are much better off today than say, 500 years ago, when one carried the equivalent of one's body weight in the form of clothes, accessories and random things that passed off as costume must-haves. It is also true that women have usually borne the brunt of the atrocities committed in the name of haute couture, although the male cast of *Bridgerton* might disagree.

However, this plaintive rant, while briefly casting its eye at history, is about something much more immediate and pressing. And yes, the pun is intended as it is in response to the new obsession with something called slim-fit. Clothes are shrunk around the assumption that men are now sleek creatures who have traded their paunches for abs. Now there is some truth to this, but it is largely contained in some gyms across the country. The rest of us, who like to exhale, continue to have thickening midriffs and slim-fit is nothing but a conspiracy not only to make us look ridiculous, but simultaneously feel perpetually discomfited. If shirts clutch our stomachs with panic-stricken urgency, trousers come in their economy avatar, as they begin below the waist and end abruptly above the ankle, all the while being tapered so narrowly that one can get cramps merely by twitching.

The problem is compounded by another design innovation. In earlier times, one's midriff modesty was protected by the fact that shirts had a substantial overlap between its two sides. I am sure there is a technical name for this, but I am talking about the strip of cloth on which the buttons are mounted. This isthmus of restraint, this plank of civilizational propriety ensured that when one sat down, and the shirt folded upon one's paunch, no skin was revealed. For reasons best known to themselves, and no doubt in the interests of moody fashion, that strip of cloth has either been removed altogether or narrowed to the point of a rumour. As a result, every time one sits down, one is exhibiting skin. Now this by itself may not be a problem, particularly if one is engrossed in the magnificence of one's own articulateness while nursing a Fuzzy Navel or like-minded beverage, but that does not happen. The spouse or the daughter is at hand, darting missile-like glances at one's exposed stomach, and ensuring that the rest of the evening is spent in striking artful poses that try and hide what lies revealed.

The Indian male stomach, it must be said, is unused to such critical scrutiny. In olden times, the bare male body excited neither comment nor interest. It was widely recognized to be a spent force and was safely ignored by all who came across it. Given the fact that we tend to regard the stomach not as an internal organ but as an external protuberance that speaks of prosperity and a life lived in close harmony with ghee and sugar, this was an agreeable state of affairs. Now, unfortunately, it has lost its anonymity and is increasingly being called a bod, which leaves nothing more to be said.

As far as one can tell, there was no provocation that has led designers to make this change. Nobody insulted the mother of the Head Designer of the Inter-Planetary Fashion Guild (based, I am told, in Milan), nor has it anything to do with global warming. One can understand that every year, the 'season' changes and old clothes must get discarded because ochre is the new black. This is all perfectly rational and fair. But to imprison people in slim-fit and then to take away the fig leaf that kept abdomens under lock and key is perverse.

If that were not enough, they have then removed the front pocket on shirts. Now it is true that the whole outrage around pockets, or, rather, the lack of these, is a subject that should by all rights be articulated by women, for they have been discriminated against for centuries on this count. The idea that any part of their clothing serve a functional person has clearly been anathema to the World Council of Gown Designers (based, I am told, in Paris), and besides, there are expensive handbags to sell, which pockets might put out of business. However, while conceding the first right of outrage to women vis-à-vis pockets, one must still protest the removal of the shirt pocket.

Where does one put one's glasses? In one's trouser pockets, where they make delicious crunching sounds if one is not careful? Sling them around the neck so that one can keep looking for them elsewhere? Hang them rakishly by the second button of one's slim-fit shirt so as to look like a gigolo? And what about a pen? Where does that go?

And what does one achieve by getting rid of the small rectangle of real estate that has such enormous functional value? What design magic is contrived by flattening out this patch of terrain? Was the pocket interfering with the flowing lines of the blue shirt that 70 per cent of Indian men wear all the time?

Is this a conspiracy or merely a whimsical exercise of power by the Global Alliance of Tailormasters (based, as you can imagine, at The Hague)? When it comes to women's fashion, it is clear that a global conspiracy has been afoot for centuries. But of late, men have had it easy. They have got rid of ties, cheerfully donned V-necked T-shirts with plunging necklines and have begun to wear socks with purple kittens on them. Perhaps men were getting soft and needed to be reminded of the coercive power of fashion. Whatever the reason, a formal protest of some kind needed to be lodged. Consider this the first salvo.

A GENERATIONAL DIVIDE?

Every generation has its own wisdom and rules for bringing up the next one. And the norms of child rearing have changed dramatically over a single generation. For one, the parent today is not just a placid noun but a harried verb. Parenting is a job – one that comes without a playbook and one that keeps an entire generation bewildered and uncertain.

The earlier mode of parenting did not involve too much conscious thought. Children grew up, as plants do. They were doted upon, to be sure, but they were also left to their own devices. What stood out was how comfortable society was with exposing them to a casual form of cruelty.

The nicknames we were given, apart from being excruciatingly embarrassing and unreasonably durable, were often quite vicious. One's flaw was picked upon and mercilessly pointed out. So, if one wore glasses, one was (in Delhi) a Chashmish or a Chokha. If one were overweight, then one was obviously Motu or Mota. Likewise for the colour of one's skin, height, or any perceived shortcomings in speech or appearance – these were instantly what one became known by.

Nursery rhymes and common ditties had this breezy nonchalance about gory happenings. For instance, a common ditty children of my time would be familiar with was, 'Motu Seth/sadak pe let/gaadi aayi/phat gaya pet/gaadi ka number 88/humne dekha India Gate.' Not the world's greatest poetry, but an earworm if there was one. Across regions, we saw the same pattern repeating. In Gujarati, for instance, we had one about a fat cat wearing a sari who goes for a swim and gets eaten up by a crocodile. In Bengali, I remember a poem about Indi Bindi Shindi, who lost their lives because they sang through their noses. In English, of course, we all know what happened to Jack and Jill and Humpty Dumpty. Even the harmless Ring a Ring o' Roses is actually about people sneezing and dying during the Great Plague.

In behaviour, too, punishment by parents and authority figures was frequent, and nobody was shy about it taking a physical form. I have been to schools where slaps, and even kicks, were considered legitimate. More innovative punishments included our entire class parading around with a 'I-am-an-anti-social-element' poster around our necks for blowing up a teacher's desk during Diwali time.

Similarly, fairy tales are, almost to a fault, all hair-raisingly violent. Little Red Riding Hood, Hansel and Gretel, and Snow White – all of them go through harrowing experiences, and while all of them do have a happy ending, these are extraordinary stories to expose the very young to.

Clearly, exposing children to harshness and cruelty was not an accident. Across cultures, the prevailing wisdom clearly was that children needed to, in a variety of ways, be introduced to the idea that the world was not perfect, and neither were they. Like all choices, this one, too, had consequences. In a world where conversations of any real kind between generations were rare and avenues for self-expression extremely limited, what we saw was widespread repression and people who nursed feelings of injury from childhood, which emerged in unexpected ways. Feelings of inferiority, once implanted, became extremely difficult to overcome. A lot of anxiety and unhappiness were the results. Equally, there was a certain resilience and hardiness – a thickness of skin – that developed for many. One took one's troubles in one's stride more easily, for one was more prepared.

Today, we conceptualize childhood very differently. Children are protected far more consciously, and care is taken to see that they develop a healthy self-image. We try hard not to characterize people based on their background, appearance, or manner. We are extremely conscious of any acts of discrimination. Body shaming, in particular, is seen as highly problematic. Corporal punishment is seen as medieval; even mild reproof by teachers causes parental agitation.

In other ways, thanks to technology, children are far more exposed to the world than was the case in the past. They have access of an unprecedented kind that earlier generations could only dream about. There is far greater confidence at a much younger age, and we see young people achieving much more even while in their teens, including building businesses valued at billions of dollars.

But there is also a growing fragility, a sense of entitlement, which, when thwarted, produces a sense of helplessness. Mental-health issues are growing at an exponential rate as internal imaginations and external realities collide. We can control cruelties of some kind, but when older children get exposed to the filth that goes around on social media, they find themselves without the equipment to process it.

Was there more wisdom in an earlier era than we gave it credit for? Is controlled cruelty a strategic tool, a feature, and not a bug? Is it too idealistic, or even foolish, to protect children in a world where cruelty has become more commonplace and public than in the past? Are we confusing a world that should be with a world that is, and is the younger generation paying the price?

It is not an easy question to answer, for even if one accepts at a conceptual level that resilience is a good quality to build amongst the young, it is virtually impossible to go back to the codes of an earlier time. Too many things have changed. But some self-awareness and self-doubt about our current approach may be in order. Every choice comes with a cost, and we are seeing those unfold right now.

Perhaps the larger, more tragic truth is that it is virtually impossible for any generation to bring up a new one without committing significant mistakes. Balancing the twin jobs of finding answers for ourselves while preparing another generation for rules that will almost certainly be different than the ones we dealt with is exceedingly difficult, and there are good chances that we will mess things up one way or another.

THE FORGOTTEN AFTERNOON

The afternoon attracts no poetry. It lies as a forgotten part of the day, a forlorn bridge between the bits that excite our imagination. We might be morning or evening people, but no one talks about inspiration striking them at 4.30 pm. In truth, of course, many great discoveries or artistic epiphanies might well have broken through our consciousness at precisely this hour, but culturally we are loath to acknowledge this.

In India, at least, we can understand the disdain that we feel for the afternoon. The sun is merciless for large parts of the country for much of the year, and escaping into the shade is an imperative. The afternoon is a time to lie low, to skulk in the shadows till the sun decides to let up. But even in the rest of the world, the afternoon is, relatively speaking, the least heralded part of the day.

The attraction of the other parts of the day is easy to understand. The morning is the dawn of new things, the beginning of a fresh chapter. The sun comes out as the day breaks and light gradually fills our lives. We are meant to rise, to shine and to get on with living our lives. In reality and metaphor, mornings represent an awakening, they reek of freshness and rejuvenation, and advertise the effects of a good night's sleep. Mornings erase, even if momentarily, the darkness of the night before and the memories that we might carry as a burden around us. The morning is always an opportunity to write a fresh story in a world born anew.

Aesthetically too, the morning is pretty. The air is bracing, unless one lives in Delhi, and the sky is full of kind light. The sun is at its most benign, and it lights up the world as if it is seeing it for the first time. No wonder so much poetry surrounds the wee hours of the morning. So many Hindi film songs, which are really a measure of the poetry that everyone understands, are about the glory of the morning.

Evenings are the time when we get to do what we really want. Going out, meeting friends, unwinding with a drink, watching television. It is a time for lovers' trysts and romantic yearning as per the many film songs that sing the glories of the 'shaam', 'sanjh' and 'sandhya-ki-bela'. The evening slips into the night, which is similarly a reservoir of meanings. If the day is all clarity and light, the night lends itself to many more subtleties. It is variously a site of sensuous possibilities, a time of loneliness and despair, an occasion to extract the most from life, a veil, a confidant, to name but a few ways in which it is imagined.

It is not as if afternoons have nothing to commend them. Perhaps the best part of the afternoon is the school bell. Nothing represents the freedom from cloistering better than the abandon with which children break out from school. The summer afternoon is no deterrent, escape is always joyful. The other time of the year when the afternoon is actually looked forward to is winters in the North. Till the sun lasts in the sky, afternoons are blissful. Or those times when, after a heavy meal, one drifts off into a torpid sleep, lost to the world. The afternoon nap is peculiarly delicious for it is time stolen from purpose and productivity. It is a defiant negation of the idea of the day as it has come to mean today. Cultures across the world, including many parts of India, have institutionalized the idea of the afternoon nap; shops in many towns used to be closed after lunch. After all, which sane person would venture out to buy things when they should have been asleep?

Even in the office, the afternoon is a slow time. Post-lunch meetings can elicit heartfelt groans. Conferences slot either the most boring or the most rousing speakers in the post-lunch 'death' slot. To counter the obvious fading of human attention in the afternoon, we now have the idea of a light lunch that stints on both calories and the mysterious substances in our food that make eyelids heavy and minds fuzzy. Of course, for a bulk of Indians, lunch in office is still a four-box tiffin affair, that can neither be hurried nor cut back on.

The afternoon cup of tea is what brings us back to some semblance of life. If the morning cup is meant to gently ease us back to the land of the living, the afternoon has a more onerous mission. It needs to startle our senses into wakefulness so that we can go back to pretending to work. The afternoon snacks, if any, are simply an added blandishment to coax us into some form of alertness.

But otherwise, the afternoon is something to run from. Growing up, the opportunity to escape into the air-conditioned arms of a cinema theatre in the 3-6 pm show was as close to bliss as one could imagine.

Our quarrel with the afternoon comes perhaps from the fact that it is the most shapeless part of the day. It is the day without nuance, without texture. It is the flattest stretch of time that we pass in a day. One where the sun keeps on climbing in the sky, doing nothing interesting. There is no meaning that one can accord to this barren stretch of time. Even as a metaphor it offers little. We talk about the evenings of our life, but what would its afternoon look like? It is neither the beginning nor the end, it portends nothing and symbolizes little. Every day, it comes and then it goes.

THE WEDDING AS SIGN

FOR THREE DAYS, IT SEEMED that a significant part of the country was riveted by a spectacle like no other – the pre-wedding celebrations of the son of India's richest man. It was interesting to note that this event had not even a trace of a ritual embedded within it; it was entirely a party in anticipation of the actual event, which was a few months away.

With an unending stream of videos that kept appearing on social media, the vicarious pleasure of participating in an event of this scale was unmistakable. To be sure, there were snide comments about the inappropriateness of such an extravagant celebration in a poor country as well as the lack of good taste on display, but regardless of whether one criticized the proceedings or adoringly followed them, there was little chance of ignoring them.

In some ways, we have been training for this. The wedding celebrations of the not-so-wealthy have also become overblown affairs with multiple events, pre-wedding videos, elaborate invitation cards, themes and dress codes. The bride and bridegroom enact a Bollywoodized imagination for themselves for the benefit of their guests, dancing to film songs every few minutes.

Is anything vulgar anymore? That particular word seems to have lost meaning in a world where everything, beginning with our own selves, is on constant display. We live in a perpetually self-congratulatory mode of existence, showing off our glorious lives to others incessantly. The only difference between billionaires and us is that their self-congratulations look a little different and they have Bill Gates in attendance.

Similarly, it seems even the filthy rich can only dream in the language of Bollywood. In that, they are also like the rest of the country, which uses that idiom to thread all their fantasies with. Every wedding strives to be a re-enactment of a Bollywood fantasy, and every celebration needs the crutch of Bollywood, whether by way of songs or, if you are lucky enough to be wealthy, the actual presence of a star. In this case, every star in the firmament was dutifully present, and performed for their hosts and their guests. There was comment in social media about the ability of the rich to buy out stars and make them dance to their tunes, in this case quite literally. But it works both ways, for they still remain the gold standard for fantasies, no matter how wealthy you are. If the stars are beholden to money, so is big money incapable of looking beyond the stars when it wants to put itself on display. Eventually, you are still known by the starry company you keep.

In an earlier time, emperors sought to achieve immortality by building spectacular monuments that would outlive them and ensure that they were never forgotten. Today, we are seeing the quest for a new kind of monumentality, one which is happy to get dissolved in the moment. All the content created around this event, copious as it was, would be erased from public consciousness in some time. In any case, that's fine, because a new bigger and better event would come around.

The desire for immortality – being remembered in time vertically – has been replaced by the need to dominate time horizontally. In those three days of the pre-wedding event, nothing else was talked about. The celebrations exhausted the meaning of celebration; there was nothing left out. The family hosted the event in a small town with no facilities, proceeding to construct them from scratch. It gathered a constellation of names from the worlds of business, cricket, and films – the only people who really matter in our consciousness – and put on a show that no other award ceremony or celebration has matched. It left nothing to chance. But it will also leave no trace of itself after some time. Remember the earlier celebration by the same family? Exactly.

It is easy to explain why an event like this is so riveting. A glimpse into the lives of the fabulously rich has always been a powerful draw. It is a fairy tale brought to life, an amplified and distorted destination for our aspirations as we gaze adoringly as someone else stretches the limits of what money can buy. What if we could have anything we wanted, what if money was not a factor in the choices we made in our life? This is a question that we only ask of ourselves in our dreams – and an occasion like this allows us to imagine a possible answer. Of course, in India it seems that whatever the question might be, the answer is always Bollywood.

It is also a sign that this India understands scale as a substitute for quality. We can see the same obsession with size in many of the new national monuments we are creating. The iconography of a new India privileges scale over beauty and obvious messaging over refinement.

It is a sign of a new India, for sure, one that sees the wealth of others as a spur rather than a sign of their own inadequacies. The envy that an event like this evokes is rooted more in a kind of wistfulness rather than resentment, and is more likely to result in a form of emulation rather than anger.

Celebrations of this kind are less about personal joy as they are about public signalling. Which is also why this event has been made so public. In an earlier time, hosting a wedding was a social duty, a way of repaying social debts often by incurring financial ones. Now it feels like an eagerly awaited opportunity to put oneself on display to an awed audience. Money is being advertised here, and as the recipients of this blitz, we have certainly got the message.

THE LIGHT IN OUR LIVES

An indelible memory of my childhood is that of my insomniac grandmother playing hand after hand of Solitaire (which she called Patience), in the light of a zero-watt bulb, while we were all sprawled on the floor trying to sleep. Her eyesight was extremely poor, and it was a miracle that she managed, by squinting ferociously at the deck of cards, to navigate her way through her nightly pastime in such dim light.

But then those were the days of bulbs that were extremely miserly when it came to delivering even a reasonable quantity of illumination, and my memory of childhood is dotted with scenes of dimly lit rooms with perfunctorily whitewashed walls. A 60-watt bulb was considered robust, and a 100-watt bulb was a shameful indulgence. The economic burden that the magic of electricity placed on us was only too evident in our niggardliness when it came to wattages, but it was also a recurring feature of our growing-up years to be admonished by our parents every time we left a room without switching off the lights. I remember many lengthy sermons on the virtues of frugality, thanks to the light bulb. Besides, stories of relatives who had assiduously studied late at night under a lonely streetlamp were a staple. The message was very clear: artificial lighting was a scarce resource to be used with great care.

Over and above the economic necessity, perhaps it was an acknowledgement of the power of the night as a primal force, a sign of respect that while we were flouting the laws of nature by illumining our abodes artificially, we were doing so with the full knowledge that this is not how things were meant to be. We apologized even as we lit our electric lamps – for some reason, always with a little prayer. That was a time when we consciously shrunk our world at night, lighting up only the most necessary parts of our lives. It was time to be home, not go gallivanting around outside. In any case, we barely had any streetlights in the small towns where I spent most of my childhood, and going out at night for any errands was a much grumbled-about event. The night felt distinctly different from the day; it was as if we lived life in two different registers.

The flashlight was an integral asset in those times. The power supply was erratic, and street lighting was virtually non-existent. In rural areas, in particular, life would be unimaginable without this sturdy companion, a fact that made Nokia one of the bestselling phones in India.

The light bulb changed civilization, of course, by being, as Marshall McLuhan put it, a 'medium without a message'. It transforms the environment merely by its presence, turning night into day, and, in effect, doubling the world we have access to. We could work 24 hours a day. The idea of 'night life' is a direct result of the bulb, yet another way in which human ingenuity has thwarted the designs of nature.

The coming of tube light was a sharp stab of abundance in the parsimonious world of the light bulb. It shone white with gauche unselfconsciousness, without any of the modesty of the bulb. It consumed less electricity, too, and hence soon came to dominate our lives with ease.

Today, of course, as one looks upon empty office buildings late at night that are ablaze with light, it is easy to see how dramatically our relationship with lighting has changed. And while it is true that the power situation in India has improved significantly, what this really points to is the change in our attitude towards lighting. We abhor darkness and have begun to find it unnatural. Darkness feels like a void, an aberration that we are no longer comfortable with. We rarely encounter darkness in our lives anymore until it's time to go to sleep. Light is a sign of space being animated by life. This probably explains the urge to leave at least one light on even if we are not at home.

The advent of LED technology has helped bring about this transformation. Lighting is now much cheaper and more versatile. Lighting methods have changed, and modern homes today can have a dazzling array of lights used in different ways. Lighting has become a lifestyle accessory, to be used for aesthetic as well as functional reasons. Today, there is talk about lighting design, which involves using light purposefully to highlight and underline different spaces that we use. There are cove lights, spotlights, accent lights, and ambient lights; a whole new vocabulary of lighting has sprung up. If, earlier, we lived by the rules of the lighting options available to us, today we paint our lives with light in the manner in which we see fit.

Along with the greater versatility of artificial lighting, there is a craving for natural light. We evaluate homes on the basis of how much natural light is available. In an earlier time, when homes had courtyards, natural light was never an issue. Today, with more and more urban life being centred around apartments, this need has become heightened. Not only do we want to be suffused by natural light, we even want artificial light to resemble the real thing.

As our lives become more brightly lit, it is curious how, in some ways, we seek out its absence. There is a market for dimly lit bars, and films and television seem to revel in producing content that is so poorly lit that it is difficult to follow what is being depicted. That's a full circle of sorts. From a time when we made do with the little light that we could afford, to a time now when we actually seek out some version of darkness.

FREEDOM FROM OWNERSHIP?

To own things was the source of the greatest joy as well as being a mark of achievement. 'Ghar basana,' the idea of setting up home, was the painstaking accumulation of objects that gave stability and meaning to life. One's place in the world got cemented by virtue of ownership. Owning things did nothing more than establish exclusivity of the right to use the thing in question, but its social meaning was so much more. One grew as one owned; the thing that one acquired became part of an expanded definition of the self.

What does it mean when we start preferring usership (an admittedly clunky, inelegant word) to ownership? The new app-based providers of transportation like Uber and Ola have revolutionized the lives of many. There are some of us today who can think about doing without a car, not for reasons of affordability but on grounds that it is no longer essential. Similarly, for travel, we now have Airbnb, which allows one's unutilized housing asset to be used as accommodation for travellers.

At a conceptual level, what does it mean for the idea of ownership? It is interesting that the idea of getting what we want when we want it seems to be becoming a higher form of possession. It raises an improbable question – what is it that we really want when we seek to own something? For ownership is, at its heart, really about control – that an object is ours to do as we please with it, at a time and place of our choosing, till the end of time. The new models of usership seem to deliver to this brief – the object in question now corresponds exactly to our desire – we get a taxi when we want it, to take us where we need it to go. It is in this preciseness of alignment between impulse and its satisfaction that a new definition of consumption is taking birth.

To own is also to simultaneously be owned. Objects occupy space; they weigh heavy and need minding. The act of driving through insane traffic, with gritted teeth and knitted brow, is part of the cost that ownership imposes on us. And then, in the case of cars, there is the question of parking. There is something cruelly metaphorical about not finding a way to extricate oneself from one's owned object. The car becomes an annoying appendage, a clingy pest that cannot be shaken off. The burden of ownership is never as heavy and as frustratingly cumbersome as it is when one is looking for a parking spot on a busy day in the city.

The joy of being able to own things begins to lose meaning in a surplus society, where the ability to afford things has no particular specialness attached to it. Consumption becomes mechanical, and excitement in owning things needs to be drummed up. The new version of a mobile phone that increasingly doesn't quite live up to expectations, the new car-buying decision which starts becoming a bit of a chore.

But ownership has its own gravitational pull; it needs built-in obsolescence to get an excuse to change things. The idea of value is like a stubborn residue, a stain that never quite gets erased from our minds. We find it difficult, particularly in this country, to throw things away. We need to extract some value from them and this isn't easy. The kabadiwallahs try gamely, but once the question of value enters the picture, objects sink into our lives with a heavier tread.

With time, we have learnt to discard things – we can think of buying a new car after five years, even three. But with the new idea of shared usership, it is possible to avoid this vexed question altogether. For here, the superfluous/underutilized and the deficient come together with a satisfying click. The negative inverts into the positive. Every socket finds a plug. And vice versa. Connective tissue welds together, with great precision, need and surplus capacity. The consumption surplus residing in unutilized objects is harnessed. A market is created out of underuse.

The declining preference for ownership potentially produces a surplus of the self. Without the baggage of attachment to things, there is more of oneself to go around. The self becomes infinitely divisible; imagine an infinite wardrobe, where one could wear the clothes of one's choice whenever one felt like it. If one could buy whatever one desired, one would have to be careful about what to acquire permanently. But now the fixed solid bits of identity could rapidly turn vaporous, as we would no longer be limited by our dominant selves – the chaps that were determining what we owned and, as a result, what we became. Usership allows our identity to flicker through possible versions of ourselves, without necessarily being held down by what we own, and what in turn owns us.

And yet, the social meaning of ownership continues to hold significance. Owning a house, for instance, has always held great meaning to one's quest for growing roots and lending weight to one's existence. However, in a purely financial sense, many argue that owning a house makes little sense in a context where rents are absurdly low when compared to the prices that houses command. The security of having one's own home and the cultural meaning that accrues on account of being a homeowner override whatever financial arguments that can be made against the idea of ownership.

We are still instinctively invested in the idea of attaching things to ourselves and extracting meaning from that sense of belonging, but technology and new models of collaborative consumption are making us more open to the idea we do not need to own everything we need. There is a new grammar of desire that is beginning to take shape, and the implications that will unfold as a result are likely to transform how we think about and lead our lives. To be free of belongings is to imagine a very different kind of world.

THE RECREATIONAL BODY

To THE WOMAN IN RURAL India who walks 10 kilometres every day to fetch water, the sight of the paunchy urban middle-aged men and women going for determined walks must seem a little absurd. What is a defining life condition for one is a self-conscious attempt to import health for another. For most of us, the walk is one of the few ways in which we exercise our bodies, used as we have become to a life which makes little demands on them. In the absence of work, we find ways to simulate it, just to keep our bodies in running condition. Make that walking condition.

We use motorized transport to travel, eschewing even the bicycle as a mode of transport, relegating it to a hobby. We use elevators to climb stairs, appliances to help us with our daily chores. We use hired help to take over all tasks that involve physical labour, if we can afford it. Products vie with each other to offer labour-saving conveniences and we surround ourselves with these. Technology works hard to eliminate work – even the smallest effort that we make is hunted down and reduced. With AI, even our mental exertions and our creative outpourings can be outsourced to machines. Progress means eliminating the effort we made to kick-start our motorcycles and dial a telephone. The idea of the 'automatic' is that of the self-fulfilling; a condition which allows us to not only eliminate all effort itself, but even the very thought of it. The automatic watch rids us of the need to wind it, the automatic washing machine of the need to transfer clothes from the tub to the dryer, and the automatic transmission in cars allows us the great facility of not having to change gears manually.

It is easy for us then to forget that our bodies are machines that transform energy into work. In the earlier days, our bodies were our primary instruments in our quest for staying alive. We hunted, grew food, cooked and cleaned and in general kept the wheels of life moving through the motive force of our bodies. With time, technology and with surplus, it was possible for us to increasingly delegate work to others, be it animals, machines or other people.

Today, for a section of the world, our bodies serve little useful purpose; these are increasingly instruments of recreation. We use our bodies when we want to and not when we need to. Societies with surpluses become increasingly drawn to sport; the body gets utilized in a manner that gives millions of spectators pleasure. Sport is an 'empty' way of using our bodies – by definition, no sport is meant to serve any utilitarian purpose. Sport allows us to expend our energies in a symbolic quest for perfection. The most exercise a child in a large city is likely to get is in sport (and in carrying her bags to school); there are no other avenues for physical exertion.

With so much emphasis on personal attractiveness, and such little real use that we put our bodies to, the body has become an end in itself. As pointed out by social scientist Chris Shilling, the body today is seen as a project that is in the process of becoming. It needs to be fashioned by diets, exercises and products. We 'work out' – having exhausted the need to do real work, we 'burn' calories, we 'build' muscles in desired parts of the body and voluntarily go on the 'treadmill' to make our bodies a work of art. In everything we do, we simulate real work, only this time to construct a version of ourselves that we are happy to see in the mirror.

As we move from the mechanical era of physical machines to the digital era of computers, we are freeing up yet another part of our bodies for recreation. The mind, which hitherto was completely occupied in our quest to build a good life for ourselves, is increasingly being freed up to pursue its own interests. Computers process information at a rate human minds can barely comprehend. A new generation is reaching adulthood not knowing how to make arithmetical calculations mentally. As computers start doing more of the 'real' work, our minds will seek more avenues for pleasure. Already, the most exciting developments in the digital world are linked to communication and entertainment.

From a time when we lived through our bodies unselfconsciously, today we are increasingly living for our bodies. The body is what we pay obeisance to; all its needs have become paramount. Every morsel we put in our mouths has to prove its usefulness. We lavish attention on the body, sculpting it, chiselling it, safeguarding it. The body is the passive recipient of new forms of stimulation. Our body today is a hobby, to be pursued for pleasure or to be perfected to gain admiration from others. To be affluent in today's world is to pander to the body; to be poor is to have to depend on it. When we don't have too much work, no wonder we need to work out.

THE UNHEALTHY PURSUIT OF HEALTH?

It is a strange paradox that as the indicators of health in India improve, the experience of being healthy seems to be declining consistently. We live longer, we have access to better healthcare (certainly for those who can afford it), we can overcome some dreaded diseases that were once considered untreatable, we are much more aware of things that are unhealthy and do, by and large, take greater care of ourselves, and yet we think of ourselves as never quite being healthy. The idea of health is a chimera, a gleaming speck of idealized possibility on the horizon, to be striven for but never to be reached. One thinks about health constantly, and almost never in a happy way.

That wasn't always the case. I had my first blood test when I was nineteen. By that age my daughters would individually have had a few dozen. It is not that one had a particularly healthy childhood; in fact, illness was a regular feature of life, but somehow that never seemed to call for any tests. One would go to the neighbourhood doctor, who would, after a matter-of-fact examination accompanied by jokes/homilies/gossip, send one packing to the compounder, who would assemble a few multicoloured pills into packets and give a complex set of instructions about how many pills to take when. Most times, one had no clue as to what exactly was wrong – the illness was a secret contract between one's body and the doctor, and between them, a negotiated settlement was arrived at.

The doctor enjoyed a position of serious divinity – no questions could be asked of him or her (in case it was a lady doctor, the preferred description for women practising medicine) except by the elders in the family, who would hang back, in the case of more serious illnesses, to have a whispered conversation and come back with statements of bland reassurance. Diagnostics were rare, and the X-ray was the ultimate arbiter of fate.

Routine illnesses did not need technical names – there were no gastrointestinal infections, just stomach upsets. More serious illnesses had names – but there were only a few that resided in one's consciousness. Measles, mumps and chickenpox in childhood, malaria, typhoid and jaundice when one was older.

Cinema provides clues to how the more serious diseases were imagined. Having high blood pressure was a bit of a status symbol, for only the older, the important and the short-tempered were imagined to be prone to this illness. Being a 'heart patient' was also the prerogative of the rich, people who wore dressing gowns and had a stern-but-kind Doctor-chacha constantly by the side. Tuberculosis, on the other hand, was the lot only of the poor, wretched or the ill-fated. Incessant coughing was the soundtrack to this narrative of current misery and impending doom. Cancer was present largely in Rajesh Khanna films, with *Anand* being one of those rare Hindi films that used the terrifyingly precise description of 'lymphosarcoma of the intestines'.

Looking back, what was striking about the engagement with health and the world of medicine was how separate it was from life. Being healthy, stomach troubles apart, was the default state, and being unwell was an aberration that got fixed by going to the doctor. Barring specialists, that dreaded species consulted only in dire times, every doctor was considered to be as good as another. Being a doctor was not a matter of degree – one either was a doctor or not –, and if one were deemed to be one, then there was no question or being better or worse. The difference, if any, was measured in terms of personal faith rather than expertise; some doctors were deemed to 'understand' a patient better. Our family doctor had not, in fact, studied allopathic medicine, but since he called himself a doctor, carried the right bag, used a stethoscope with familiar ease and gave injections with due gravitas, was revered highly by the entire family.

Categories of illnesses were rudimentary – and one operated on very little knowledge. Without the ability to Google one's symptoms, being unwell meant entering a flat zone of ignorance, one which left the patient no room for confusion. There was little one could do except go to the doctor and do as one was told. The world was a simple place, full of ignorance and simple-minded faith. The individual was exempted from most responsibility – there was dim awareness of the importance of hygiene, but food was as yet an unmarked terrain without being dotted with the minefields it is today.

In reality, illnesses were more frequent and lives of many near and dear ones were lost because of the rudimentary nature of medicine that was practised a generation ago, but the overall experience of health was not filled by anxiety and self-doubt. One did not feel responsible, for one was free of knowledge and unburdened by any sense of control over the situation. The idea that one could prevent illness, therefore, was alien. Now, we spend so much time and effort in the endless pursuit of healthiness, not in response to illness but as we lie in wait for it to come to us, an inevitability one must prepare for. Being unwell was an act of surrender, rather than a journey of struggle.

Today one can always do more – there is a better doctor to see, a more expensive test that diagnoses more accurately, a newer diet that gives results, an exercise regime that works, a food group that can be avoided, a procedure that helps, and then there is the world of alternative medicine – homeopathy, ayurveda, aromatherapy, acupuncture, acupressure, reiki, even vaastu. So little time, and so many things to try. The number of enemies has increased – and these include the most fundamental ingredients of life: air, food and water – as have the weapons at our disposal. Of course, each of these weapons can also act as enemies. Trying to be healthy is to be engaged fearfully in constant battle and a pandemic like Covid certainly doesn't help. A battle which, by definition, cannot be won. And one which is very, very expensive.

THE SLEEP THAT FORGOT US

We FELL ASLEEP. DRIFTED INTO the arms of Morpheus, or we nodded, dozed off into another world. We sank into sleep, succumbed to it, embraced it, yielded to it, were lulled into it. The language is clear – sleep was an overwhelming force at whose mercy we lay.

And sleep used to be the answer. To aching limbs, to heavy thoughts, to days that had taken more than they gave. It was the soft edge at the end of the page, the kindness that came without asking. If we couldn't sleep, it meant something was wrong. The body knew. The mind protested. Sleep was what we lost when life became too much.

Now, sleep is the problem. We chase it, coax it, measure it, fear its absence. We lie in bed with eyes shut and minds lit up – scrolling, planning, remembering, regretting. The bedroom is now a digital orchestra, full of unpredictable performers. We no longer fall asleep. The mind doesn't shut down – it simply shifts tabs. We attempt it – like a test we haven't studied for.

There are too many things to do instead. The night, once a natural dimming of the day, now pulses with options. One more episode. One last scroll. One more dart into other people's lives. The beep of an incoming message that might be important. Sleep has rivals now – faster, louder, brighter. Why surrender to darkness when there is so much still calling to us?

The body, faithful for so long, is no longer trusted. We set alarms not just to wake up, but to remind us to go to bed. Modern life does not heed the signs nature gives us – sunrises, sunsets, silence, fatigue. We craft our own life rhythms. We wear rings that tell us how well we slept. We outsource instinct to devices, listen to voices that tell us how to breathe, when to stretch, when to stop thinking. We do not sleep – we manage the idea of sleep.

There is no true night anymore. Only the dimming of screens, the cooling of rooms, the switching from active light to ambient light. Our cities flicker, our bedrooms glow. Even our dreams feel half-remembered, as though performed under surveillance. Sleep used to be a place we entered. Now it's a condition we try to simulate.

When was the last time you woke up feeling fresh? When you leapt out of bed, raring to get on with it – instead of dragging yourself up and coaxing some life back with tea or coffee? The reality is that we are overstimulated and under-rested. The mind buzzes long after the world dims. There is no wind-down, only a crash. And even then, we hover. We nap with guilt, rise with doubt. We carry the stress of the day in our bones, in the tightness of our muscles that refuse to relax. Our minds have taught our bodies to forget how to sleep. We store the day in our bodies, and sleep isn't able to prise it loose.

There are, of course, people who have a medical problem with sleep – those who simply cannot find a way to drift off. But increasingly, the rest of us are turning into amateur insomniacs. Not quite sleepless, but never truly rested. Hovering on the edge of wakefulness, like guests overstaying at the gates of sleep.

What was once effortless has become a regimen. Weighted blankets. Chamomile teas. Breathing apps. Melatonin rituals. Sleep is now curated, stage-managed, fragile. It must be earned, prepared for, supported by accessories. One wrong pillow, and the night is lost.

There is a quiet tragedy here. Not loud enough to mourn, but enough to notice. That something as elemental as rest, as ancient as the tide, now needs to be taught to us. That we require podcasts to lull us, and scores to validate us. That we wake up more tired than we were when we lay down – not because we didn't sleep, but because we didn't sleep well enough.

There are a few aggravating people who just fall asleep. They board a flight and they pop off. Just like that. One second they are absently flipping through the desultory charms of the airline magazine, and the next you hear a gentle snore. These are the lucky outliers, those whose bodies have refused to learn the ways of being. It is remarkable – and increasingly rare. The ease of it, the instinctive trust, the body knowing exactly what to do without permission or preparation. It feels like a superpower from a simpler age. A time when sleep wasn't optimized, only obeyed.

For the rest of us, we have turned sleep into a mirror. We want our dreams to be productive. We want our rest to be efficient. Sleep no longer belongs to the night – it belongs to the day that follows, as a prelude to performance.

And yet, once in a while, magic happens. When our bodies fall off our minds. When day sags into night. When the thoughts unspool. When the world falls quiet and the body forgets. Not every night. Not often. But enough to believe that sleep hasn't left us completely.

We didn't lose sleep all at once. It slipped away gradually – through glowing screens, through clenched jaws and ticking thoughts, through our hunger for more and our fear of missing something. Sleep didn't forget how to find us. We forgot how to let go.

It used to be a surrender. Now it's a performance we wake up from, hoping we scored well.

THE MODERN BEARD DECODED

To be a man in today's team, one needs to wear a beard. Or so it would seem going by the thorny visage of so many in all walks of life. From Narendra Modi to Virat Kohli, public life is rife with men sporting large quantities of hair on their face. For some, it has been an enduring part of their identity, while there are many others who have a beard because everyone has a beard. Like all forms of personal affectations, the beard is essentially a form of communication that broadcasts a sense of who one is and who one wishes to be seen as.

The sage's beard that Mr Modi wore for a period made its intention quite clear. Whether or not it was a nod to Rabindranath Tagore, given that it coincided with the Bengal elections at the time, the intended message left no one in doubt. Over the years, Mr Modi's projected image has moved from being a hands-on man of action to being a wise oracle who is above the fray. Creating a persona that reminded Bengal of a favourite was an election gambit, which did not exactly turn out as he might have wished it to.

The sage's beard communicates profusely by its abundance. White and overflowing, it is as if the flood of wisdom that emanates from the oracle is being allowed to flow untrammelled. Two otherwise opposing codes sit together – that of age and abundance. Normally, age brings in its wake sparseness and diminution. Things thin out, shrivel up and shrink, except notably for the flowing beard. The lushness of the sage's beard is a sign of one of the few things that are seen to become more abundant with age – wisdom. In the sage's and the guru's beard, age becomes synonymous with baked wisdom, representing an effortless wellspring, of deep understanding that gushes out without any deliberate effort.

Rahul Gandhi's beard, on the other hand, could be construed as an attempt to acquire some gravitas, to walk away from the 'Pappu' label that has stuck to him with an ease he must find exasperating. Read in conjunction with his Bharat Jodo Yatra, the beard was to signal a generational shift, in maturity as well as physical appearance.

On the other end of the spectrum is the beard most in vogue today, the kind worn by Virat Kohli. After years of aspiring to hard-jawed gleaming chins, the tide turned a few years ago and it became mandatory for men who had come of age to sport a more hirsute look. The beard in vogue is carefully groomed, fastidiously maintained and scrupulously displayed. It is a sign of fussy self-absorption, rather than careless disinterest in one's appearance. It speaks of a masculinity intent on fetishizing itself, a uniform to be worn to be in trend.

Along with the modern preoccupation with sculpting the body, this is a way of enacting masculinity, a performance that is carefully orchestrated. Like the bell-bottoms of the 1970s, the beard today is merely a sign of the times. It is worn on the outside in every possible sense. It uses a device usually seen as a return to a more primitive idea of masculinity to make a more contemporary statement. The hipster beard, in particular, is the ultimate expression of the idea of beard as costume. Across the many forms it takes, this beard is part homage, part parody, as it grafts another identity from another time and places it on to oneself.

The beard is, in many ways, an attempt to reclaim the glory of masculinity in a time when men feel under pressure from the increasing presence of women in public life, but simultaneously, it is so transparently a costume that it undercuts itself. While all masculinity is an act of performance, the beard today is much more consciously so. By amplifying what is a specific sign of maleness, and yet according to it the kind of careful attention that was historically associated with the feminine, the modern beard is an act of self-aware bravado.

On the surface, the current look is the polar opposite of the metrosexual, but structurally, the difference is not vast. This is masculinity worn on the outside, putting on an exaggerated display while confessing to its inadequacy. The modern beard, in all its varied forms, represents the taming of the beard and its conversion into a processed cultural product. A whole regimen of grooming products, which once languished in commercial wilderness, has sprung around the beard.

There are several other kinds of beards. The activist's beard is a site of restlessness, of active dissatisfaction, It is unkempt and straggly, determined to resist order, as befits a dissident fermenting ideas and fomenting trouble for the establishment. Of someone too caught up in the weighty issues of injustice and discrimination in the world to bother with appearances. The beard is a sign of individuality, of not caring enough about the things that don't count while caring deeply for the things that do. Of course, given that it has been the time-honoured look for intellectuals, there is conformity, merely of another kind.

The stubble is an interesting creature for it revels in its neither-here-nor-there-ness. At one level, it is a sign of a masculine overflow that could neither be tamed nor get fully realized. The unshaven, underslept look is a sign of a mind in turmoil, lacking equilibrium. The 'majnu' look made popular by Bollywood captures this state. The designer stubble, on the other hand, is an artful declaration of underpreparedness. The graininess of skin and the roughness of texture act as an advertisement for a masculinity that is perpetually a work-in-progress, not having come to rest. The designer stubble is the beard in its Calvin Klein underwear, balancing raw masculinity with chic sophistication.

The beard was the refuge of the weak-chinned. Today it is the pride of anyone with a chin. The beard wearer has a deep relationship with his own facial hair, and takes it extremely seriously. While at one level it is an outward sign that aligns itself with the times, it is also a deep expression of an inner felt reality. The current prevalence of the beard (virtually every Indian cricketer, for instance, sports one) will fade as most grooming trends do, but as gender turns even more liquid, the beard will continue to be both an anchor and a site for experimentation.

THE RETURN OF THE BICYCLE

Recently, a colleague bought a bicycle. Not just a bicycle, but a helmet, knee pads, new clothes, including shorts that hugged his thighs an awful lot, and in all probability, new shoes, too, made no doubt with the latest aerospace technology to withstand the damage that pedals are known to inflict on shoes. He is part of a new movement that we see in many parts of India, where groups of people, young and old, have rediscovered bicycling and go for many rides across improbably large distances. The bicycles, too, are things of technology, and come at prices that are suitably impressive; after all, they have to go with the new clothes that one has bought. In its new avatar, bicycling has been imagined as an exciting adventure sport, full of lurking danger to one's head and knees and needing streamlined attire to cut the drag from the wind.

All of which feels faintly ridiculous to a generation brought up depending on the bicycle for basic transportation. Cycling was an extension of one's body – one spent most of one's days in communion with it, not in a Zen-like state of post-adrenaline bliss, but a practical backside-grinding-on-narrow-seat sort of a way. The equipment at one's disposal was the robust black Hercules/Atlas/Hero bicycle, available in ladies' and gents' versions. There was the other, more exotic, 'sports' version, with its fancy colours, streamlined shape and flimsier framework, but that was not regarded as being solid enough by most. Owning a bicycle converted one's status on the road; the ability to move at three to four times the speed of walking meant that in a small town, nothing was more than half an hour away. That meant freedom as well as the burden of many more household chores that one could be relied upon easily for.

The bicycle itself is, in some ways, a great advertisement for the idea of a machine in that it serves back the physical force we apply in a multiplied form, by using some rudimentary principles of physics. The bicycle produces speed largely through knowledge; it has no 'black box' where any magical technological transformation takes place. You push at something, a wheel transfers the motion to another through a chain, and the bicycle moves. The bicycle represents technology at its flattest and most self-evident. Like a lever or a wheel, it is barely more than a scientific principle brought to life in a surprisingly useful way.

For equipment that has such few elements, a surprising number of things could go wrong with the bicycle. Apart from the regular need to fill air in the tyres, a pursuit that took a considerable amount of effort, 'punchers' were frequent and needed a primitive combination of a trough of water in which an inflated tube was immersed to locate the leak, and a crude rubber patch that was melted on to the puncture, so as to cover up the leak. The chain was another source of frequent trouble, with a distressing tendency to come off, just as greater force was applied to the pedals. The pedals themselves could dismantle themselves quite frequently, and the brakes, too, could be temperamental, losing traction, particularly in the rains. Owning a bicycle meant that one needed to be at least a little comfortable with the mechanical – there was no escaping working with one's hands and getting them dirty when using a cycle. There wasn't enough distance between the rider and the machine – unlike with other machines, one could not even pretend that it was too complex to try and fix it oneself.

But for all that, cycling gave a sense of oneness with the road that other vehicles could not really match. The machine responded totally and only to the rider's actions, and this gave one a sense of control that was enjoyable. Riding downhill, with one's hands off the handlebars or taking a curve at a fast clip while ringing the metallic bell furiously were full-bodied pleasures that were easy to revel in. The feeling of exhilaration felt when the weather was glorious, the road open and one's body was fresh, was difficult to replicate. On the flip side, riding 'doubles' uphill on a hot summer afternoon, carrying a younger sibling for a few kilometres, evened up the slate quite well. After all, the bicycle did not promise escape from reality, it only helped navigate it a little faster.

The idea of accessible mobility has always been a deeply empowering one in India. Personal transportation frees up the individual from the collective both in thought and action, and allows for new imaginations to get unlocked. The role of the bicycle in Hindi cinema underlines this sense of openness and freedom that the lowly contraption brought to us. The idea of a group of young girls off on cycles on wide open vistas for a picnic, only to encounter a group of personable young men (often also on bicycles) while singing a happy ditty, was part of the imagined world of freedom that bicycles gave one access to. That the bicycle was used as a vehicle to escape the city and its oppressive familiarity was a sign that the idea of being in control of one's own movements had intrinsic value and that for all its functional uses, the bicycle opened a door in the minds of its users.

As times have changed, the middle class has no need for the bicycle in its quest for personal mobility. As a thing of recreation, it needs new bells and whistles. After all, it must help us consume a vision of ourselves as beings transformed visibly by our new passions. Hitherto-routine activities are being reinvented as exotic new pursuits; running needs equipment and mobile apps, eating out becomes an occupation involving specialized experts, knowing what wine to drink with what has an exotic French name, and in order to get on to a bicycle, one must look like an athlete in leotards.

CHAPTER 4

Urban Living

Modernity without Content?

Modernity strides into cities with a swagger, but often curdles into parody.

It improves specific parts of the city while blighting the whole.

Our urban spaces reflect aspiration without imagination, structure without soul.

From builder flats to pastry shops, we ask: Can you have form without feeling?

THE NEW PUBLIC SPACES

Using paper towels in a toilet at an Indian airport feels surreal to those who have grown up in another India. There is a wholly unfamiliar sense of crisp hygiene that accompanies its use and one can only imagine how many illnesses have been prevented by this one simple facility. The filthy communal towels of another time spring to mind, when we swapped germs with each other with cheerful impunity.

Growing up, a visit to a public facility of this kind was a battle between two primitive urges – the pressing need to relieve oneself against a fervent desire to protect one's senses from olfactory assault. Toilets in these spaces were filthy, smelly, and did not concern themselves even remotely with the question of hygiene. The problem for women was infinitely worse. Public spaces of all descriptions – airports, railway stations, markets, stadia, public lavatories, offices – were unselfconscious repositories of the sights and smells of our collective lives.

This has begun to change, particularly in many public spaces in the larger towns. And clean and well-maintained toilets are only part of the story. New public spaces increasingly have a new aesthetic, with order and cleanliness being key pillars of their design. Although their origins are by no means organic, having been transplanted from global sources, with time, modernity becomes contagious as one public space influences another. The change seen is in proportion to the affluence levels of the users of these spaces – malls and airports lead the way, while the railway station shows modest signs of change. Platforms have started getting escalators but the toilets in trains continue to deposit their fertile produce on railway tracks across the country.

In many cities, the differences among the three parts – the old, the intermediate and the new – are becoming quite pronounced. The old city created spaces where the dominant presence was that of people, for these were spaces designed for close human interaction. Barring a few cities, where the older part of town is being reconfigured as a consumer product by converting it into a touristy simulation of itself, in most cases, the old town has simply stopped being the centre of business activity. Designed to be navigated on foot, it still bustles, but more out of habit than need.

The intermediate city was modern once, but over the years has achieved the rundown and highly lived-in look that most Indian spaces eventually start tending towards. Unlike the closed nature of modern public spaces, the intermediate city is full of structures that are open – markets in colonies, public parks, schools and colleges of newer vintage being some examples. Modernity here is signified by a basic level of organization, and the presence of some rudimentary common facilities.

Today's modern city creates spaces that begin by cutting themselves off from the environment around them, and constructing an artificial internal habitat that can be built from scratch. The outside world ceases to exist, and a climate-controlled bubble where time and space lose texture and shape is created. Commerce is at the heart of most of these spaces; the idea of development involves more opportunities to consume. In a branded environment, even familiar names feel like facsimile reproductions – extensions of choices made popular elsewhere.

The coming of these new kinds of spaces has meant that over the last few years, urban Indians have had to re-train their eyes. While the new aesthetic of the public space can legitimately be described as derivative, it succeeds in achieving its primary goal – replacing the messy and chaotic with surface visual order. Glass is everywhere, and straight clean lines are the new standard that is aspired to. If the palace was the ultimate visual benchmark earlier, today it is the mall.

As our eye changes, so do our homes. The desire to unclutter our living spaces, and to wear a veneer of slickness, can be seen in the way the new apartments are imagined. The use of glass and marble, the growing popularity of modular kitchens, and the popularity of veneers of all kinds point to the overflow of influence from the public to the private. Shape is being imagined more fluidly, and the home is beginning to speak on behalf of its residents more deliberately.

It is also true that the overhauled public spaces are for the most part not truly public. Only a certain section of society gets access to these, either on account of affordability or by virtue of being from the right social class. Genuinely open public spaces, where people from all sections of society can mingle, are rare. Modern public spaces achieve their modernity in part by becoming less public.

The new public spaces of today emit a striking absence of any message. The use of glass as a sign of modernity is an admission that modernity does not need content; its aim is to signify nothing more than its intention to be modern. It gathers no references or allusions in its fold nor does it speak of the place or the people it is meant for. By being a line of demarcation, rather than an instrument of communication, it serves as an inarticulate monument to itself. It is not the past, and the future that it represents is one where there is little to touch or feel. But the stickiness of a past that would not let go is being successfully shaken off.

With time, perhaps public spaces will evolve from merely erasing the past to creating more enriching experiences. Mumbai's new airport is a great example of using a public space to create a stunning gallery of diverse artistic experiences. Here, space is infused with meaning. It is eloquent and distinctive. Bengaluru, too, has designed an airport that creates an organic, welcoming feeling. Today, it would seem that when it comes to designing new public spaces, the choice that needs to be made is between order and diversity. Perhaps, letting go of this binary might be a good starting point for creating more meaningful and enriching modern spaces.

THE BAZAAR AS IMPULSE

It is the destiny of every public space, no matter how large or grand it is to begin with, to end up looking like a bazaar and sounding like a railway platform. Visiting the international airport in Delhi after a while revealed that it had turned into a version of the neighbourhood Monday market. Ditto for the domestic section of the Mumbai airport. The shopping area that was once the preserve of large stores set sparsely amidst lavish space was now punctuated with little stalls selling knick-knacks, including the mandatory hairbands. At Delhi airport, there is a section officially called Delhi Bazaar, which looks and feels exactly as the name suggests.

The same phenomenon can be seen in many malls, too. They start out as projects in grandeur, that look and feel 'international' in that vast empty spaces are allowed to stand, but with time, they turn into a mish-mash of the old and new, local and international, organized and decidedly disorganized. It is as if every space in India demands squatters, entities that carry an air of intrusive intermediateness. Encroachment is more cultural imperative than commercial necessity, and is not merely physical but also conceptual in that established and codified categories are disrupted. Kiosks, stalls, booths – call them what you will – spring up with a ferocious and untidy energy and seem to speak to the Indian buyer in some deeply instinctive way. Even the fancy mall cannot help but host small vendors who sell a variety of knick-knacks from its hallowed portals. These are called 'pop-ups' but that's just another word for a bazaar.

The neat order, symmetry and scale of a well-designed space seems to cry out for a viral outbreak of disorder and division. The tendency is to fragment space, to fill it up with the most vibrant and unruly form of life. At one level, leaving space empty seems like such a waste. The purpose of space, it would seem, is to be filled with some sign of activity, preferably human. Emptiness seems to get equated with barrenness, and there is an urge for it to be filled up with something that reeks of energy, even chaos. The default design philosophy seems to be that of disruptive bisection, with any space getting successively divided with increasingly abrupt intrusions. In traffic, this takes on the manifestation of vehicles leaving a whisker's space between each other, refusing to grant the other an inch of personal territory. While waiting at a traffic light, leaving even a small empty patch of empty space between your car and the one in front invites instant honking from those straining at the leash behind you.

The idea that any space is left uncovered even briefly is seen to be an unforgivable oversight, and invites admonition. The need to cover up all available space is visible at its finest in advertisements put out by the government. Advertising convention, without question originating in the West, makes a case for objects to be set in relief, so that emphasis on the important can be provided. This point of view is summarily rejected here, as space is conquered ruthlessly and every inch of it covered up – this is most striking in the case of some hoardings where, regardless of considerations of the nature of the medium, which is invariably viewed from a distance and while one is moving, the entire space is covered by text so minute that it could not be read even if a ladder and microscope were to be simultaneously employed.

The interest lies in utilizing the available real estate that the empty space represents rather than serving the main purpose of the exercise – communicating to an audience. Visiting cards and invitation cards tend, when designed locally, to follow the same principle, that of florid abundance. Similarly, no new colony retains the air of a quiet suburb – that image is too restful to be allowed to remain. Houses with massive areas too contrive to look cramped – the idea of not constructing on space available for aesthetic reasons is deemed wasteful. Builders vie to squeeze out as much space as they possibly can, and when they can't they make up new categories such as 'carpet area' and 'built-up area', which allow them to claim space that doesn't quite exist, at least in a way that is material. Space is not only fully utilized, but invented. It is also freely encroached upon – every house vies to expand itself territorially, either by way of an unauthorized balcony or simply by putting plants and extending one's property.

Part of the impulse has to do with eking out value from everything. It is also in part a surrender to time, in that there is an acknowledgement that with time, needs will grow as will appetites, and space, being finite, will inevitably end up being used. There seems to be an inability and an unwillingness to acknowledge the integrity of any original conception; everything is seen to be subject to negotiation. Part of the reason why all our cities, including all the new spaces within these, eventually end up looking scruffy and unruly is this – no boundary is seen to be sacrosanct and no design inviolable. Greed encroaches on all public spaces. The modern in India is destined, more often than not, to eventually look squalid, but equally, it is likely to feel more alive.

In some ways, space seems to be equated not with physical presence but with human absence. The amount of empty space is translated in terms of units of human absence, which must eventually be filled. In physical terms, too, the human body seems to be the pivot around which the idea of space that is deemed necessary is imagined. Spaces that depart too much from human-sized dimensions potentially create discomfort, and even anxiety. The urge to fill up space might have to do with it being seen primarily as a way of accommodating human beings. This is a democratic instinct of a deep kind, for here, the human impulse overrides institutional order, but it is also a recipe for continuing disorder, which subverts the intent to create a neat and shiny future.

DIVORCING OUR STREETS?

THE STREETS HAVE INVADED THE restaurants. Chinese Bhel, Vada Pav Sliders, Pav Bhaji Fondue, College Van Spring Rolls, Bread Pakoda with Teriyaki Glaze and Potato Sphere Galangal Chaat – these are just a few of the menu options that we are likely to find today. The new kind of Indian eatery seems to revel in a playful take on the foods that the streets have made famous.

It is perhaps just a passing fad, a new distraction that will enthral us for a while before quietly expiring. Or it could be a sign that we are beginning to integrate our influences with a new confidence. We own our past, without becoming beholden to it, while at the same time feeling confident enough in our grasp of the global to be able to play with it. Think of it as a double subversion – with our primary allegiance being to our taste buds. We pick and choose the best parts of all our options and mash them together without embarrassment.

Fusion food extracts the street from our lives and relocates it in an exotic form of play. The city becomes an affectionate joke, to be consumed with a wink, between taco shells. The menus of these restaurants burst with a particular kind of creativity as our uncapitalized past – our little sins of the tongue – gets a coating of our newly discovered global selves. We sneak in the pleasures we have grown up with into the pleasures we have learned to enjoy.

However we read this new burst of creative energy, it seems quite clear that the street is beginning to recede from our lives, particularly in our larger cities. Not just in terms of food, but even as an essential part of our experience of urban living, the street is no longer as central to large cities. The coming of malls, the growing incidence of gated communities where 'the hawker menace' is controlled, the rise in personal-vehicle ownership, and our new imagination of what public spaces should look and feel like are some of the reasons why this is happening.

A recent visit to Karol Bagh, one of Delhi's premier markets, and the place where much of my adolescence was spent, was a deeply dispiriting experience. The once-bustling streets carry more memory than energy. There are still shoppers around, but the awareness that this is no longer the place to be infects everyone. And this is true of many other traditional bazaars in the larger cities, which have begun to sag with a lack of self-belief, even as the modern malls bazaarify.

A sanitized form of the street and bazaar is being made available to us. We can sit in fancy restaurants and eat a cool version of a street food instead of standing in a street rubbing elbows with strangers or while sitting in a 'sweet shop' and devouring samosas and chutney with a battered steel spoon. We can shop in air-conditioned comfort at a mall, but feel more comfortable if it is noisy, crowded and appears to be 'filled up'. We cannot escape the street, for it stirs our blood like nothing else can, but we can tame it.

To be sure, some traditional street spots become nostalgic monuments, must-dos on a list of a city's hot spots. This is an exaggerated homage to the past, a very conscious act of consuming, with great care, a replica of a cherished experience. Every city has its appointed places of pilgrimage, but this is no longer a natural way of life. We now act as tourists in our own home, as we look upon these as artefacts to be marvelled at.

Nothing underlines the drying up of cities as much as the gradual decline in the number of neighbourhood street vendors. The neighbourhood hawkers, advertising their merchandise or services with a distinctive aural signature, are harder to come by. Of the range of services available at one's doorstep, which included the locksmith, cobbler, knife sharpener, raddiwallah, kalaiwallah (re-tinner of brass utensils), pillow and mattress fluffer, carpet seller, vegetable- and fruitwallahs, among many others, only a few survive. The city rarely comes visiting anymore.

The street vendors were the rivers of a city, flowing with services and merchandise. Seasons came to us through these daily messengers of merchandise. They brought to our lives flavours from the city and beyond, and made us all citizens bound in trade. They represented the aggregate collective memory and stored wisdom of the city, a moving map of its desires and tastes. As a fluid, fluent, time- and market-tested chronicle of a city, street vending operated as an organic document of a lived reality.

A city starts dying when its streets lose meaning. It becomes a shell of functionality, a discrete collection of commercial and residential quarters without any dialogue between its parts. In effect, the city secedes from itself in little islets, choosing to trade its specific character for a homogenous form of modernity. It now belongs to its users, who reconfigure it according to their needs, rather than to its residents, who worked with and added to what the city had to offer. It disowns what got it here and borrows a destination that it envies. The past, other people, other modes of living become unfamiliar exotic objects to be briefly cooed at admiringly but otherwise to be pushed away to the periphery.

The balance between the old and the new, the raw and the ordered, the artisanal and the manufactured, the small and the large, the real and the simulated – this is what will determine the true health of a city. The city must gather its past, and all the people and the ideas that have made it what it is, and integrate this into its vision for the future. The street, which is the city's most accomplished theatre of change, needs to be a central part of its future.

THE VANISHING HORIZON

Moving from the heart of a metropolitan city to a suburb changes one's life in many ways. Although Gurugram is by no means a pastoral paradise where wheat fields sway in unison to an unheard melody, it still gave us a sense of freedom that one hadn't felt for a long time in our otherwise pleasant Delhi neighbourhood. Given that Gurugram is, on the whole, a soulless collection of tall buildings with a lot of glass, this was somewhat unexpected.

Our new home is admittedly set in a more open area, but on reflection it appeared that the real difference was made by the fact that from where we are now, we can see the horizon, and this has somehow been vastly liberating. When one looks far enough, one encounters a hazy sense of nothing. The big cities of the day deny us the horizon, unless one lives in a sea-facing apartment in a coastal city. This has arguably a strong, if invisible, effect. The cityscape traps us inside itself and gives us no out. One human contrivance leads to another; like a dictionary where one word can only be expressed in terms of another, we are caught up in the language of the city, unable to find any external reference. The city becomes the sum total of our experience, and it becomes a natural way of life.

Even the eye gets hobbled – take the experience of New York, where magnificent skyscrapers huddle so close to each other that we can never see them except in slivers of eyeshot. There is no vantage point from which the building can be admired, for the city, far from affording the sight of the horizon, refuses to let the eye travel as far as the next building. Catching a glimpse of the sky becomes an achievement. This is true of most large metropolises, where, barring deliberately constructed green spaces, there is no escaping the embrace of the urban shroud.

Without natural reference points around which we wrap our lives, urban living encourages a certain kind of abstract thinking, one that depends on language and ideas brought alive by it. It is its own metropolis, crammed with its own structures, fences, traffic signals and potholes. Conversations in the city revolve around the price of real estate, the growth in the economy, the valuation commanded by the latest unicorn – all second-order human-made contrivances with no connection to the physical or the natural. The urban mindset is more than just a physical experience; it represents an inexorable movement away from the natural rhythms of living – the urban reshapes every element in our life. When to wake up, when to sleep, when to eat, what to eat, what to talk about, what to watch, when to work, what to call work – all of these ideas get redefined. Time and space take on entirely new meanings. The time it takes to commute has less to do with the distance we need to traverse and more to do with how many other people will be on the road at the same time. Traffic, that product of other people's exertions, rules our everyday life. Space, too, takes on a peculiar grammar – 1200 sq ft 2 BHK, for instance, is a highly intelligible form of code that shapes our sense of space. Every inch of space is stretched in order to eke out utility. Space and time become precious commodities with differential values attached to them.

And then we have the other city, one that is infinite in scope and from which we do not seek escape, the internet. The digital makes the urban feel bucolic, for here, the world is made not out of stuff, but of flickers of meaning on a screen. In this rimless world, without shape or form, the idea of the horizon becomes meaningless, for here everything is within reach, regardless of how far it is.

The reason why the urge to escape to nature is so fundamental has to do with the strong need to escape ourselves and the products of our exertions. The humility that comes from finding ourselves in the midst of magnificence that we played no role whatsoever in creating, is welcome. The beach precludes argument, a mountain sunrise shuts up discussion. The valorization of nature is understandable as there is so much to run away from. It is no surprise that increasingly we have become tourists of the eye, for it is the eye that seeks succour. We feast on the sights of nature, on the travels that our eye becomes capable of. Nature today is imagined as the docile dispenser of serenity and beauty, and its other side, full of feral unpredictability, is papered over.

The horizon has the magical quality of making us feel alone; a small speck in an endless space. The sky meets the earth not with a resounding crash, but in ambivalent fluff. Just across here, there and that other place, one can see the blurry line that signals to us that infinity is a destination, at least from where we stand. The sunrise and the sunset are the best advertisements for the horizon, for here, instead of sitting in smug infinity, the horizon comes alive in a blaze of colours. The sun descends, yolk melting fatly on the horizon, and rises in a zeal of orange. The sea is particularly hospitable to the sun, as are the hills. The world appears as if in Cinemascope; the word yonder comes alive.

The horizon is both an anchor and an escape. Aircraft need an artificial horizon so as to fix their bearings. Always within reach, never within grasp, it is endless end, of a world that goes on and on simply by virtue of being round. It cements our expectations, rooting us in an illusion of finiteness while at the same time advertising itself as an illusion, urging us onwards to the next horizon. It becomes a symbol of how far we can see, how wide our imagination can stretch and what the future might hold for us. We search for new horizons, but perhaps should be grateful if we can catch a glimpse of the horizon we have.

THE BUILDER FLAT: MODERNITY WITHOUT CONTENT?

Across the country, a new kind of habitat is being created. As the city spills over from its original boundaries and moves skywards, more and more Indians are coming to terms with the idea of living in flats. In a place like Mumbai, this has always been the case, but today, even in small-town India, multi-storeyed buildings are mushrooming, and the flat is emerging as the modern way to live. For many, this shift is now so much a part of the accepted reality of our lives that it no longer carries any significance, but in reality, the changes it sets in motion can be profound.

The dominant mental model of the home has been as a place of origin, as a seat of belonging. This is why the home in India has been a highly unselfconscious space, one that accommodated all the angularities of one's preferred mode of living. The home was a sprawled space, gathering objects that were assigned places depending on the purpose they served. It was an organism which grew seemingly on its own, gradually acquiring layers of use. In most traditional homes, space wasn't measured; one rarely knew how large or small one's living space was. Space seemed to expand or contract around one's needs. The home was imagined inside out – it was a space built around the people who lived there.

The builder flat is constructed the other way around. It is conceived as the new grid within which lives are being relocated. Created by the inexorable arithmetic of space as currency, the builder flat delivers a template that acts as a solution to one's housing needs. The space is determined first – the lives of the residents who occupy it have to fit in into this preconfigured arena.

In that sense, the builder flat privileges lifestyle over one's life. It begins by an act of non-belonging. The owners are airdropped into a new life, and then have to find their place in it. It is a new skin in which the old body must find a sense of home.

In order to help a prospective buyer imagine the final product, every new building development uses a 'sample flat', which is fully done up and populated with furniture. This has become the default imagination for the new home – this dressing up of space with the veneer of surface modernity. This brand of interior design has a great preference for neatness and slickness. Nothing juts out, surfaces are evened out and glossified. The eye slides over everything that it sees – the modern 'designed' flat comes without memory or reference, the primary aim is to start anew by leaving the messiness of the past behind. The builder flat has marble floors and straight lines. Everything is exposed and all space is rendered useful.

Memories do not stand in a straight line, even though the way we measure time is linear. Memories defy chronology, they leap about and arrive unannounced. The builder flat does not allow for this untidiness, not to begin with anyway. Here the personal is tucked away behind a screen. The modern is a denial of memory rather than an evocation of a new one. It marks the beginning of a new journey. Here one is meant to strive to become oneself by jettisoning the accumulated luggage of the past.

Living in a flat and being responsible for one's own home from scratch creates a new experience of the self. In the builder flat, one arrives abruptly at the present, having bailed on the past. The builder flat is, in many ways, a no-man's land where one catches one's breath and idles in neutral. It opens up the possibility of making choices that were unavailable otherwise. It allows one to embark on a journey towards being an individual and gradually learning to make choices. The task of building one's own life in one's own home calls for making decisions that involve an awareness of one's preferences, tastes and personality. The builder flat provides a start by putting together all those elements of modernity on which there is a general consensus, and even some on which there is not.

A good example is found in the number of flats that now have an open kitchen that abuts the living room. Borrowed from the West, this is an idea that is far removed from the reality of Indian kitchens, where 'tadkas' and masalas impose themselves on one's senses. That so many people are open to this idea suggests that the desire to submit to a 'modern' life without asking too many questions of it is considerable.

The new habitat of the middle class also creates new anxieties and a desire for new affiliations. The community of the old needs to be replaced with a new kind of community. Here proximity is by itself not enough – being someone's neighbour is an elective position; one chooses who to be neighbourly with. Apartment living makes all actions deliberate – there are few things that are given, that one must do. The experience of living in a crowd while being relatively anonymous, of being in plain sight of so many without necessarily feeling observed, is a completely new sensation. To have one's action freed from the relentless scrutiny of those who appoint themselves as stakeholder in one's life can be a liberating feeling but equally, it creates a void in feeling significant that needs to be filled.

The beliefs of the past, which were steeped in so much certitude, now need to be renewed without help from an enabling environment. The self-conscious preservation of the past becomes a project, as does the desire to acquire new skills. The search for new anchors and for a new sense of belonging is only likely to intensify. New modes of living create new opportunities but also open up new gaps. The idea of being an individual is gradually getting constructed but it brings in its wake anxieties springing from an unfamiliar feeling of rootlessness. The builder flat promises freedom from the past, but offers little by way of filling this void. It offers modernity without content, replacing textured memory with neat surfaces. A new ecosystem is being created and as yet we can grasp only the bare outlines of the changes it might bring with it.

THE HOME IN TRANSITION?

Architects treat walls with a distressing amount of disdain. To them walls are nothing more than reality clearing its throat, words written in pencil with an eraser in hand. Walls can be shifted, torn down, converted into glass dividers, so that space, light and air circulation, those abstract ideas that they owe their real allegiance to, can get to do their thing. Architects can make space dance, and get it to do things that seem quite magical for the layperson. This realization came to me while going through a process of redoing our apartment, and finding both a great sense of wonder as well as an inarticulate but stubborn resistance to change. Having grown up with the idea that rooms in a home are settled existences, that cannot simply be rearranged – it is as if the material basis of all reality gets challenged when walls begin to move around.

But then the idea of buying a home is in itself a contradiction in terms. The idea that any space can arbitrarily be called home simply because of a commercial transaction, that a word tingling unbearably with meaning can get so abruptly attached to a space that one owes nothing to and has no connection with, is a little uncomfortable. But then we now transact in homes, selling and reselling them, indeed 'flipping' them as if they were hamburgers, and talking ceaselessly and animatedly about property prices.

When we buy a home, we are in effect stuffing a space devoid of meaning with an enormous amount of ourselves. But eventually a space becomes home only when we start living in it, when it becomes a natural niche in which our life curls up and sighs. The idea of home has to do with a space where we can live without being aware of ourselves. To be at home is to be asleep, in a state of blissful unconsciousness, snoring, flailing about, muttering guttural dreams, snatching memories of foetal embrace.

The home used to be a place we could never own, only belong to. Where do you come from, we were asked. We 'hailed' from somewhere – we had a 'permanent address' that we were asked about when filling any form. Even when the joint family with its headquarters at the ancestral home began to gradually fragment, its role as the emotional command post of one's life stayed put. This permanent home is where we came back to, literally in annual holidays and otherwise in our minds whenever we thought of a place of anchorage.

As a child of the Nehruvian industrial project, my childhood lay scattered over towns that my father got posted to. A product of seven schools, three colleges and twelve houses, every home came with an expiry date. While we were there, each of those places was home, but it was easy to have an acute sense of one's own insignificance. It was clear that we were passing through the structure we called home – it was ours, without that word carrying any trace of the idea of ownership.

As a space, homes did not follow any templates. Things settled around people. Space sprawled without a plan. Rooms were organized, if one could use the word, because of someone's convenience. The refrigerator could be in the bedroom because an elderly aunt who could not move around much liked her water cold. A large table lay grazing idly in a room because the grandfather, long deceased, used to write there. The lumpy sofa, grey on the inside and eventually also on the outside, was bought at the time of the war, although which one was a matter of some debate. Different rooms were painted in different colours at different times and stayed that way. A part of the house accommodated miscellaneous things that were just too messy to be organized. Space by itself did not carry a premium. Even in a small house, there were parts that were never used.

The formal delineation of space began perhaps with the idea of the drawing room a generation ago, but the transition was an awkward one. The idea that one whole room had to be kept aside only for receiving visitors was a difficult one to come to terms with. A room was empty space and should ideally be used as needed.

A site of identity, rather than a seat of adornment, what went into a home had more to do with memory than aesthetics. The home was more culture than personality. When one thinks about the showcase, still a standard feature in many Indian homes, it is striking how things deemed worthy of showcasing were often little odds-and-ends of personal memory, marking events of some significance. A squeaky toy bought from one's first trip abroad, a souvenir picked up at a honeymoon, a plaque honouring some obscure achievement, a laughing Buddha statue which, for some reason, can be seen in every nook and corner of the country. It is as if even when one wants to find ways to show off the self, one could only lapse into memory, a gallery of recollections rather than a collection of artifacts.

The architect's dazzling vision has won and the walls in our new apartment have moved. Without question, the new space it has created is much more useful. And the act of moving things around has made an alien space seem familiar. The home may no longer be the womb where we came from, but as a nest that we build for a reason, for a length of time, it still feels like home.

LIVING THE HIGH LIFE?

About nine years ago, we moved into a condo in Gurugram. It was done after a lot of moaning and foot-dragging, having to give up our first-floor home in a south Delhi colony. The idea of moving into a condo felt like moving into a synthetic world, a bubble of manicured sameness.

Much as one wanted to hate the experience, that is not what happened. We found condo living to be, above all, extremely convenient, which, at a certain stage in life, feels disproportionately important. The shared facilities are a boon, the club might be a glittering mirage but serves as a reassuring presence should we want to use it. There are the usual lifestyle trappings – a gym, pool, club events and common celebrations. It is everything that we feared it would be – a small island of privilege determined to make itself as self-sufficient as possible, and yet it vastly reduces the burden of managing everyday life that urban living imposes on you.

The condominium is a social enclave that stacks people on top of each other, exchanging the fluid interaction of the self with the outside in a regular house, for the contained order of people similarly endowed. It is bound together by a level of affluence and not much else.

To those living within it, there is an option of what to plug into and what to opt out of. There is a lot of social interaction for those who wish it, but it is easily possible to be a recluse and have nothing to do with one's neighbours. In an earlier time, neighbourhoods were like an extended family, with a good measure of dysfunction thrown in. There was an implicit reciprocity in a neighbourhood; we were bound together – if by nothing else, then by gossip – and ever-intrusive eyes that made your business everyone else's.

Apartment living was the first truly modern version of city life. A place where people didn't know each other and had little in common (notwithstanding the fact that even here, religion, caste and diet have often played a role). Condos have taken that essential template and added layers of icing to it. The attempt is to offer its residents a life that borrows in equal part from hotels, clubs, restaurants, supermarkets, chemists, and even hospitals.

The social aspect of condos is important, for given its density of population, it is not that difficult to find like-minded people. Interesting connections are possible to make, and, if desired, one can avoid the social isolation that has otherwise become the norm.

As a design, it thrives on compression. It stuffs a large number of living quarters in a small space and then mitigates the loss of room by adding on facilities that had largely become inaccessible in a city.

The condo offers what so much of the upwardly mobile affluent class seeks – not just a life, but a lifestyle. It offers form to the idea of success, translating it into a set of desirable activities, including those that are otherwise the preserve of more developed nations. Hanging out at the club, taking a lazy swim, running on the jogging track, working out at the gym – these provide a graspable handle on what the good life means, a life that normal city living denies.

In some sense, the condo tries to restore to the city everything that has been lost – social interaction, a sense of community, the ability to engage in leisure activities – but does so by cutting off its connection with the outside world.

Condo living gets a bad press in general. It is seen to be elitist; an enclave of privilege that works hard to set itself apart from the other. There is much truth to this. The mental formulation that this is a place for people like 'us' is dependent on being clear as to who is the 'them'. Hawkers are not permitted; help is frisked on its way out, and often arbitrary rules exist about keeping out people deemed 'undesirable'. Single people, particularly women, face challenges in finding a place. The condo operates as a fiefdom with its own boundaries and rules; the horrific stories that periodically emerge from condos where the owners brutally ill-treat the staff is an outgrowth of this sense of entitlement. In a larger sense, when more people retreat into these islands, the pressure to improve other public spaces and facilities diminishes.

And yet, the truth is that all urban living is not that different. Condos merely complete the process of social cleaving that has been set in motion in urban India. From a time when we all shared the same form of public transport, went to the same markets, saw the same films at the same theatres, ate the same street food, bought wares from the same vendors who roamed our streets, already the world has been divided up.

The older colonies vie with each other in enclaving and isolating themselves in the name of security. Malls cater to a defined segment, multiplexes not only charge the earth, but screen films designed for that small audience, fancy supermarkets have an in-built 'keep out' sign for those who cannot afford it, and e-commerce has made going to physical shops itself optional.

The attractiveness of condo living is a part of a larger shift in the meaning of the home. From a time when it was seen to be a place of mooring, the source where we came from, the home is now a destination, something we can own for our own edification. We evaluate homes on more utilitarian grounds – what can it do for me, what does it say about me, what kind of life can I lead here, who does it place me in the company of. Condos are designed to answer such questions, which is why they are likely to be the future of the city.

MISSING THE MOON

For one remarkable evening, the entire nation was moonstruck as we followed the descent of Chandrayaan-3 on the moon's hallowed surface. The idea of sending a spacecraft to the moon, our most enchanting neighbour in the universe, has always held magic, and we were all under its spell in that moment.

But that was an aberration. For the most part, the moon barely registers as it goes about its business and we go about ours. The moon has more or less disappeared from the lives of those who live in large cities, in small flats with smaller balconies. The moon does not preside over the night, having been tucked away behind some buildings. Our windows look often at other windows, and at night the sky is a snatch of black somewhere in the background.

This wasn't the case in an earlier era and still isn't the case as one steps out of the city. The other day, I saw the moon for the first time in a long time. It was more beautiful than I remembered – a blaze of luminosity falling out of the sky. It was in the hills, where the moon is still an arm's pluck away and where stars come out of hiding in a giddy rush. It was not quite Poornima, and sitting in the open in the well-lit night, it was impossible not to be mesmerized. The moon looked huge and implausibly round, and the fact that its magnetic pull controlled the rise and fall of tides seemed easy to believe.

Moonlight has a magic of its own. Sunlight is the default setting for the idea of light, particularly in a tropical country where the appearance of the sun comes unaccompanied by any question marks. The sun is always out and lights up the world in a flat, matter-of-fact way. The moon casts light more enigmatically, with its own cadence of waxing and waning, and sometimes disappearing altogether behind clouds. Moonlight doesn't just render things visible; it imparts a quality to everything it touches. Things seem to sparkle with their own essence under the moon, something that has made the moon so attractive to poets and writers of lyrics for Hindi film songs. It was a sign of ethereal beauty, a witness to the little games lovers played; it presided over union and heartbreak, ached with separation, marked time occasionally with indifference, and acted as a confidante for the lonely. The moon connected the individual with the universe in a way that no other natural object could. One felt kinship with the moon, never with the sun or the stars.

Nothing unified the world in quite the same way as the moon. We marked our days through our nights, giving time a lunar name. In lunar calendars, time grows out of life, with every day marked by an individual and independent character. Poornima, the night of the full moon, was imbued with a sense of fertile celebration, while Amavasya, the state of moonlessness, was seen with trepidation as it underlined the power that nature, always a fickle friend, held over us. The moon had many powers, not only over the oceans but also over the bodies and minds of animals and humans. The full moon made us wild and primitive – madness (lunacy), after all, has some lunar origins.

The moon is not that useful anymore and lives on in our imaginations as a vestigial habit. Its light carries little meaning, for the city is ablaze with its own, and it is difficult to tell a full-moon night from a moonless one. It is no longer a marker of time. Time itself has lost rhyme; it now refers to nothing else outside of itself. It offers no proof and comes with no markers. Day and night do exist, of course, but in a globalized world, with decreasing meaning. Time is now a purely conceptual entity, a convention that we have collectively agreed to submit to.

Its mysteriousness, too, has lost lustre. The moon was once beyond human reach, but as fables have it, it was made available to children crying for it by casting its reflection in a bowl of water. Even the landing of Chandrayaan on the moon serves to make it more prosaic – yet another hitherto-unfathomable presence that the human race has managed to vanquish. Flags have been planted on the moon, and, in the ultimate sign of mastery, samples from the moon have been tested in our laboratories.

Science has been nature's ally in demystifying nature and its complexities. Gradually, nature is being erased as a point of reference for our real lives, residing instead as screensaver on our virtual ones. The internet is humankind's most ambitious rejoinder to the natural universe. Here is a universe of another kind, hewed out of human imagination, living in a space constructed by electronic signals. The digital marks an independence from the physical and takes the separation from the natural to its logical end.

With time, it seems that our sources of wonder are diminishing. Once, we marvelled at everything, often out of ignorance, but the world seemed full of things much larger and more mysterious than what our minds could grasp. Now, technology produces wonder just as easily as it destroys it. We still seek wonder in other ways: in new gadgets with frequent updates, in fantastic stories of the superhuman and the otherworldly, by making nostalgic artefacts out of our past, by converting nature into a monument, by using the word 'awesome' an awful lot, and by clicking on links that promise us that we will be amazed or blown away by what we are about to see.

And yet, in the midst of all the change brought about by human progress, the moon's gravitational pull on our imagination, while buried under layers of indifference, emerges out in the open like it did during Chandrayaan's landing – it still entrances us as it always has.

DEATH BY AIR

IT HAPPENS EVERY YEAR. AS winter recedes and the AQI slinks back to its non-catastrophic levels by being merely deadly, the conversation around it begins to ebb just a little. Like so many other things we deal with, we adjust to it, accord it some kind of place in our lives, and move on muttering. Soon the muttering will also stop, as winter gives way to spring, and patches of blue can be seen occasionally in the sky.

Pollution might just be the single biggest threat to our health and our lives. According to IQAir, in 2023, 42 of the top 50 most polluted cities were in India. But if you were to follow our political discourse, you would think that apart from being another stick to beat some local governments with, it has no place in our political calculations. No senior member of the government has deemed it worthy to take serious note of it, and the same tired symbolic steps are taken every year to make a lame attempt at pretending to act.

While pollution might be the biggest problem many parts of India are facing, there is an even bigger problem that needs to be tackled first. It is the indifference with which this problem is being treated. Of course, the government takes the biggest share of the blame, but it is by no means the only stakeholder that is complicit. As voters, we don't think it is important enough to make it an election issue. Our interest in it is as transient as the intensity with which we worry about it the few days in a year that we do. The media also wakes up in alarm at precisely the same time every year and then goes to sleep when the AQI goes back to 300.

Why does this subject evoke such indifference? Why do we feel alarmed only when cities are shrouded in a toxic smog that you can cut with a knife and sing Happy Birthday to? Other governments, notably China, faced the same problem but acted with prompt determination and managed to substantially transform the quality of the air, so why can't we? Even here, solutions have been placed on the table by many knowledgeable experts, so it isn't as if the government doesn't know what to do, however difficult that action might be. The magnitude of the problem warrants it.

Part of the problem lies in the nature of the issue. Unless it is truly extreme, the problem is not visible. It is literally all around us. Breathing is the single most natural human activity. We are hard-wired not to notice it, unless we are sitting cross-legged in a yogasana doing anulom-vilom. Trusting our breath is a central human need, for otherwise, every breath would be a minefield. Learning to distrust water was difficult enough; thinking about the dangers of breathing is just too exhausting.

A bigger issue is that a natural reaction among a large group of people about pollution, or, in a larger sense, the environment, is an air of masculine disdain. It is seen as an effete concern of those who are fragile, who do not have the grit necessary to deal with life's difficulties, and who need to be protected from every little eventuality. The sense of 'it's not such a big deal' is bolstered by the fact that, barring those that suffer from respiratory issues and react adversely to bad air quality, for most others the consequences are long-term in nature. By the time we figure out that we should have been worried, we needn't. We might well be dead.

There is, of course, the other reality to consider. For a significant part of India, navigating everyday life is difficult enough without needing to worry about the toxicity of the air. There are many more problems that are more immediate and pressing that make the prospect of a future decline in health not a particularly compelling issue. It is unlikely that this section has the inclination to care about this subject.

For the others, the most urgent action that is needed today is to attack this institutional and individual indifference. Having a measurable index for poor air quality is a start, but the problem with numbers is that very high ones desensitize us to those that are merely high. Once we have seen numbers cross 1,000 in news reports, a 500 feels tolerable and 300, the level at which other countries shut down schools, feels positively healthy.

What we need are private sector campaigns round the year that keep the issue top of mind. Hospitals need to show a running scoreboard of people suffering from respiratory disorders. Air purifiers should have an in-built alarm that starts going off when a certain threshold is crossed (this is being done in the case of vehicular speed; we hear a beep when we cross 80 kmph and then a constant sound when we breach the 120 kmph barrier). A siren that goes off when a certain level is breached. Signboards everywhere that track air quality. We need a protocol for when to shut down schools and offices so that work visibly suffers when the situation is bad. Importantly, this protocol should be based on international norms where even an AQI of 151–200 is classified as very unhealthy and demands significant restrictions. Mask advisories need to be issued, and smartphone apps with clear instructions on what to do at what level need to be designed and circulated.

The overall idea is to convert an abstract potential danger into a tangible reality. We need to disrupt normal life so that there is a cost attached to our indifference, particularly for people who are in influential decision-making roles. And all of this is needed not to solve the problem but to try and ensure that the real problem is taken seriously. Politically, socially, and economically, it is time to make this issue matter.

THE TERRACE – A MOUTHFUL OF SKY

As THE TRAIN HURTLES PAST the interminable outskirts of Delhi, the geography falters and then fragments. Scale shrinks and life becomes a spray of composite humanity. Small plots, narrow houses, some without any plaster cladding, huddle together in animated proximity. People, shops, houses, rickshaws, cows, streets, garbage, electricity poles, and wires are a smudge of activity to the moving eye. Neighbourhoods here are a babble of space and a jumble of time. The only snatches of space that can be seen are the terraces that every house, no matter how small, seems to have. The ubiquity of the terrace sparks off memories going back to childhood.

The terrace was a space that rose above our lives, pushing outwards into the sky. A site of retreat, a little hideaway from chores and the relentless embrace of middle-class families. A place to escape to, and steal a quick smoke. A place from which to look longingly at the latest object of one's affections in the neighbourhood. A place you would find in a Ghulam Ali ghazal where assignations quivering with risk took place.

The terrace came alive particularly in the winters as we gravitated upwards. As long as the sun was out, the terrace was crammed full of activity – people either lounging around, sitting on charpoys, eating 'chikis' and shelling peanuts, standing and gazing at the world, drying clothes and pickles, knitting sweaters absent-mindedly while gossiping over endless cups of tea, and, when the time was right, flying kites.

One ran onto terraces when the first rains of the season came, drawn irresistibly by the tentative patter of drops that soon became the insistent tattoo of real rain. In summers, the only time one ventured onto the terrace in the day was to put clothes out to dry or to retrieve them, feet stinging on the burning floor as one hopped hurriedly to complete the chore. When the sun went down, the terrace became much more welcoming. Sleeping on the terrace was always a relief, however hot the night might be. The early mornings were sweet as the heat abated enough for one to feel the need for a sheet, till of course the sun had its way and we were all up, and then one floor down, back to earth to resume regular life.

Implicit in the idea of the terrace is a different understanding of space and time. Rooms have a purpose, they house things that are used. A room has a grammar of use, for things in it are arranged in a certain way for a reason. A chair sits here, and a sofa is placed symmetrically against another. The terrace is space left over, kept fallow for activities of a sundry kind to spill over into. Apart from being a place to dry clothes, it serves no specific fixed purpose, and its commodiousness allows for a variety of uses. Sometimes the centre of activity, and on other occasions accessed only to check if the water tank was indeed empty, or if the television antenna needed a good twist till the picture downstairs improved. Time, too, takes on a different quality on the terrace, as it is more directly aligned with the natural rhythms of the day. The sun, the moon, the rain, and the wind – these are what determine how we use this space.

Of course, there was always an element of purpose in the terrace. In Delhi, for instance, the 'barsaati' was a fixture in most 'kothis'. While the name conjures up the wonderful idea that some room has been made for the rain to beat down on one's home, it had a more practical side to it. So many young people – a gaggle of bachelors or tentative young couples beginning their journey towards real adulthood – have made their start in the one room that was perched on the terrace. The barsaati was the first step in the act of becoming a householder, a toehold in the urban sprawl. It gave the young their own space, and made up in sky what it stinted on land. '*Thodi si zameen, thoda aasman,*' as the Gulzar song goes.

There were other pauses of space that dotted the landscape. The 'aangan', the patio, the courtyard, the chowk, the balcony, the verandah, the dusty garden, apart from the terrace. Little outbreaks of freedom, zones where the inside and the outside met while preserving the integrity of both. Each served a slightly different purpose, but each was a way of leaving one's life ajar for the outside world to come in for a bit. The private was always a little public, and nature was never a complete stranger.

The train approaches a city, and as the landscape becomes more upmarket, the houses become larger, signs of life rarer, and the terraces invisible. In the flat of today, the terrace is a right to be bought and used exotically. The terrace is a premium facility, one that could house a bar, a garden, or, in the case of the really well-off, a swimming pool. It is no longer an overflow of space, the remainder in a maths sum involving division, but purposeful real estate, to be accounted for in calculations.

As our new compulsions of space have taken over, the homes of today have no room for these lungs of our life. On the other hand, we do have social media, which kind of plays a similar role. Twitter (now called X), is the public square where all of humanity washes its dirty linen. Facebook is the patio of today's times, as we hang out of our virtual balconies and gaze at our timelines going by. We are voyeurs all over again, nosy neighbours intensely involved in everything that everyone else does. In some ways, nothing changes. But the terrace was a place purposefully empty, waiting for us to fill it in with whatever else we wanted from our life. That kind of emptiness seems to be a luxury today.

HIGHWAYS OF CHANGE?

ROADS FEEL A CERTAIN WAY. Every highway has its own character, its own little quirks. One gets to notice this best when one drives down the same road regularly, but infrequently. As a document of change, the road is quite articulate, and travelling year in and out on the same road is instructive, for it helps frame change sharply.

The same does not quite happen in the train, for the landscape around railway tracks changes far more slowly. For one, unlike the highway, which is constantly subject to change, both through neglect and design, railway tracks are lines drawn into eternity, and even the landscape around them has an air of settled finality. The rhythmic movement of the train lends an air of comfortable predictability to the experience. The outside is a visual backdrop that rattles by without drawing any attention to itself. On the road, one notices much more and reacts more immediately to a constantly changing context.

Of course, along with the road, one changes too. From a time when the bus was the primary mode of travel to one where becoming a squished passenger in a squashed car felt like heaven. Then, the car stopped getting stuffed with people, it stopped overheating and breaking down at routine intervals, and air-conditioning, that divine human invention, made its way into our lives. With time and greater comfort, one also grew more impatient with the slightest inconvenience, so overall, the grumpiness factor in the car did not change significantly. We found newer things to grumble about. Something called legroom, which is never quite enough. And suspension, which is too hard or too soggy. And, of course, other drivers who are cursed colourfully for being reckless road hogs, even when they drive exactly as we do.

In my own case, the road I am most familiar with happens to be the one connecting Delhi with Nainital. From a time when it was a thin rope apologetically wriggling its way through the landscape to now, when, for the most part, it is a four-lane assertion of self-confident authority, the road has come a long way. Passing through crowded market towns (Hapur and Moradabad, in this case) was a nightmarish prospect that was much dreaded and the crossing of which produced celebratory relief. The obstacle course – two major and two-to-three minor level crossings to negotiate, one of which could sometimes take hours to cross. Of course, the logic of level crossings in India is that the most obnoxious behaviour gets the most reward. The hunt for toilets was often white-knuckled, as the women present in the car could testify. The men, of course, went anywhere. Petrol pumps were very few, and on some stretches, a single miss was enough to guarantee disaster. There were a few places to eat – usually dhabas, some celebrated, others dodgy, the odd shabby government tourist facility, and one enterprising entrepreneur who had set up a large complex, complete with almost clean toilets, and a wide choice of attractive but mediocrely cooked food. An option that was usually favoured was to carry packed meals. This meant that a shaded spot by the side of the road was found and an elaborate meal laid down on some bedsheets.

Of course, the modern has brought with it its own set of obstacles. The level crossings have virtually disappeared, but they have been replaced by the equally diabolical device called the toll booth. A toll booth is a breakdown in conversation. It is an invitation to collapse. A spectacle of chaos, argument, and, in some cases, gunfire. People cut into lanes, honk impatiently at the vehicle in front, and find reasons why they are too important to have to pay the toll. Of course, the builders of highways rarely account for the fact that when fast-moving traffic encounters a dead stop, a pile-up is inevitable.

Now with the introduction of the national FASTag system, which allows us to breeze through the toll booths, things have certainly changed. Even now, of course, one could have the misfortune of being stuck behind someone who decides to argue that the toll is not applicable to them, but otherwise things are a lot better.

The toilet situation has improved significantly, and this is a big development. However, the availability of toilets and the usability of said facilities are not always aligned. There is a curious Indian indifference to toilets, and it is not uncommon to come across spanking new structures that stink gloriously. For women, every new toilet experience is an expedition into the olfactory unknown, and the person who goes first becomes the reluctant pioneer for the rest.

But overall, with time, the highway journey has become easier. Although most journeys continue to be punctuated by sights of impossibly mangled vehicles even now, four-lane roads have made travel a little safer, not that there is still any guarantee that some truck won't come careening down the wrong side of the road. Some of the comfort also comes from being able to leap over reality – flyovers that skirt the issue, and bypasses that take the long way around nowhere. Unlike an expressway, which skims over reality and sidesteps habitation and where all dialogue with the emotional landscape of the country ceases, traditional highways, in their spruced-up avatar, produce a hybrid form of reality – some intense contact with civilization peppered with long periods of abstinence. But even with these, over a period of time, highways make people disappear. Eventually, everything becomes a blur of metal on tar.

The highway experience has become more ordered, within the bounds of the kind of order India is capable of producing. It has gained in comfort what it has lost in texture, but on the whole, things are far easier. The time it takes to reach the edge of the urban has stretched significantly. Reaching the great wide open, with fields luxuriating in space without getting hemmed in by a building of some sort, now can take close to a couple of hours. But the feeling of release when one does finally hit the open road, continues to be as exhilarating as it always was.

Popular Pursuits

The Power of Melodrama

We don't merely consume drama – we live it.

Our national pastimes – cricket, Bollywood, music and celebrity – have morphed into personal mythologies, where fandom becomes identity and emotion finds its loudest echo in the public square.

Melodrama, it turns out, is our national operating system.

THE POWER OF MELODRAMA

Growing up, one remembers longing for our cinema to become more realistic, or, at the very least, a little less ridiculous. At one stage, virtually every film made was a lost-and-found potboiler that featured more or less the same dialogues. We have got our wish to a certain extent. The films of today try harder to tell a single story, populate them with characters that go beyond Kishan and Bishan, two friends who became enemies for a while until one sacrificed his life for the other, and steer clear of some stock devices, including heroes disguising themselves by wearing pencil-thin moustaches and ripping them off come climax time to reveal their inner Jeetendra. Of course, no one can still accuse Hindi cinema of stark realism, but, on the whole, today it bears greater resemblance to reality than it did in the past, with due apologies to the *Grand Masti* school of film-making.

But something is lost in the bargain. A couple of months ago, this realization about Hindi cinema was brought home to me thanks to my Iraqi-born cabbie in London, who, after giving us a 30-minute lecture on the relative merits of Amitabh Bachchan and Dharmendra, bemoaned the fact that the films of today are just not the same. No emotion, he said, hollow like Hollywood. Where did the stories full of twists, turns and coincidences go? When did the emotional crescendos give way to life-sized depictions of what we go through every day? People are boring, myths were not.

Much as a part of me is grateful that the repetitive tedious melodramas of yore have died out, it is also true that watching movies is not the full-bodied experience it once was. More interesting cinema is being made today than in the 1980s and 1990s certainly, but one's involvement with it is not the same.

We are outside the film when we watch it today; we consume it with cautious discernment. Reviews are scanned, opinions sought, and critiques discussed. The delight of an earlier time, the unrestrained glee with which any and every film, however bad, was lapped up, is now a distant memory. Cinema at its best today is thoughtful entertainment, but it is not quite undiluted magic.

The role of melodrama was to dissolve us in a collective soup of feeling. Everything had heightened meaning, and we, as audiences, were nothing. Something big was always at stake, heroes were never really representing only themselves. Mothers died coughing, sisters were thrown out of their marital homes, fortunes were usurped, the family's honour was hanging by a thread.

Cinema was able to stir up emotion using devices that were standard; you could see them coming from a mile. The dialogue-baazi, the rubbing in of indignities, the amplification of the sordid, the setting up of overly neat archetypes, the need to repeat everything loudly thrice – barring our TV news channels, we don't see these kinds of devices anymore in popular culture.

Mere paas ma hai. Kanoon ke haath. Khandan ki izzat. The innocent tawaif. The father's heart attack. The doctor-chacha's advice to go to a hill station. The reformed vamp wearing a white saree in the last shot. The long dialogue-soaked death of heroes. *Yeh shaadi nahi ho sakti.* Pagdi, vardi, khoon, mamta, parampara, wafa, me-lord, dua not dawa, kalmuhi – all gone.

In this world, everything was fraught with consequences. People were suspended in culturally determined roles that they could not detach themselves from. Nothing existed on its own, no event or person had any agency as such. One acted because one had to, and one paid the price because that was the rule. But nothing was matter of fact; the cost of everything was spelled out, and the joys fairly quivered with bliss connoted by exactly one particular set of musical notes.

Hamming was and continues to be a game that the film plays with an audience. It allowed the viewers to insert themselves emotionally into the narrative, by emphasizing that this was an enactment, not real life, which is why it was worth so much. Theatricality was the burden carried by the culturally significant. The actor's role was not merely to make the character believable, but to make the culture it resided in desirable.

Those who cringe at this kind of cinema stand outside the narrative; and the whole game is not meant for them. These are people who cannot let go of a sense of self-awareness even for a moment, they are unable or unwilling to immerse themselves in the emotional tides of their surrogate psyches represented on screen. They are too aware of the surface absurdity of what is being shown, forgetting that the film is trying to speak not to the individual but to something more primal that resides inside us.

There are good melodramatic films and there are ordinary attempts that don't come together. These tend to use melodrama without belief, as a formula. Emotionally powerful representations need the belief of the maker, they need the willingness to embrace the fullness of the encounters that unfold on screen. The great melodramas could be watched over and over again. There was nothing to reveal, but enough to experience. Memories do not fear repetition, myths grow with every retelling. The films were meant to evoke sentiment, not to tell a new story. Ironically, those films are missed on grounds that the films of today 'do not tell a story'. In truth, what is being said is that the films of today do not travel down sweeping arcs of emotion, they lack the dizzying highs and plunging lows that made watching films an emotionally vertiginous experience.

But while there may be occasional pangs of nostalgia, there is no going back. We know too much, and cannot unlearn what we know. We cannot become putty again, and so we will discuss cinema and make our points, and disagree with each other's 'takes'. We own our movies now, they don't own us.

THE ANGER OF THE STRONG?

RRR, PUSHPA, KABIR SINGH AND *Animal* – what is common to all these films is an exaggerated form of masculinity that lies well beyond the pale of reality. Now, Indian films, however fantastic they might be, have always spoken some emotional truth. Like advertising, Indian cinema is a lie that speaks the truth.

The much-discussed 1970s phenomenon of the angry young man came from a larger social reality of a generation that felt orphaned, having been abandoned by father figures and having lost any sense of direction. Which is why so many Amitabh Bachchan films, in particular, dealt with this subject. In film after film, Bachchan's character is let down by a father-like figure, whether it was *Deewar*, *Shakti*, *Sharaabi* or *Trishul*. The emotional resonance of Bachchan's archetypal character resounded beyond the confines of any one particular story – it spoke for a generation. The films were violent, the character was self-destructive, there was an overt display of masculinity, but there was a deeper reason that drove it.

Today, what we see is the detachment of violence from emotional purpose. The anger behind the spectacular acts of violence comes from outside the script. It is in the air, and it seeps into the narrative as an external agent. It relies on the audience sharing this unstated reservoir of frustration and plays to it without too much explanation. The anger comes from different apparent sources. In *Animal*, it is the cold father figure, in *Kabir Singh*, the girlfriend who married someone else, in *RRR*, it is the anger of an oppressed community. In each case, the anger feels overblown and contrived. The violence itself is the symbol, perhaps the most important one.

The other characteristic of today's films is that the violence is fantasized. Now, in a certain sense, all cinematic violence is a form of fantasy. Real-world violence is far less spectacular and much clumsier. But if beating up a dozen people in a warehouse was over-the-top, what we see today goes far beyond the fantastic. Dozens, sometimes hundreds of people are massacred in gory detail, limbs are torn, eyes gouged, and heads separated from the body in slow motion. The pornography of violence, where it is feasted upon, blood running from one's mouth, is unlike anything we saw in an earlier generation.

What is central to these stories is not mere violence, but an unhinged expression of male anger. The need to go beyond the limits of understanding, to plumb the depths of a primal rage that needs to bear no relationship to the trigger that caused it, is somehow an essential part of these films. What it does, in effect, is to give licence to leave all ideas of a reasonable response behind. Male anger becomes self-justifying, its presence itself being a sign that it needed to exist. This is rage at its infantile peak, a screaming anger that knows no context and respects no boundaries. It is narcissistic in the deepest possible way and comes from a place of an imagined centrality in the universe.

What is represented is the anger of the strong, rather than that of the weak. Even the manner in which violence is enacted underlines this. The desire is not merely to overcome or overpower an antagonist, it is to decimate them, to pulverize them into a state of non-being. The intensity of the violence, the need to go beyond the mere outcome of victory, comes from a desire for strength that cannot be challenged. The alpha-male depictions are part of this need to experience a kind of mastery over the world, where the weak know their place and accept that their role is that of supplicants. The celebration of inequality, of designating people as alphas who have a right to lord it over others, is accompanied by a belief that an essential feature of masculinity is anger. And that the acceptance of the legitimacy of this anger is the natural order of things, one that is ordained. In this scheme of things, the weak will follow, and women, while professing disgust, will be attracted to this kind of excessive masculine display, even if it involves licking the boots of the protagonist as a sign of love.

Where does this need come from? At one level, it is the fantasy of strength which comes out of the comfort of being part of a majority that also enjoys the explicit backing of a state that is not shy about using its muscle. But a major source of this anger lies perhaps in the changing equation between the genders. There is a reason why so many of these hypermasculine films go out of their way to assign a secondary, and often degrading, position to the women they depict. The reassertion of male superiority, of underlining traditional gender roles, becomes an important project at a time when the contrary is the reality. Women are exercising far greater power, showing agency in domains that were once restricted for them, and challenging men in spheres where they reigned supreme. The desire to put women back in their place is an animating motivation for a lot of these films.

What does this mean for us as a society? At one level, we could see these films as a fantasized response to an unstoppable change. Men will have to adjust to a new reality where they are no longer presumptive masters of the world that they live in. Let the men have their toys while they can, could be one response. The other would be to worry about where this kind of cinema will take us. Given that politically, there is great comfort with maintaining more traditional gender roles, this emphatic assertion of masculinity might take us back in time. When the strong feel the need to justify their existence through a brute show of power, it is time to worry.

BOLLYWOODIZING OUR LIVES

Just the other day, the calm in our residential area was shattered by loud music coming from a nearby school that was celebrating Republic Day. Barring a five-minute lull that included the playing of the national anthem, the soundtrack for the morning consisted entirely of upbeat dance-worthy Bollywood songs. To be fair, most of them could be classified as having some patriotic sentiment, although there were others where that connection was extremely tenuous ('Jai ho,' for instance, which, barring its rousing title, carries not a trace of patriotic feeling in the rest of the song). It would appear that without the help of Bollywood, we have no vocabulary in which to express the idea of patriotism, or, at a more fundamental level, the idea of celebration itself.

But then, Bollywood is everywhere and one uses the label deliberately. It isn't cinema, which has always been deeply influential in India, but the bloated commercially packaged version of the culture that has come to represent it, that is everywhere. Bollywood has become shorthand for a way of living life by amplifying crude pleasure, accessed cheaply.

Every celebration in India somehow ends up becoming a Bollywood dance. Every function needs a Bollywood star. Stars from any field need to dance at functions. Media summits that apparently transform the world with earth-shattering cerebral dialogues cannot do without a few Bollywood-types to represent the 'youth'. Every awards show requires people wearing shiny leotards gyrating in a simulation of coordination. Public parks and monuments have been taken over by the 'wedding shoots' of newly married couples, as they enact Bollywood-inspired scenes of romance in slow motion. Across the country, 'baraats' are becoming the norm, no matter what the original customs might have been, and everyone dances to film songs on the street. The wedding today is nothing but an extension of what in the older days would be labelled a 'dream sequence' in films. Fantastic sets, impossibly bejewelled people glittering from every part of their bodies, a willingness to break into dance at every available opportunity, and an obsession with the self that would be pathological if it hadn't been so thoroughly normalized.

The kawadias who walk days on foot have trucks accompanying them that blare Bollywood music from giant speakers. Talent shows are full of tiny children bumping and grinding to suggestive songs, egged on by beaming proud parents, unmindful of what they are making their children do. Bhajans are cheerfully set to the tune of 'Munni badnaam hui, darling tere liye' ('Bhakt phire maara maara, o maiya tere liye'), or 'Choli ke peeche kya hai' ('Mata ke dil mein kya hai'). This creeping Bollywoodization of our landscape has largely gone unchallenged.

Cast your mind back to the controversy around the film *Padmaavat*. The most puzzling aspect about the whole episode was why an outfit like the Karni Sena would object to a film that did nothing but glorify, and that too in the excessive idiom of Sanjay Leela Bhansali, all that passes for traditional Rajput values. The film was a paean to the codes, values, symbols, rituals and people that the Karni Sena apparently represents.

Perhaps the provocation, such as it is, is not provided by the content of the film, but the fact that it got the Bollywood treatment. Revealingly, Maharajkumar Vishvaraj Singh, son of Mahendra Singh Mewar, reportedly called it a 'historic fraud to portray an incorrectly attired courtesan-like painted doll in the song as the very "queen" the film purports to pay obeisance to'.

But then per Bollywood standards, the queen is the heroine, and heroines have to dance. This film is reverential in its intent of everything the Karni Sena holds dear, except that it is hard-wired to show its reverence in the idiom of Bollywood. This means that every character is, above all, a supplicant to the viewer. The reason why item songs have been invented is to get rid of any artifice whatsoever – these songs are not situated in the story at all; they are just airdropped into the film to pander to the viewer. Rewarding the spectator in every scene, enabling an owner's relationship between the key character and the viewer, is the implicit rule that successful commercial blockbusters must follow. Touched by Bollywood, even what is presented as sacred becomes a commodity – a shiny one perhaps, but a commodity nevertheless.

But while that controversy is now an infinitesimal speck in the overcrowded rear-view mirror of our social media feed, it raises a larger question: should the coarsening of our everyday lives not offend us a little more than it does? Can we not find new currencies of expression that draw from more diverse sources? Growing out of an imagination colonized by Bollywood may be a good starting point. What is particularly surprising is that even as Bollywood struggles, in the face of the competition provided by OTT channels, to retain its hold over our consciousness, its pervasive influence has not waned.

THE ETERNAL VOICE

Many years ago, I was sitting in the lounge-cum-restaurant at Delhi airport, those days on the first floor. I had my back to the door, and was, amid the usual hubbub that marks such public spaces, immersed in my phone. Suddenly, like the parting of the sea in some stirring mythological tale, a hushed silence swept over that large bustling space. Lata Mangeshkar had just walked in, along with a couple of other elderly women. She quietly slipped into her chair, drawing absolutely no attention to herself by her actions, but it was a lost cause. Nothing else existed but that reverential silence, almost religious in its certitude. Celebrities routinely cause a stir when they appear god-like in our midst, but this was something different, this instinctive sense of gratitude.

How do you remember someone like Lata Mangeshkar? How do you acknowledge someone who has been a presence in your life virtually every single day of your existence? How do you separate her influence from the rest of your life? What do you say about someone who has filled in gaps, transported you to feel emotions that don't come easily, filled you with awe, moved you to tears? It is almost like an important part of one's back story has slipped away.

My earliest memories of Lata's songs came through my mother, who had a habit of singing as she went about her household chores. Unlike my father, who had the same habit but was innocent of the concepts of melody and metre, she could sing and Lata's songs were a favourite. Of course, the transistor was always on and so, like for every other Indian at that time, Lata Mangeshkar was just an omnipresent fact of life. Like what Ramanujan said of the Mahabharata, no Indian has ever heard Lata Mangeshkar for the first time. I was a fan before knowing

I was one, and with time, the admiration only grew as the songs took on more specific meaning.

What made it possible for Lata to be so dominant for so long? Part of the reason lies in the peculiar institution of playback singing, which allows us to focus on the song, and not the singer. It is also true, as is widely believed, that along with her sibling, she used her power to thwart the prospects of potential rivals. But eventually, it was her voice and its ability to stay unsullied by the march of time or her life experiences. It may have lost some of that sparkling freshness which leaps out at you in her early years, but it did not change in character or texture.

Perhaps it was the little-girl innocence in her voice that sat well with the idealized conception of the woman in Hindi films. Lata's voice captures all emotional nuances but for knowingness. That was Asha's domain – the articulation of the more complex feelings of desire and worldly disappointment. Lata's finest songs come at the junction of pain and longing, and evoke a woman who is afraid to want what she does. Although Lata has sung songs of every possible genre, melancholic wistfulness is what she does best.

Her voice has often been compared to water. It has the same transparent quality, it flows effortlessly, ascending and descending notes with fluid ease. It has the universality of appeal, the ageless ability to speak the truth, and, like water, is able to quench thirst in a way that nothing else can. Her songs communicate with a directness that gets to the heart of the emotion that they seek to evoke, which is perhaps why she was the preferred choice of so many music directors, however diverse their styles might be.

It is usual to talk of the passing of an era when someone important dies. But in Lata's case there can be no passing. Lata did not belong to any one era, and her music will continue to cast spells as it always has. In that sense we haven't lost her – she had transcended mortality quite a while back.

A MUSIC OF WHOLENESS?

THERE IS SOMETHING COMPELLING ABOUT refined gentleness. So compelling, in fact, that even in these polarized and angry times, it manages to rise above the vitriol that characterizes so many of our public conversations, and makes us recognize its quiet power. In the persona of Zakir Hussain, we saw this power on display as he managed to remain one of the few people about whom virtually nobody had a negative thing to say.

What made him unique wasn't just his virtuosity with the tabla, though that was extraordinary enough. It was his ability to make music that reached what one might call a substrate of oneness, a place that transcended rather than denied differences. In an age where identity is worn as a badge of differentiation, Hussain's music suggested a more profound truth – that the deeper we go, the more connected we feel. We simply outlast and outpace differences. That what lay beneath all the things that we believe define us was something far deeper and infinitely more valuable – something words and labels could not begin to describe.

Consider the ease with which he inhabited seemingly contradictory spaces. Here was a classical tabla maestro who could sit behind a Western drum kit with complete naturalness, an accompanist to orthodox purists who could just as easily collaborate with experimental fusion artists. He was equally at home in a traditional mehfil and a global jazz festival, in an austere classical recording and a playful advertisement for tea that became part of our cultural memory.

In his case, belonging to one label or another seemed to be no struggle – he simply followed the music to its natural destinations. His music suggested a deeper authenticity that made such movements across cultural spaces seem natural rather than self-conscious. He was every inch an Indian artist even as he became a completely natural global citizen, suggesting that these identities need not be at war.

Unusually for a classical musician, for decades he was the face of a brand of tea, in what was a truly inspired collaboration, and yet he was never deemed to have sold out to the forces of commerce. He was a young heart-throb who came closest to generating a rockstar-like reaction among his audience, and yet the adulation, while gratefully acknowledged, did not seem to change him in any way.

The secret perhaps lay in his chosen instrument and role. The tabla, in the classical tradition, is primarily an accompaniment, its artistry lying in enhancement rather than domination. His role was to help the music discover what it wanted to become. As the guardian of time, his tabla spoke when it needed to in the manner that the music demanded, in whispers or as thunder. This is a peculiar kind of genius – one that finds its fullest expression in making others sound better.

He managed his superstardom with grace, never allowing it to overshadow either his art or his role as an accompanist. He represented the face of the tabla; in mainstream consciousness, these two were synonymous, but he always took care to shrug off superlatives by calling attention to the other maestros of the instrument who were not as well known.

This quality extended beyond his music. There was a grace with which he embraced people from all walks of life, and the genuine warmth with which he engaged across hierarchies of fame and status suggested someone who understood that true artistry lies in connection rather than performance. In an era of carefully curated public personae, his humility felt neither practised nor strategic but as an overflow from his natural persona.

An aspect that made his passing feel wrong was that he embodied a sense of youth regardless of his age. His mane, even if it had become less lush with time, was still a joyous accompaniment to his music, bouncing along as he weaved his magic on the tabla. His visage was never burdened, never lined with cynicism; the aura of youthfulness that he exuded was rooted not in time but in innocence. There was a refusal to let the outside world intrude on and taint the sacred pact he had with music.

In his art, we saw the possibilities of differences becoming reasons for dialogue rather than division. He worked across the spectrum of musical expression – from the most orthodox to the most experimental, without compromise or dilution. With his music, he demonstrated how tradition, when deeply understood, becomes a way to exercise freedom rather than act as a confining cage. His mastery of the classical form was so complete that he could experiment freely without ever feeling restrained by tradition.

This has implications far beyond music. In a world increasingly anxious about cultural appropriation and authenticity, Hussain showed how true cross-cultural dialogue might work – not through superficial borrowing or defensive preservation, but through deep understanding and genuine respect. The numerous collaborations that marked his career weren't just musical experiments; they were demonstrations of how differences might be bridged without being erased. Whether performing with jazz legends or classical maestros, what emerged wasn't a reduction to the lowest common denominator but an elevation to new possibilities of expression.

What was most remarkable was that he managed to do this without ever making it an overt cause. There was no preaching, no messaging about breaking barriers or building bridges. The transcendence of differences emerged naturally from the music itself, from its ability to reach that substrate of oneness where our constructed divisions reveal their ultimate insubstantiality. The music did the talking; words were not needed.

What made Ustad Zakir Hussain so special was that he embodied the power of wholeness through everything he did and represented. In some ways, he exemplified why music occupies such a special place in our hearts, and why it can reach places that nothing else can. Music makes us better than we deserve to be, and Zakir Hussain brought us face-to-face with our better selves.

THE VIRAT KOHLI PARADOX

Virat kohli has had an exceptional career along with its attendant ups and downs. His record is exceptional, across all formats of the game. As he rides off into the sunset, one format at a time, how will we remember his legacy?

In the last few years, Kohli has outstripped all heroes of the past, and yes, that includes Sachin Tendulkar, in terms of performance. The numbers tell an eloquent story and it feels as if he still has some gas left in the tank. He has matured at a personal level, too, having channelized his earlier impetuousness into a highly productive form of aggression on the field. He seeks out challenges, vying to insert himself into the toughest situations in order to test himself. When he was captain, too, he had found a way to make his aggression work for the team, and the results had followed.

As a player, he operates at peak fitness, having chiselled his physical appearance to a point where he looks like a compendium of flattering contemporary adjectives. He is married to a top Bollywood star, and promotes any number of local and international brands – and, as expected, basks in the attention showered on him by adoring fans wherever he goes. His performance is still spoken of with awe. The six off Haris Rauf in Australia, his heroics in the 2023 World Cup in India, they all add up to a stirring story.

For all that, something is missing in our relationship with Virat Kohli. The crowds do chant his name when he walks in to bat, but he does not make our heart stop. He can be applauded, but his success is somehow not our success in the same way as with other players in the past. He evokes awe, but does not evoke superstition. Sachin, Dhoni, Sehwag, Dravid, Ganguly, Gavaskar and Kapil Dev in earlier eras – were some of the players who enjoyed a deep connection with fans that Kohli does not quite have. Many might contest that, but Kohli does not get under our skin and stir up our emotions the way the greats of an earlier time did. We make up in fulsome praise what we cannot in emotion.

Part of the reason lies in the fact that cricket itself does not evoke the passion it once did. Too much cricket, peppered with too many sixes, too many 300-plus scores in one-day matches accompanied by the exact same commentary that was born in the early 1990s, has robbed cricket of some vitality. Watching cricket is a habit, but the involvement is becoming more passive. In most cases, even diehard fans keep track of the score, rather than follow it actively. One series blurs into another, and one tournament erases memories of previous editions.

But the larger reason is that Virat Kohli lacks a narrative. His performance works for him and the team, and by extension for the country, but it does not reveal any cherished truths about us as a collective. It does not feed into any deep-seated anxiety, nor does it help us believe in an incredible dream. Sachin Tendulkar spoke to a nation's need to be taken seriously. He was our cherub who could take on the world effortlessly. The Sachin narrative was always about us, never about him – we owned him and willed him to succeed.

To some extent, the extended loss of form Kohli went through a couple of years ago and his subsequent recovery did create a sense of sympathy for him, but it was of a generic kind. The redemptive arc of hero-fallen-on-bad-times finding his feet again is a familiar one and is not specific to him. We miss his aggression as a captain, but again in a low-key way.

Dhoni and Sehwag, in their own ways, spoke for the nothing-to-lose fearlessness of small-town India. Dravid's narrative was a more archetypal one. The idea of commitment and integrity honed till it shone bright, offered us hope that decency is still relevant in today's transactional times.

Virat Kohli does not have the same effect on us – he does not tap into a larger storyline. He has a story – of his transition from a hot-headed brat into an aggressive but mature sportsman, but it is one that lacks both cinematic scale and an emotional hook. He makes us admire him, but what we really want is a reason to admire ourselves. Here, the Kohli story falls short. By the time he hit his stride, India had already reached the pinnacle of the sport more than once, and we did not have that much to prove to the world through cricket. His journey does not easily represent something larger, and Kohli's greatness turns statistical far too easily. Kohli is a superstar we admire, but not quite a symbol that we need.

Which is why, when the BCCI, in its usual inscrutable way, decided to sideline Kohli in a less-than-gracious way, he garnered some support but there wasn't the kind of outrage that would have been evoked if the same action had been taken against someone like Dhoni.

It is unfair, but true. For in Kohli's efforts there is not a trace of selfishness; he does not allow his celebrity status to intrude into any aspect of his performance. He gives more than what can be asked on the field for the Indian team. 'There is no enough to Kohli,' as the sublime Rohit Brijnath put it.

Sometimes, being a hero has less to do with one's own achievements and more to do with what the audience lacks. Amitabh Bachchan became a superstar because his audience wanted a voice for their repressed feelings. Sachin became a liberalization-era hero because the country wanted to see a more assertive self in the mirror. Today, it is possible that Kohli's brilliance does not give us the answers we need, or perhaps cricket has itself stopped being a vehicle of anything more than itself. At its best, cricket is a thrilling spectacle, and Virat Kohli its headline act.

SUNNY DAYS FOREVER?

THERE IS SOMETHING ABOUT SUNIL GAVASKAR that makes him a permanent presence in our lives. He burst onto the international scene over fifty years ago and has never stopped being a part of our lives ever since. Barring Lata Mangeshkar and Amitabh Bachchan, there is no other Indian public figure in any sphere that has had the same longevity as him. If, for the first sixteen years, it was as a cricketer who was India's ticket to be considered a rival worth respecting, for the next four decades and counting, it has been as a commentator who has become the voice of Indian cricket, through all the changes that it has seen.

If Virat gave the Indian team a ruthlessness of spirit, and an ability to win and keep on winning, Dhoni made victory feel like a right to be accepted as a matter of course, Sachin showed us that we could not only win but dominate the best, Kapil proved that we had what it took to win at the highest level, Gavaskar was the one who made us feel that we belonged on the world stage. At a time when the Indian team had a fragility about it that endured in spite of occasional flashes of brilliance, Gavaskar was the one pillar that could not be shaken, not even by the very best that the world could throw at him. And he did this not by grit or determination alone but by showing the kind of technique and class that the game valued the most. He played the game the classical way, and he played it better than almost anybody else at the time.

For years, the only person standing between the pace attacks of the world and the Indian team was Sunil Gavaskar. To be sure, there were others. We had the artistic flair of Vishwanath, the brave obduracy of Mohinder Amarnath, and the willowy brilliance of Dilip Vengsarkar, but none of them came close to matching the consistency and the sheer volume of runs that Gavaskar racked up.

To be an opener in the time of Roberts, Marshall, Holding, Garner, Lillee, Thomson, Imran, Willis and Hadlee was to be a gladiator in the time of tyrants. Relentless hostility was the defining trait of fast bowling then, and nothing we see today comes close to that. Unprepared pitches, no helmets, shoddy protective gear, no restriction on the number of bouncers – this was not a time for the faint of heart. Fear was a palpable emotion experienced by even the most seasoned batsmen. Being an opener was then perhaps one of the most unenviable jobs in the world.

For some, correctness is a prison, a set of confining rules that limits one's freedom and provides a formulaic answer to everything. For Gavaskar, correctness was a source of freedom. The technique seemed an inborn trait rather than an acquired skill. Balance, posture, poise, patience, certain straightness of carriage, these came naturally to him. Which is what imparted beauty to his game, rather than mere technical exactitude.

Gavaskar made smallness feel like a work of art. Everything flowed smoothly, in a compact package. The cover drives, the straight drives, and the flicks were a combination of precision and elegance as if they were always meant to be. His height seemed to offer him protection against the quicks, and once he cut out the hook, he looked relatively undisturbed by all that was dished out to him. Watching Gavaskar play was a lesson in correctness made beautiful, the technical turned fluid.

He was perhaps the only cricketing superstar who left the stage on his terms, without having the big question, that has so dogged others, dangling ominously in front of him. He retired while having a good run with the bat, and he stayed retired thereafter.

As a sporting hero who has stayed relevant for over fifty years, Gavaskar paints a complex picture with many shades. At one level, he is the voice of palatable wisdom that has managed to stay effortlessly contemporary by avoiding the old-fogeyness that can afflict the wisest of the accomplished. He is the one constant in a world that has changed beyond recognition. Cricket is nothing like what it was in his time, and yet Gavaskar goes on. He plays the role of providing a sense of continuity to Indian cricket without it lapsing into sepia-tinged nostalgia. His inherent pragmatism makes him comfortable with young and old alike, and it helps that he looks pretty much the same as he always has.

What is interesting is that while he has played the role of the person bridging generations, he has always very much been his own person. There is a streak of individualism, of always knowing where his interests lie, and a willingness to exercise a certain part of his personality to maintain distance from others. He was the first player to recognize the commercial potential of cricket and has never shied away from fighting for what he believes is his due. He is also politically adept; the fact that he managed to stay relevant even through all the muddy transitions that the BCCI has gone through speaks for both the respect he commands and his ability to stay on the right side of things.

His career, too, has been dotted with instances both of uncharacteristic loss of self-control and difficult relationships with some teammates. The inexplicable 36 not out compiled batting through 60 overs in a World Cup match or the petulant walk-out against Australia that could have led to more serious consequences but for the timely intervention of the Indian manager, are well-advertised cases of these lapses.

In Gavaskar, the Indian middle class has found a voice that manages to reconcile individuality and self-interest with classical ability. He played cricket the way it was meant to be played, with everything right about his technique, while living his life, till today, on his own terms. Ambition, correctness, political acumen, selfishness all come together in the package we call the Little Master.

He is not a cardboard cut-out of a hero, as no human being is. But over fifty years ago, he began the journey that has culminated in India becoming the top-ranked team in the world. It all began with Sunil Gavaskar.

A WORLD BEYOND THE MEN IN BLUE?

HARMANPREET KAUR, MITHALI RAJ, SMRITI Mandhana, Jhulan Goswami, Shafali Verma – the fact that so many of us can reel off these and many more names of women cricketers in India is quite remarkable. So far, women's cricket had been a lurking background presence in our lives. There was familiarity with names like Shanta Rangaswamy, Diana Edulji and Anjum Chopra, but most cricket fans would not have seen them in action. The first time India featured in the Women's World Cup finals, in 2005, barely anyone noticed. In a larger sense, for any sport other than men's cricket to get attention at the national level has always been a struggle. There have been many champions from other sports who have been celebrated in their time, but this has rarely translated into a deeper interest in the sport itself.

But things seem to be changing. Over the last couple of years, we have seen many new names emerge with great regularity and occupy their places in our mantelpiece of heroes. Saina Nehwal, P.V. Sindhu, Neeraj Chopra, Mithali Raj, Sardar Singh, Srikanth Kidambi, Sakshi Malik, Dipa Karmakar, Nikhat Zareen, to name but a few, are part of a long and growing list. Is there something real and durable about this trend, or is it the transient celebration of one-off performances?

In a vast majority of cases, interest in a less popular sport spikes as a result of an impressive performance by an individual or team or when some international recognition is forthcoming. The desire to feel good about oneself produces a hunger for heroes to celebrate and any available and plausible instrument towards this end is welcomed. In most cases, the names that attract a blaze of attention slowly fade away once their moment passes. Interest in javelin, gymnastics and boxing has not grown significantly post the stellar performances of Neeraj Chopra, Nikhat Zareen, Dipa Karmakar and Mary Kom.

On the other hand, kabaddi has, without the benefit of any stars or global recognition, been reimagined in a dramatic fashion. A sport that was familiar but was not followed in any organized manner has now become one that is more commercially viable than many others that had a better chance on paper. From nowhere, we have a sport with new fans and a spanking new pantheon of stars.

There is reason to believe that India is on the verge of a reinvigorated engagement with sport, one that goes beyond its traditional obsession with the men in blue. Commerce is a key driver – the part of India which experiences a surplus economy has a growing appetite for new forms of diversion and gratification. Sports other than cricket become potential opportunities that are extremely attractive for the market. The intervention of the market and the infusion of money, however, do not automatically translate into enhanced popularity for any particular sport. The easy way out is to model all market interventions on the lines of the IPL, and this approach has failed as often as it has succeeded. The kabaddi model, on the other hand, uses some elements from the IPL but is original and bold in its conception. It has had the luxury of being able to reimagine the sport, instead of merely repackaging it.

The other new player in the equation is popular culture. Films about Milkha Singh, Mary Kom, M.S. Dhoni, and movies like *Dangal* and *Chak De! India* have tapped into the storytelling potential of sport. This is the new mythology of the times, a new canvas to paint heroism on. Tailwinds in the form of a rising tide of nationalism that is worn on the sleeve also help things along. After all, sport is the least violent way of expressing a competitive form of patriotism.

The recasting of sport as entertainment and of sporting victory as personal validation for the spectator makes it easier for sports that were on the periphery to become more popular. In such a construct, the precise nature of the sport starts becoming less important. As long as it is easy to consume, satisfies needs of entertainment and validation, and is presented on a scale that appears significant, an audience for it potentially exists. Given the explosion in the availability of personal media, there is a growing market for subjects to offer one's opinion on. New nodes of interest allow for the proliferation of views, and sport is a huge beneficiary of this hunger to constantly shower adoration, commentary and vitriol on a growing list of subjects.

Earlier, interest in a sport tended to come from within – one tuned into the sport itself, understanding its particular grammar and enjoying its intricacies. Today, we follow various sports and its stars for a variety of reasons that do not necessarily lie within the sport itself. We don't have to enjoy the sport per se, as long as the stories that it tells and the outcome that it delivers makes us feel better about ourselves. Post IPL, for instance, cricket is followed by many who don't have any particular interest in the game; just in what surrounds it.

Purists can argue that an overly commercial and outcome-oriented view of sport robs it of its essence, and that packaging and glitzy promotion end up homogenizing all sport, but in the short term, given the abysmal condition of most sport in India, any change is good news.

THE RETURN OF KABADDI

Watching kabaddi on television is an interesting experience. Watching it after many years, and seeing it in a more modern avatar, combines the pleasures of familiarity and strangeness, allowing an opportunity to feel old feelings and see new things about the sport.

Kabaddi is a team sport without equipment, something that sets it apart from most other sport. It works at a primal level, in that its operating unit is the span of one's breath. One hangs by the thin thread of one's breath as one sets off to raid enemy territory, hoping to 'tag' someone from the other side and to rule them out of the contest.

Although kabaddi follows a structure common to many sports, that of sequential penetrative forays into the other side in order to breach their defences in the form of a goal, wicket, basket or, in this case, a 'tag', it has a somewhat different rhythm. Here, attack and defence are not separated, as they are in sports like hockey, football and basketball, but happen simultaneously. The hunter is simultaneously the hunted and every raid is equally an opportunity to bring down a member of the attacking party. Every time the attacker goes off on a raid, one cannot be sure of his return; he could return triumphant with prey or be ruled out of the game, making the job that much more difficult for the home side.

All sport is a metaphor for life as it is a flirtation with death, and kabaddi is no exception. It converts a primitive hunt into a structured pastime using the most primal sign of life there is – one's breath. One lives by the radius of the breath, and dies by it. The death, too, is a graphic enactment of sorts – one runs out of breath, flailing to reach the safety of one's own side as one drowns amidst a pack of defenders.

Playing kabaddi is a thrilling experience; no other sport can quite capture the sense of danger that one feels in the nostrils, a heady mix of attacking zest and watchful fear. Watching it, too, has its rewards. It is television-friendly, in that the playing arena is easy to contain on a television screen and the action happens in discrete steps that are easy to follow visually. For the layperson, too, the sport is easy to get initiated into, for it works at a primitive level; victory and defeat are not technical contrivances but visually obvious outcomes.

The idea of reviving interest in kabaddi through the launch of two professional leagues was a bold one. The attempt to breathe life back into a local sport and do it with a genuine seriousness of intent by throwing all that modern marketing can deliver at it, is one that needs enthusiastic endorsement. And it seems to have worked. Even though the larger question of how to promote sport in India continues to be a challenging one.

It would seem that the IPL has become the default model for many sports striving to establish themselves in a country that seems saturated with cricket. The IPL is a system that is designed to exploit an existing passion by making it easier to consume. It reorders what already exists by using the principles of compression and acceleration and it surrounds this 'new, improved' product with glitter and glamour so as to heighten its value as a spectacle.

What works for cricket might not work for other sports. Promoting any sport needs much more than packaging. Sustained interest in any sport cannot be determined by how much entertainment surrounds it, but by how much meaning lies imbued within it. This is a process that needs to be carefully nurtured over a period of time. People need to be made familiar with the sport, its rules, conventions and meanings. They need a shared vocabulary to describe the sport and its constituent actions. They need to know what to admire and what to bemoan. They need a framework of intelligibility and comprehension, as well as a language of criticism. The sport needs to be populated with enough significant events (sixes, fours, wickets, catches, run-outs, fouls, free kicks, penalties), and should allow for discussion and controversy. It needs to provide a basis for belonging, for the attachment of identity. It needs a narrative storyline, and, above all, it needs heroes that it can celebrate and hope to emulate. Over time, it needs its own history and mythology, stories that can be told in smoky bars with halting voices.

Strategies to promote any sport need to come from within the sport rather than outside it. They need to capture the unique flavour and the motivations that surround the individual sport rather than covering it in a haze of celebrity smoke or standardized advertising glibness. The development of any sport needs time and genuine interest in the content of the sport. The problem is that the way the market constructs sports promotion, most often too much investment is made too quickly, resulting in a desire for quick returns and the setting up of inevitable disappointment.

Contrary to appearances, developing sport is not fundamentally about commerce or entertainment, but about infecting people with passion and belief. It is not about a big-bang-one-time generic effort but a highly specific one that gathers gradual momentum. That means not worrying too much about viewership or the commercial viability of the sport in the short run but finding a way to enjoy it and give it an ever increasing place in our lives. Sport needs the market, but equally, the market needs to understand how to engage with sport. In kabaddi, the opportunity is real, and the effort to revive interest in it truly brave, but it needs belief more than slickness. And there is much to believe in when it comes to kabaddi.

CHAPTER 6

COVID

The Revenge of the Normal

When the world was forced to pause, India, too, found itself suspended in stillness.

But even disruption seeks equilibrium. Covid may have stopped time, but it also accelerated change – reshaping how we worked, consumed, and even thought about what really matters.

THE REVENGE OF THE NORMAL

Normal is boring. It is one of those clichés of our time that forswears anything that is deemed normal. Normal is ordinary, it is dull and uninteresting. It lacks imagination. Normal is a state of inconspicuousness. Of fitting in. Of not being challenged in the things we take for granted. No wonder we try our damnedest to avoid being normal. We cultivate interests, fashion a persona, or, in the world of online primping, invent multiple personae, present an amped-up version of ourselves on social media, engage in exotic travel, eat all kinds of food from places we cannot locate on a map. In short, we strive to prove that we are extraordinary, and that we lead awesome and epic lives.

There is another problem we have with the idea of the normal. Historically, the normal ended up celebrating a state of stasis. By creating a set template of what was deemed socially acceptable and what was not, it fostered discrimination, often invisible. It became a form of tyranny – a standard applied to describe those who fit into a common conception of how reality should be and exclude those who did not. We normalized divisions, ascribing a sense of naturalness to them. Race, caste, sexual orientation – all of them thrive on a fear of the abnormal. The abnormal is terrifying. It stands out, and seeks an ugly form of attention to itself. The new is feared as is that which is not easily classifiable.

Historically, anything that was a hybrid, lay between set boundaries and was unclassifiable produced an anxiety and needed to be delegitimized. The concept of dirt as 'matter out of place', an idea often attributed to Mary Douglas, captures this suspicion of things that are 'out of place' and the tendency to classify these as contaminants.

Today, there is a concerted pushback to the kind of hard boundaries that defined identity. We celebrate the fluid, the intersectional and the hybrid. There is much greater openness about accepting influences and behaviour of all kinds, and fixed labels of any kind are increasingly being shunned.

And yet, as we lived through pandemic-battered times, all we wished for was that things return to normal, for them to be classifiable and graspable. When we talked about the New Normal, we were actually pining for the return of the Good Old Normal. The meaning of normal that we were referencing was that state of being where we could act unthinkingly. Where every action of ours was not laden with a potential consequence, where doing the most ordinary things naturally was not taboo. Where we could stroll into crowded malls, take the Metro, land up fashionably late at a rocking party, catch up with colleagues after work at a bar, put an arm around a shoulder or toss a hug at someone. It was desire not for an extraordinary experience, no yearning for the epic or the awesome, but simply for that which we did not need to think about.

Instead, during the pandemic, we had to watch our every step. If the doorbell rang, we had to gear up to open it. If we used a lift, we had to wear two masks and pray that no one else entered it. If we were in a car all by ourselves, we had to wear a mask because a court had deemed it to be a public space. If we opened a door, we had to sanitize our hands. Every action had to be forethought and post analysed.

Never before has the ordinary been romanced in quite the same way as during and post the pandemic. To be sure, we have always been nostalgic about the good old times, that time in our lives when we didn't have much but somehow things felt more real and purer, but this is a different kind of feeling. Nostalgia normally has a moral value running through it, for we equate scarcity with simplicity and mix up the rudimentary with the pure. Today, there is no higher consideration – what we miss is the simple act of being ourselves and doing whatever came naturally. The past is not seen as superior, just more convenient. What we miss is the idea of a past continuous tense, one where things simply stayed the way they were.

It is understandable, this urge to return to normal. A crisis of this kind shakes all foundational assumptions we have made about how our lives will be. We need normal. Life would be unbearable if every day was actually a new dawn. We need our dawns to be old, and gravity to work boringly. We need a rhythm to our lives, we need to be able to think selectively.

There are other aspects of the ordinary that we have learned to appreciate more. Families actually behaved like families during the pandemic. They shared not only limited space but time, love, care, attention, they were with each other in contexts that they hadn't been exposed to earlier. Food gave us inordinate pleasure, both the cooking and consuming, the cleaning up not so much. Old games were played, and new irritations identified. In a highly constrained playing field, we rediscovered the joys of simple everyday pleasures.

What made this yearning for the normal more poignant was that the pandemic did not seem to have a sense of an ending about it. It seemed to abate only to return unpredictably, with sudden ferocity. We alternated between periods of hope and despair, and all the while the strong need for things to become normal became that much stronger. Today, normal is not boring, it is reassuring.

WHAT DID COVID REALLY CHANGE?

Now that COVID is comfortably in our rearview mirror (fingers crossed), it is interesting to look back on what it has changed in the long run and what it hasn't. So many predictions were made at the time about the sweeping effects that this pandemic would have on our lives. And there is no question that humanity collectively went through a traumatic experience that it had no precedent of. But despite this, has anything significant really changed?

Things that were already changing have accelerated in speed and deepened in impact. Our embrace of the digital world, which accelerated significantly during the pandemic, seems to have continued for the most part. Shopping online feels far more natural now, even among audiences that were slow to warm to the idea. Quick commerce is a product of the pandemic in many ways.

However, not all online businesses have sustained the momentum; in cases where the adoption of digital means was purely a substitute for the real thing, the effects of the pandemic have ebbed. Education is a prime example, and the edtech sector is testament to the fact that once it was possible to go back to schools and colleges, the spurt in online learning has died down. However, what it has left behind is a greater openness to digital modes of education, again something that had already begun to happen.

The other big impact of the pandemic was normalizing working from home. The technology was always available, but its adoption skyrocketed in a time when there was no other option. Working from home changed something fundamental in our mental model of work. It was previously taken for granted that work could happen in a certain way, and maintaining the distance between office and home had become an article of faith. This despite the fact that this distinction had been trampled upon by technology, which ensured work permeated every moment of our lives.

Today, we see an ever-increasing number of businesses going back to the pre-pandemic mode of working from office. Employers have been pushing for this, for they believe that having a scattered workforce reduces focus and intensity. The employees are not so gung-ho about returning to the office, having experienced the freedom that working from home afforded them.

This is not a problem that will resolve itself soon, for the younger generations that are entering the workforce are even more certain that they want to retain as much personal freedom as possible while employed. Chances are that the movement towards more flexible work conditions, which had begun well before the pandemic, will continue, perhaps at a slower pace, but inexorably, nevertheless.

In each of these cases, it is not that things have not changed at all but that the shifts don't feel fundamental. There has been a shift towards more comfortable clothes, but again, this is balanced by a renewed desire to dress up, something that was denied to us during the pandemic.

Being cooped up indoors for a long time seems to have left a deep impression; the desire for outdoor experiences has certainly returned with a vengeance. Increasingly, as more functional needs get met digitally, the outdoors have taken on a more recreational role. Eating out is perhaps the biggest beneficiary of this trend, with families tumbling out of their homes in search of newer culinary experiences.

The pandemic also created a need for looking at optional ways of living away from the madness of cities. The lure of smaller towns where the pace of life is more relaxed has become more real, with more people evaluating this as an option. A place like Goa has felt the full force of this need, with so many people from larger metros seeking refuge here, often to the detriment of the local populace.

A subject like mental health also seems to have become more mainstream. For a lot of the people, the experience of being confined, accompanied by the anxiety induced by a phenomenon that they had no previous experience of nor the mental wherewithal to deal with, created mental issues they had not encountered before. A subject that was often dismissed as the weak person's inability to cope suddenly became more real and personal.

It was generally assumed that the pandemic would change our attitude towards making us more careful and receptive to preventative healthcare. I am not sure that this has happened; it seems that we have slipped back into old ways. Perhaps we are a little more careful about the idea of diseases that are contagious, but a significant shift in attitudes has perhaps eluded us. The other much heralded change, that of a more equitable distribution of household responsibilities between the genders, too, seems to have gone back and embraced familiar patterns.

What has emphatically not changed is our love for travel. Again, the quantum of 'revenge travel' that we saw in the immediate aftermath of the pandemic seems to show no signs of abating. A lot of social conversations tend to focus on food or travel. Similarly, the need for other people's company continues to be as robust as it always was.

What we learn from our experience with the pandemic is that while human beings are quick to adapt to sudden unfamiliar situations, that is by no means our preferred state. Eventually we only end up retaining new behaviours if they deepen existing shifts that were already underway or if they expose an area of simmering discontent. The changes we have seen are those of degree rather than direction. Overall, it is fair to say that what the pandemic underlines is that change does not come easily to human behaviour. Even when subject to extraordinary pressure over a reasonably long period of time, the human tendency is to go back to familiar modes of living our lives. There is something stubborn about our happiness and misery; we seem loath to change either. We adjust instantly, but we don't change that easily.

LIFE AFTER COVID: TIME FOR A RESET

A PANDEMIC DESTROYS MANY THINGS – apart from taking millions of lives and leaving a large number of people substantially impaired both physically and psychologically, it shakes a society's confidence in itself and the future that it imagined. But simultaneously, it also destroys some old set-in-stone perspectives and throws up opportunities to be able to see the world in a new light.

This is the time for a reset. Of a new way, that sheds many habits of the past, habits that fed on themselves and assumed the form of inevitability. Over the course of the pandemic, we were made to go back to first principles, and discovered that so many of the things we assumed as being necessary were, in fact, quite expendable. In the name of normalcy, it would be foolish to return to old ways without reflection, to repeat without reinvention.

Our work lives, for instance, were vampires of our time and attention. Time for oneself and the family were seen as leakages from productivity, which needed to be apologized for. Every leave application came accompanied with both guilt and trepidation, even though what we were staking a claim to was our own time, earned following the rules of the world. Maternity leave rules in many parts of the world are still shockingly exploitative, and the idea of men taking time off for childbirth is still regarded as a fringe fad.

Why does one need to go to office every single day? Work had become synonymous with going to office rather than with accomplishing tasks. Why commute just so as to mark one's presence? In a large metropolis, we spend two to three miserable hours every day just getting to work. Why travel outstation for work? Virtual meetings are far more efficient – everyone is on time, the meeting starts when it is meant to, and we get to wear shorts all the time.

Why must one necessarily live in a large city? The costs of living in a bustling metropolis are increasingly outweighing the benefits. True, access to education and healthcare is highly skewed in favour of the metros, and there is a certain allure to the idea of being at the centre of action. But, on the other hand, there is traffic, pollution and an overall sense of being under siege that makes our shoulders sag and puts a permanent frown on our faces.

This is a good time to look at options. Was the hometown we left behind as being too quiet and lacking in opportunity really so? Or is it simply a more serene hideout with great Wi-Fi that allows us to breathe large gulps of clean fresh air? Besides, India has changed and what were derogatorily dismissed as small towns have transformed beyond recognition. Technology, in any case, does make geography less relevant.

The other big change we can make to our lifestyles is to get much more selective about consumption. The pandemic underlined how we can make do with so much less, without any visible effect on any aspect of our well-being. Consumption is an important part of our lives today, but the opportunity is there to consume more meaningfully so as to derive richer pleasure from it.

The other transformative change that we need to adopt is to invest significantly more in public health. The danger of slipping back into old ways now that the threat from the virus has abated is very real. The current system is too well enmeshed for it to change easily. The next pandemic could come anytime, a mutated form of Covid could evolve more rapidly than imagined, and we will end up being just as unprepared. Without a far more robust and equitable public healthcare system, any focus on economic development will be rendered meaningless.

An infectious disease like Covid does not discriminate between those who can afford good healthcare and those who can't. Anyone can get it. Protecting a few, while ignoring the needs of the many, might work in the case of lifestyle diseases, but is worthless in the case of an all-embracing pandemic. Changing our approach towards public health is a matter of survival, nothing less.

The other change that was forced upon us during the pandemic was a rediscovered regard for science. While there were sections of the population that stubbornly resisted the wisdom on offer from science and preferred to rely on their own highly original theories, the rest of us found ourselves reacquainting ourselves with the power of the scientific method. In a world where, let alone science, even facts are losing their primacy, the return of a scientific temper could well be the single most important gift that the pandemic could give us. If we allow ourselves that.

Perhaps the biggest opportunity for a reset comes from embracing change of a more fundamental nature. If the pandemic did teach us something, apart from how to wash our hands for ten minutes, it was the fact that at the end of day, what we have is each other. A crisis of this kind is truly a great equalizer. The virus does not recognize privilege or rank. While the privileged still have better access to healthcare facilities, no magic solution is available to those with better means.

There is a need to recognize that the world is not merely connected but interdependent, that no matter how successfully we can isolate ourselves in gated complexes and lose ourselves in virtual thrall on sundry screens, in a moment of crisis we all need each other. Local communities were the primary coping mechanisms that came to our aid at this time of crisis.

After the stifling and fearful time spent under the shadow of the pandemic, it is time for some naivete and innocence. For us to believe that the crisis did leave in its wake some hope of a new beginning. And perhaps a better way to lead some important parts of our lives.

OTT IN WFH TIMES?

Thank god for OTT platforms. Navigating the pandemic without having these options would have been exceedingly difficult. The OTT format is ideally suited for these WFH times. Our days have lost shape, and time has come unstuck from its otherwise predictable and orderly routine. We can create little pockets of time in the middle of the day in between Zoom calls and household chores. We can sneak in a programme or two at times otherwise considered impossible. The anytime access to a wide range of programming provides back-up to a day that lacks its previous definition, and serves to fill gaps that might pop up.

For socially inept people like this author, OTT channels are, above all, a conversational boon. Whenever one is racking one's brain to figure out how exactly to make 'small talk', that mysterious skill that some possess effortlessly and others regard as bafflingly arcane, now there is a universal answer. When in doubt, talk Netflix. What are you watching nowadays? And then the conversation has a set script that unspools itself without any additional effort.

The interesting thing about streaming sites is that there is a sense of a common pool of content that virtually everyone can have an opinion on but equally, the range of options is so wide that the prospect of making new discoveries is always present. Conversation is possible on both fronts – what one thinks of the shows one has seen as well as what shows one is missing.

There are cloudbursts of interest around some new happening series – the names keep changing, but the phenomenon is the same. These become common reference points for a period of time, and attract a blizzard of opinions. Articles are written about these, counterpoints are mounted; some are watched with admiration and awe and others exist to be cringed deliciously at.

Discovering new options, finding treasure troves in cultures beyond the Hollywood-inspired networks that we are otherwise used to, is a special delight – Nordic noir, Malayali cinema, K-dramas, Turkish fantasy extravaganzas, true-crime documentaries, Australian sleeper hits, morose British police procedurals – one's viewing portfolio can be diverse and rewarding.

Quite a journey from the days when TV channels were our only options. TV viewing had its own grammar. For one, programming was fixed in time and place. You could watch a movie or a serial only at its appointed time, and you could watch on the one TV set that most households owned. It was difficult to keep track of every episode of one's favourite serials, for life had a way of intervening. There were re-runs but these were usually at awkward times and could not be relied upon. Of course, some films could not be avoided try as you might – *Sooryavansham* and *Indra: The Tiger* are names that will haunt us for the rest of our lives.

The OTT channels give us the power of both stock and flow, unlike the past, when the only options at our disposal were the ones that were aired on TV. As the number of channels increased, we had much more horizontal choice. At any given point in time, there were many options to choose from, but we had to choose from a limited menu of what the channels decided to air at that particular moment. With OTT channels, we have a stock of programming options that is more or less permanently available to us. Our choice set expands dramatically as we have a library at our disposal, to pick and choose from at our convenience.

What we get is greater mastery over time. We can luxuriate in it, as we languidly pick viewing options that interest us; we can crunch it up as we binge-watch our way through shows; we can start a series, get bored of it, and pick it up again when the mood strikes. The mode of viewing is a significant change from the passivity of TV, where we had no option but to surrender to what was served to us. There is a new sense of agency in the

OTT viewership experience, both in terms of watching what we want when we want to, as also discovering things to watch in the first place.

The kind of programming we see on these platforms strikes a refreshingly new note. The idea of a serial on chess, or a documentary on an unhinged sub-culture that collects big cats, or a feature about Indian arranged marriages would have been no one's idea of riveting television, and yet they have become sensations in the streaming world. The subscription model ensures that while programming is aligned to the market, every show is not a source of independent revenue and hence is allowed breathing room to experiment. Of course, it is important for shows to do well in terms of viewership, but the creators do not suffer the same level of anxiety in their conception because of this relative freedom. This is most noticeable in the kind of content that is being produced in India, which is a big departure from what was dished out on mainstream TV channels.

There is also the confidence that compelling stories will eventually get discovered because word-of-mouth has the power to light up the darkest corners of any catalogue. Unlike cinema, where there is an urgent need to get people to the theatre in the short window available on the movie's release, or even in television, where viewers need to tune in at a specific time so as catch the show early enough, content on the OTT platforms can allow viewers to find it. Discovery can be a gradual process.

What is being enabled is for us to feel like a collective as we respond to the same entertainment stimuli in similar ways across the world, as well as individuals as we discover the extremities of our own appetite and the contours of our taste. In these constrained times, we are what we watch.

WHEN THE WORLD STOPPED FLOWING

THE LOCKDOWN WAS AN ALTOGETHER novel experience for the world, something that no one had any preparation for. It was a frontal attack on notions of mobility and connectivity, which form the foundations of our lives today.

That such a move caused dislocation and a great amount of distress was not surprising. After all, more than ever before, today's world is premised on the idea of flow. The world is intricately connected and is increasingly premised on seamlessness, easy instant access and speed. Money flows, goods move, we are in a constant state of motion. The digital is nothing but the ceaseless flow of electronic bits of information. In a larger sense, we have been moving from a world premised on stock, on accumulation, to one based on flow, getting things on demand, when we need them. Uber, Airbnb, the rise of the gig economy, all point to a world where the fixed gives way to the fluid and ownership gets overtaken by the idea of 'usership'– in effect, a place of dwelling or an automobile is made functionally fluid.

We also increasingly visualize our world as a flow. The GPS gives us an out-of-body experience of locating ourselves on a moving map. Deliveries are tracked, vehicles are tracked – in a surveillance economy, our actions and movements are relentlessly tracked. Every motion becomes significant, every key stroke revelatory. If, earlier, we revealed ourselves to the outside through discretionary and discrete actions – for example, when we bought something, complained about something or applied for something official –, today, we are a continuous stream of information that keeps flowing out involuntarily. This is what allows the business of modern life to function.

Covid was a disruption, thus, of a fundamental kind. We couldn't move, not across countries, nor domestically, not even in our neighbourhoods. The goods we needed didn't move, our work came to a standstill, our leisure hours were spent cooped up indoors. The flow of our salaries became uncertain, the rhythm of daily labour was disrupted. A world dependent on the idea of flow found itself locked down, frozen in several forms of immobility. Revenues for businesses dried up, supply chains stopped moving. Even digital commerce, which needed the flow of the physical world, found itself hamstrung when things stopped flowing.

We were forced to go back to the older idea of stocking up, of using resources frugally, of making do with what we had at home, including people. We needed to value owning things again, of using what we really needed and doing so frugally. We learned to covet experiences over possessions, and found to our surprise that scarcity multiplied rather than diminished meaning.

The pandemic, on the other hand, was a flow. It moved rapidly from person to person, colonizing clusters, and spreading at speeds not usually seen in the physical world. Not only did it flow, it multiplied exponentially, mocking our new-found obsession with making things go viral. Everything that we found valuable about the seamless flow of our lives was negated by the ease with which the virus flowed. It streamed itself naturally from one host to another, hitching a ride in our bodies, feasting on it.

The other flow that continued to thrive was that of information. The digital marketplace needs the physical world as its back end, so we found it spluttering at a time like this. But pure information flowed seamlessly. We were besieged by it, as we looked hard at it, hoping to find some answers. It was our tormentor and our saviour, for we could not escape it just as we could escape only because of it. Without the ceaseless flow of social media and the entertainment provided by the streaming sites, we would have struggled to cope with the lockdown. At the same time, we were locked inside this torrent of information about the pandemic from where even momentary escape was difficult.

Information itself was a pandemic of sorts as it galloped ahead of reality. We were infected by doubt, by fear, by crippling anxiety, even if the virus had not harmed us. It colonized our waking hours, making us die a little in anticipation. We devoured information and were in turn devoured by it. It kept us alive while killing us a little every day.

So there we were, trapped between the two flows that made us shrink even more into ourselves. The disease was invisibly snaking its way towards us, and the swirls of information were surrounding us with dread and a sense of imminent foreboding. We were now afraid of everything that we were meant to trust. Friends, public facilities, even hospitals. Not only people, we feared residues left by people. Things that were designed to be touched were now potential enemies; otherwise, a doorknob lives to be gripped and turned and a lift button's only purpose in life is to be pressed.

As we look back on those days, we realize to what extent we take constant movement for granted. Everything in our world flows, in real life and virtually, and when a lot of this ceaseless movement stops, we are at a total loss. We found a way to cope, but it brought home to us as to just how fragile the world we live in is. The ease with which we have gone back to our old ways does not bode well for the future.

CHAPTER 7

Work

The Changing Meaning of Work

The workplace is no longer a place. Work now has a constantly shifting address and meaning.

Twenty-somethings run the world, Gen Z employees bring a whole new way of thinking about work.

The very idea of productivity has been rewritten in the age of hustle and hashtags.

THE CHANGING MEANING OF WORK

Among the many new careers that have sprung up recently, none is perhaps as curious as that of a water sommelier, whose job it is to understand different kinds of bottled water and guide presumably confused consumers about which kind of water to drink with what kind of food. Nobody in their right minds could have foreseen the possibility of this being a legitimate job, and few perhaps still do. Even a traditional sommelier – the one that helps us choose the wine in a fancy restaurant – performs a function few would have thought of as a function. And yet, not only is it a profession, it is very highly paid and comes accompanied by pomp, a touch of hauteur and a lot of reverential self-regard.

The phenomenon of influencers – people who essentially tell us how to consume – is one of the most attractive professions for the young today. Very often, the skills needed are nothing more than a photogenic appearance, an easy communication-friendly personality, and an ability to perform utterly banal actions like opening a package and gushing over some new product. Unboxing videos, zany product reviews, reaction videos – these are immensely popular new formats of communication that wield enormous influence today. People with a large number of followers are monetizing their audiences and earning significant sums of money.

Work is whatever we agree to call work and pay for. And what we are choosing to call work is changing. One pattern that can be seen quite clearly is the growing energy around the act of consumption as against the historical centrality of the act of production. As production becomes relatively routine and automated, the excitement is shifting towards developing the ecosystem around consumption. Earlier, we worked hard to make things so that we could consume them. Production was the credit side of our life and consumption the debit. There was a science to production, there were important sounding professions that involved doing things that looked like work. Consumption, on the other hand, was either an indulgence or a chore. We earned money through production, which was spent by acts of consumption.

That has been changing for a while, and is poised to change much more dramatically. Over the years, the service sector has been the fastest growing part of economies in most parts of the world. The idea of 'service' is really about catering to the many intangible, and often inexplicable, needs that human beings have. Given that human needs take new forms and shapes all the time, new, hitherto-undreamt-of jobs have a good chance of being born. And going forward, this movement is only going to intensify. Increasingly, we are seeing the rise of jobs that were not thought of as jobs till recently. Apart from sommeliers, today we have personal trainers, event managers, wedding planners, beauty advisors at retail outlets, fashion bloggers, life coaches, DJs at parties, app developers, data miners, gadget reviewers – all jobs that have come into being recently.

In a digital world, consumption becomes a kind of production. That easy separation between production and consumption is changing, as is the meaning we attach to both sides of the equation. In a digital world, production becomes simpler and consumption more complex and layered. How to consume, what to consume, what new meanings to attach to consumption – these are the new civilizational questions of the day. Identity descriptors, too, are moving from what we do to earn a living (our occupations), to what we spend our time and money on (our interests). Newer professions are working to sharpen the pursuit of consumption. Whether it is data scientists looking to map the implicit preferences of every individual, or curators helping other consumers refine their acts of consumption, the direction is unmistakable.

Becoming expert consumers could well be the next frontier of work. Like in the case of production, consumption needs its own specialists. The two currencies of our age are time and money, and learning how to spend both better is becoming an increasingly more significant pursuit. We have already started filling up time more deliberately. Work takes time, and a lot of the work we do today is to help others directly consume time. Entertainment, sport, shopping, surfing the internet, using social media – these are all ways of consuming time. The more we are able to place value on ideas rather than things, representations rather than reality, the closer we get to a world where our primary preoccupation is consumption. Buying things has a limit, even if it may not feel like that. But buying ideas or symbols is potentially limitless.

Along with this shift in emphasis comes the possibility of new ways of imagining how we make money. The origins of the idea of the Universal Basic Income may lie in the need for a form of a guaranteed social safety net but in effect, it lays the ground for an economy where we are paid to consume. Conceptually, it is a device that provides us a certain minimum standing as consumers. Could we inhabit a world tomorrow where we are paid according to our ability to consume and to aid consumption? Could we get paid simply to provide data about ourselves? In an economic system perpetually hungry for consumer demand, jobs are arguably plausible excuses to give people money to spend on things, and, with time, we will dream up new excuses.

The future of jobs may look very different from what today's reality looks like. The threat that automation poses to employment, however, is a real and pressing one; the changes being spoken of will take much longer to unfold. But in the long run, the idea of jobs is fluid enough to take on new forms in line with newer contexts. Jobs are cultural inventions, and we will invent new occupations. What kind of world would this translate into, and how desirable it would be, is another question altogether.

WHO RUNS THE WORLD? TWENTY-SOMETHINGS

THE WORLD IS BEING RUN by twenty-somethings. Strictly speaking, that is a bit of an exaggeration, but it would seem that in a few years' time, it might well be true. Giant businesses are being built by people who cannot buy a beer in Delhi. A bunch of kids are dreaming up ideas, hiring people much older than them, negotiating tough deals with a bunch of cut-throat investors, and generally reimagining the world as we know it.

Apart from making older people look ridiculous, the emergence of this new breed of leaders also dramatically challenges the idea that doing certain kinds of jobs requires qualifications, the relevant experience, and a host of qualities that are deemed absolutely essential by management consultants (delegating effectively, getting hands dirty, being good listeners, leading from the front, reinventing oneself frequently, and so on). These young people not quite out of college seem to rush into everything and find it remarkably easy to do all the things that we have been told are very difficult.

And they are not the only ones who pose this question of us. The idea that only people with the proper education, requisite experience and formal training can, over time, become capable of handling ever more complex tasks is something that gets challenged in different ways all around us. Politicians, for instance, run ministries without having a clue about the subject that they are final arbiters of. There is no formal training that they undergo. They might not be the finest advertisements for a lack of qualifications, but as we have seen in the past, having highly qualified leaders does not necessarily translate into meaningful action either.

Young scions of business families are routinely parachuted into top management where they get to lord over professionals who not only have eye-popping qualifications, but have spent weeks sitting in various training programmes painstakingly 'developing competencies' and working on their team building and leadership skills. By and large, this model works just fine, for if it didn't the market would have ensured that only professionals ran companies.

Could it be that the idea of competence is, in part, a device used to determine who gets to leadership positions when there are no other means available to figure this out? So, when it is possible to either elect people through voting, as is the case with politicians, or with lineage, as is the case with family business, we rely on these methods. When such universally transparent and culturally incontrovertible methods are not available or seem inappropriate, we turn to an invented system based on the notion that competence and capability need to be acquired systematically by going through a certain institutionalized process.

Or is the very idea that management is a standalone discipline that can be taught, by itself a somewhat dodgy proposition, constructed as a way of establishing a certain kind of order? Reading popular management texts, business self-help books or even the newspaper supplements that peddle what passes for strategic wisdom, seems to confirm that management science consists largely of wrapping some staggeringly self-evident clichés in waves of self-important language.

Among the business bestsellers on Amazon at the time of writing this piece are titles like *Rising Strong* (by the author of *Daring Greatly*), *The Rich Employee*, *Strengths Finder 2.0*, *Platform: Get Noticed In A Noisy World*, *10-Minute Declutter*, *Get What's Yours*, *Getting to Yes* and that old faithful, *7 Habits of Highly Effective People*. At the considerable risk of judging books by their titles, it would seem that these texts seem to represent a discipline that is less about science and more about assorted short-cuts to become successful, without having to tax the intellect mightily.

The management myth arrogates to itself great complexity, which requires strategic vision and other such lofty skills while simultaneously valorizing concepts that even half-wits would find rudimentary. This is why organizations go to great lengths to hire really smart people and then go to even greater lengths to ensure that this smartness is rarely put to use. The truth might well be that there is nothing that requires deep intellect in managing organizations; however, it does require sophisticated life skills, which does not need any great formal training.

Perhaps something fundamental has changed. As new ideas become the dominant source of energy in any ecosystem, the power of the management myth begins to subside. In a world where settled structures based on size, history and power are the dominant forces, being qualified is of great value. One has to fit into a complex framework that already exists, and that is not easy. A stable system needs order, and a predictable set of processes. But a world founded on ideas is fundamentally a more unstable one. What matters here is the power of the idea – ecosystems follow ideas, and capabilities develop in the gap that exists between an idea and its execution, or can be bought off the market.

The opening up of the digital space, which is, in many ways, a completely new universe that needs to be colonized, has thrown up a new set of pioneers who are known more by their ideas than by their antecedents. These are creators, not managers, concerned more with building news ways of imagining the world rather than with efficiently distributing scarce resources over competing priorities. That they are as young as they are is no accident, for the freshness of perspective they bring needs them to be free of the stifling order embedded within the very idea of organizations. They will, in time, develop their own clichés and find their own mental prisons, but for now, it is time to acknowledge the coming of a new order.

THE POWER OF PAPERBOAT WEALTH

Elon Musk has every right to change Twitter's name to X, even if he has no reason to. After all, he paid a ridiculous sum of money to acquire a new toy, and if he can't play with it as he chooses, what would have been the point? From a strictly business lens, his reign as the owner of this influential social media app has at best achieved mixed results, but that hasn't deterred him in the slightest.

Boring analysts may point out that the Twitter name and the symbol were vital assets that were not only an embedded part of our lives but had also become part of our everyday language. It is the rare brand that manages to build such an inventory, and to fritter it away makes little sense. And that, too, for no good reason except a vague yearning to be an everything 'super' app, a desire that has not been translated in even the smallest way so far. And then there is the new name X, which is about as generic as it gets with its forbidding masculine symbol that is the antithesis of a sweet little bird. But apparently, this is all part of a plan – one more move in the 4-D chess that this genius plays that mere mortals like us cannot understand.

Musk is the wealthiest man in the world, and he has undeniably built and been associated with some of the most innovative businesses that we have seen. PayPal, Tesla, Starlink, and SpaceX – that's an impressive body of work that has helped him build his wealth. But it is equally true that most of this wealth is based not on the profits his businesses generate but on how they are valued. Like a lot of wealth in the new economy, this is paperboat wealth – money that lives in ink and trembles when the weather turns foul.

We have seen that in so many other businesses, where valuations can be halved or even slashed to a fourth in a matter of months. This is the kind of wealth that multiplies as easily as it dwindles – Byjus, Ola, OYO, Pharmeasy are some names that come to mind. One day it just appears, and another day it could be decimated.

What this kind of wealth promotes is both a sense of infallibility and a disdain for the kind of norms that governed wealth earlier. Traditional wealth is built over time and comes with attendant responsibilities. Money accumulated over time is weighed down by the effort that goes into gathering it. It often means having to oversee a large workforce over many years. Industrial wealth was built on the backs of factories, colonies, and entire settlements set up by entrepreneurs. It meant tracking the market, dealing with competition, and keeping track of consumer and cultural changes over decades. The progress it made was often incremental, and the owner accreted wealth over time. This kind of wealth is inherently conservative and, more often than not, views any change as a threat. The gravitational force that this wealth is embedded in comes from its dependence on many aspects of society.

Start-up wealth is weightless and comes with little responsibility. The only stakeholders are VCs and private equity firms, which are the key forces that have created the ecosystem that produces this wealth. The whole idea of valuing businesses for their future potential is based on a system where each individual player is hoping to sell off its investment to the next link in the chain for a profit. Its accumulation is much more rapid; people have made billions in just a few years. When wealth is so easily attributable to an individual, and that too in such a short period of time, it is understandable that it is far more individualistic than traditional wealth.

What it creates is a sense of immunity from consequences. Wealth comes from intense effort in a limited domain for a short period of time without the involvement of too many players. It is easy to feel invincible as the distance between stimulus in terms of one's actions and response in terms of wealth creation is so direct and dramatic.

Also, there is a sense of freedom from money and its trappings. The traditionally wealthy get used to money; their lifestyles are fashioned around the certainty of wealth. There is an entire ecosystem that springs up around them that feeds off this energy. For start-up wealth, money is a thing of abstract wonder. It has not carved out a place for itself in the lives of the newly wealthy. It comes and goes easily and thus does not impose the kind of burdens and checks on behaviour that traditional wealth does.

It helps that the dominant medium of the time allows for a direct conversation between founders and a worldwide audience. If, in an earlier time, businesses communicated through carefully fortified bunkers like advertising and PR releases, today it is the individual entrepreneur who has access to millions without the need of a mediating instrument or agency.

It is as if the dominant attire of wealth today is a T-shirt and not a suit. It speaks in a casual, almost flippant, manner and does not overly watch its words. This is both a source of innovation and courage for money, which can today take on causes that traditional wealth has been too conservative to tackle. It can be directed outward at the problems of the world rather than inward towards accumulating it for personal gain. On the other hand, it can back unhinged ideas, fuel dangerous fantasies, and breed volatility of a kind that owes little responsibility to any institutions. We are seeing a little bit of both today. Billionaires playing with their toys is usually not a problem unless what they think of as a toy determines how the world thinks about itself.

SEVENTY HOURS TO NATION-BUILDING?

Mr Narayana Murthy's statement urging young people to work up to 70 hours a week in the interests of nation-building evoked a storm of response, both in support and against. Many other entrepreneurs jumped into the fray, echoing his sentiments, while the reaction from those the message was targeted at was less positive.

The statement could be read as a reaction against the prevailing trend of young people drawing sharp boundaries between their work life and their personal time. Post Covid, the return to office has been somewhat reluctant, and even otherwise, there is a clear recognition of the limits of what a job can ask from you.

On the other hand, there are any number of instances of young founders who work maybe 90 hours a week; indeed, Mr Murthy, despite his age and his stature, is reportedly working 80–90 hours a week. Many such industry doyens are leading by example; surely, that should be reason enough for the younger generation to take his advice seriously. It is also true that India is poised at an interesting juncture, from which it can take off and accelerate growth. Why should such well-meaning advice from a respected industry veteran evoke such negative reactions?

For one, the advice can come across as a way of wanting something for nothing. If employers want people to work harder than what is contractually agreed upon, then they should pay more. Over the years, a narrative has been built around work, which glorifies working long hours and squeezing out personal time. This kind of culture is presented as a sign of passion. Essentially, what it means is that employees work far beyond what they are meant to do, in the name of commitment. The relationship between employer and employee is somehow seen as something deeper and more sacred than a mere contract for using a set of services. And yet, when it suits the business, employees can be fired at will. The deeper relationship is prone to evaporate quite quickly.

At its core, the problem lies with our mental model of employment. What if we were to think about it differently? Let us call employees capability entrepreneurs – businesspersons who sell their time and expertise for a stable income. They agree to forego some of their freedom in exchange for the continuity that comes along with a steady job. Now, as businesspeople, they have every right to maximize their profit and reduce any inefficiencies. Spending more time than contracted is potentially an inefficient use of their resources, and they have a legitimate right, like any business, to optimize their input. It is possible that working harder and putting in more hours might bring them greater profit; they might get promoted faster, for instance, but that choice is theirs to make. We don't expect businesses to embrace inefficiencies in the name of nation-building; for instance, no one thinks that Infosys should hire more people than it needs in order to reduce unemployment and help the country, so why should we expect the employee to act inefficiently?

It seems that being matter-of-fact and clinical is fine when we use the label 'business' but not so when it comes to 'employment', although they are intrinsically far more similar than they appear to be. The newer generation of employees sees through this intrinsic hypocrisy, and traditional business resents this. It is also true that the rewards that accrue because of this work are wildly disproportional. It is easy for entrepreneurs and founders to talk about working hard, for they get the rewards to match. It is instructive that in the sector that Mr Murthy is from, starting salaries have barely moved in the last few years, while CEO compensation has multiplied manifold.

It is not that people do not wish to put everything, or, as business jargon puts it, 110 per cent, into their work. If inspired, and if they feel that they have an emotional stake in the organization, employees do go above and beyond the call of duty in their work. But for this to happen, it is necessary that the organization create an atmosphere that builds a shared sense of ownership. Companies cannot demand this of their employees; the responsibility is theirs to create such a culture.

More than anything else, the desire to make this generation work harder flies in the face of the current social reality. Far too many forces are pushing the world in the opposite direction. The operative part of the shift is that it is not that this generation will work less, but that they seek much greater control over their time. They have seen the older generation spend the primary part of their lives immersed in their jobs while missing out on the other parts of their lives, and there is an understandable reluctance to walk down the same path.

They also challenge embedded norms that are not logically defensible. Why should an employer have the right to intrude on time that they do not pay for or even acknowledge? Why should people feel guilty about prioritizing their family's needs over those of work?

What we are seeing play out is a clash not just between two perspectives, but between two eras. The older world has a mental model of employment rooted in an environment of scarcity. The employer held disproportionate power and could dictate terms that the employee had no option but to accept. More subtly, business created a narrative of commitment and passion that the employee willingly bought into. Today, it is not that jobs have become that plentiful, but there is a much greater sense of opportunity. Employees are willing to chuck up their jobs for reasons that an older generation will think of as quite trivial.

The onus is squarely on business to find a way to inspire and engage this generation. Admonishing them for their lack of dedication is unlikely to have any effect. That ship has sailed.

HOW HARD SHOULD HARD WORK BE?

HARD WORK NEVER KILLED ANYBODY. Or so we heard repeatedly growing up. Clearly, that does not ring true these days. Every few months, we hear of the tragic passing of a young fresher, allegedly of overwork. And we ask questions about the nature of work culture.

It has almost been a central belief across cultures that hard work, in all its forms, is, by definition, good. We have grown up hearing about its desirability and have been admonished repeatedly by parents and teachers against laziness. Students who spent hours studying, often staying up nights, were held up as role models, and scathing comparisons were drawn with the rest of us. An often-repeated line that most of us would have heard was that 'this was the time to work hard; after all, we had the rest of our lives to enjoy ourselves'.

Of course, as we discovered, the 'rest of our lives' had no place for enjoyment. The workplace valorizes hard work even more. And curiously, it puts a premium on working beyond the mandated and paid-for amount. Treating the job 'just like a job' is apparently a horrible crime. We are meant to go 'above and beyond' and work 70 hours a week for our own good without getting paid extra for it.

What is strange is that this idea sits at odds with how we market the fast-changing world we live in. In a primarily agrarian society, one could understand the emphasis on hard work, for our bodies were virtually the only machines we had access to, and life was exceedingly hard. Backbreaking work schedules were the only way to navigate everyday life. Everything was a chore – farming, drawing water, collecting firewood, washing clothes, cooking, looking after children. With few support systems, it was impossible to survive without working really hard.

In an industrial society, working hard took on a new form. People became cogs in a machine, each with a designated and repetitive role. Individuals lost control over their lives; the physical workload was punishing, but there was also a measure of order. Work hours were regulated, and extra hours meant extra wages. The coming of trade unions helped harness the collective power of the workforce and allowed them some leverage for negotiating better terms.

With the coming of the knowledge economy, where the body is not exercised at all and it is only the mind that is at work, one would have expected the codes of the workplace to change. But, surprisingly, we use the same yardsticks that we used in agrarian and industrial societies to measure work of a completely different kind.

We have had so many technological instruments that have come to our aid in the workplace post the arrival of the personal computer, and yet there is no change whatsoever in our workload. On the contrary, what has happened is that work has vampired our leisure time by making us accessible and answerable at all times. The future is meant to give us even greater freedom as AI transforms the world, but how many of us truly believe that work cultures will change?

Greater leisure has been glittering on the technology mirage for decades now. The promise of having more time to devote to other, more important, parts of our lives has been held out to us in every successive technological epoch.

For those who hark back to the past with nostalgia about how hard they worked in their youth, it is important to recognize just how different the world is today. Unlike the past, where the line between work and the rest of our lives was sharp, today it is virtually nonexistent. Letters took weeks to reach the intended receiver; planning cycles were stretched over months, if not years. Once we got back home, we were truly home. Today, work consumes not just a part of our lives but all of it. Pressure is constant, and it is no surprise that there are so many diseases of modernity around us that were virtually absent in an earlier time.

And work is just part of the pressure felt by the young. Making one's way in today's social landscape is no picnic either. The self has to be burnished and put on display, not just once in a while but every single day. And then there is the pressure that is exerted by one's peer group. The promise of reaching dizzying heights by following the recipe laid out by the 'winners' in this world seduces so many others to strive beyond their capacities. The 'hustle culture' that is looked up to encourages this 'winner-take-all' sentiment.

The great illusion that the white-collar workforce carries about themselves is that they are not 'labour', that they are a higher category of beings. This leads to an expectation that they create about themselves that, as part of 'management', they carry an additional responsibility that goes beyond what is officially their remit. The corporations are only too glad to feed this delusion by creating a range of symbols that emphasize their superiority – fancy titles, important-sounding language, training sessions. There is an elaborate protocol that serves to obscure the fact that all employees are part of 'labour'.

At its heart, the problem lies in the combination of a vested business interest on one side and an internalized feeling of guilt on the other. Cost structures of organizations have been optimized around the assumption that employees will deliver more than what they are paid for. Every new benefit from technology is offset by reducing the workforce so that the pressure on existing employees remains the same.

An intern's death is not an isolated case. While death may not be the outcome in thousands of other instances, the toll that the valorization of hard work extracts is real. Hard work is important, but life is even more so.

DROWNING IN AWARDS?

IT IS GETTING EXTREMELY DIFFICULT to avoid winning an award. Social media is full of people who have been recognized in one way or another and they are as profuse in their humility as they are insistent on sharing the news with as many people as they can. Entirely new categories of awards have sprung up, making sure that none of us feels left out. If, earlier, winning an award meant that you had to be the very best at something, today such exacting requirements feel dated. Awards are no longer given for doing anything remarkable, but merely for being wonderful.

Many things have changed. For one, the number of awards has mushroomed. Every corporation, media house, institution – and there are companies that exist only to give awards – confers these recognitions. They then expand these categories in ways that make exclusion difficult – one can be awarded for being a Changemaker, a Disruptor, an Innovator, a Tastemaker, a Man of Excellence, a Champion, a Paragon of Style, or for being Influential, Impactful, an Out-of-the-Box Thinker or someone utterly Unstoppable.

Movie awards now have graduated well beyond the traditional categories rewarding cinematic excellence. We now have awards that range from the Most Stylish Performance to the more blindingly self-explanatory ones like the Nothing to Hide Award (conferred in 2018 to Kriti Sanon). And finally, awards are no longer given to individuals one at a time; categories like 40, Under-40, or The 50 Most Influential Achievers have ensured that democracy prevails in the Land of Eternal Self-Congratulation, too.

Awards are taken seriously by those who get them. The others clap perfunctorily. There are, of course, industries like advertising that exist largely to win some awards – their main line of work is a bit of a distraction from their true pursuit. In the world of films, too, despite the transparent worthlessness of most awards, feuds have raged on account of someone not getting a recognition that they thought was theirs.

Many companies have figured out that awarding people who are important to their business is the most efficient sales promotion tool at their disposal – after all, large customers might balk at being given an open bribe, but who can resist the charms of being anointed the Pharma Supply Chain Inspiring Leader of the Year? To receive such an award in an audience of peers at a glittering (never gleaming or shining or iridescent) ceremony is one of those innocent joys of corporate life that it would be cruel to deny. For employers, too, awards are a good motivational tool that keeps their people feel recognized on the cheap.

A new breed of awards has sprung up that has monetized our hunger for recognition. Media houses now are ready to confer grand sounding trophies on all those willing to pay the price. We can now buy awards, or, more accurately, contribute to the advertising effort of the media title in question in return for the recognition that they have determined that we were worthy of.

What drives this hunger for recognition is, at one level, not a particularly complex question. As human beings we need validation, and we seek it from everyone that we interact with, in one form or another. Institutionalized recognition gives us a sense of worth over and above what is due to us. It is a form of surplus that we crave – something that goes beyond the transactional exchange of performance and reward. Awards pull us out from the crowd and make us feel special. They convert our own perceived specialness into public news. Even if the award has been bought or otherwise managed, the winner revels in the effect it has on others.

What has made this need for awards more pressing is the nature of social media, which demands that we present ourselves with ever greater urgency and self-importance. We are all media figures now, with our broadcast channels. As celebrities in our own imagination, we need an incessant flow of good news about ourselves to continue to make the point that we are indeed special. Everything is fodder for this machine – our Bermuda-clad pictures from the Maldives, the ornate manner in which we present our homes and our costumed selves during festivals, big and small achievements of our progeny, lavish marriages that we attend, articles that we might have written (including this one), and, of course, the latest trophy to grace our drawing-room shelves.

We don't even need any achievements, or events, to toot our own horn. On business sites like LinkedIn, every small act of common humanity becomes an inspirational story. Every random opinion is presented like a timeless quote. Banal pieces of utterly trivial and self-evident advice are shared as life-altering wisdom.

We are both subject and audience – we would have to be, otherwise the whole enterprise falls apart. We need to pander to the other's need for validation if we hope to receive it in return. The currency of superlatives requires a two-way exchange.

What is wrong if our need for validation is met in this way? In earlier generations, praise was tightly controlled and needed to be prised out of the clammy hands of a boss or older relative. In India, in particular, so many children grew up hankering for some recognition from an authority figure, recognition that seemed always to be withheld, with sphincter clenched. Why should any form of encouragement, however banal, be looked down upon if it helps people feel better about themselves?

The problem is not with the intent but with the nature of the recognition. Like all forms of preciousness, it has value only if it is rare. Overuse exhausts meaning. As awards become more commonplace, and as the mystery around them wanes, they become the small change of our lives, instead of the milestones that they once used to be.

THE SOCIAL FACE OF BUSINESS?

'In an emergency, anywhere in India, someone from our side will be with you within an hour.' This was how two Indian entrepreneurs, involved with the textile industry, were trying to communicate the scale of their business in a recent conversation. They did not talk about their sales, or the number of outlets they serviced, nor did they use statistics about the number of people who bought their product or the millions of metres of fabric that they sold. They chose to bring alive the scale of their network by focusing on a possible human need, one that would strike a resonant chord with almost anyone, even those who have no interest in textiles or in business itself. Having someone to depend on in a crisis anywhere in the country is a thought that is wonderfully comforting. To use such a human need as a measure of business success was an unselfconscious action from their side, but remarkable all the same, for it showed what their mental model of business was.

In the view of traditional Indian business, the market (bazaar) is not an impersonal device that merely helps make money but a living organism, one that serves a very real human function. The market lives not as an alcove of commercial interest, but at the centre of a community's social life, and serves purposes far in excess of making money. Scholar and author Rajni Bakshi describes this model of the bazaar as 'a more socially-embedded market culture – based on a broader, more well-rounded view of human nature'.

Personal life and work are part of an organic whole, without a great need felt to draw sharp boundaries. The family is involved in the business seamlessly, and roles shift fluidly according to need. Money is handled with great care, but the business often does not know exactly how much surplus it generates. One's word is a cherished commodity and personal reputation is everything. Oral contracts are inviolable, and some flexibility is shown in accommodating each other's needs, for relationships and trust count for more than anything else. This is what makes it possible for traditional structures like the commodity markets to function with very low levels of default.

In this model, disputes are dealt with using a communitarian notion of justice, rather than a legal one. The use of informal mechanisms and unconventional instruments abounds. One might pay a penalty, forgo opportunities, perform an act of penance, endure shaming and social boycotts – the range of punitive and corrective actions is a large and inventive one. The parameters of the social, rather than legal, hold sway. The overall purpose is to further the cause of the community, rather than focus narrowly on individual gain.

The modern market has, in contrast, been built on an impersonal vision of reciprocity, one which converts the idea of long-term interdependence into a series of short-term encounters, clinical in nature and transactional in spirit. The currency of money, the act of putting a price on everything, makes the market a mechanistic apparatus, one which gives us predictable relationships between input and output and allows for scale and replication. Documentation becomes key, as does the separation of the personal from the professional.

At the heart of this mental model of markets lies the valorization of the professional, who is seen as a commercial hit-man, using his skills to deliver secular outcomes for a business – growth, profits, market share. To the professional, the world of relationships and informal mechanisms is an irritant, for it renders the achievement of commercial goals far too context-sensitive, rather than uniform and predictable. The allegiance is to the task given, and any acknowledgement of the larger context is carefully filtered out. Ethics need to be consciously articulated, for a natural sense of the moral is difficult to grasp in such an impersonal construct. In some sense then, the idea of the professional is constructed in opposition to that of the social.

The corporation as a structure further distances business from society by atomizing ownership, thereby detaching its purpose from any identifiable human motivation. Shorn of any larger responsibility and detached from any social ecology, it is able to pursue a single goal and serve the largely invisible shareholder. This extractive view of business exacts costs from all the contexts that it is embedded in, including the natural environment and society.

This is beginning to change. Armed with a voice on social media, consumers are pushing business to integrate more with social concerns, and it is responding in its own way. We see more corporations waking up to their social role and professing a deep interest in society. Every corporation and brand seems to be looking for a larger purpose and is chasing a cause of some kind. Advertising is full of pious declarations of social action – suddenly, business seems to be as focused on saving the world as it is on boosting its bottom line, and perhaps the two are not entirely unrelated.

However, the problem lies not with intention alone, but with the mental model of business itself. Without reconciling the personal with the commercial, attempts by business to don a more human face seem contrived, nothing more than a new advertising peg. Business still operates in a realm of its own, with only a token nod to the human needs of its stakeholders. The fact that in the USA, the crucible of market capitalism, there is no paid leave that is guaranteed for maternity (federal law mandates twelve weeks of unpaid leave) is a pointer to how business cannot accommodate a need as fundamental as childbirth.

This is not to argue for a wholesale embrace of the traditional way of doing business, for it is not equipped to handle the complex needs of today's business context, but to acknowledge that there is much to learn from it. We need to be reminded that business has always been a human network that exists for a collective human purpose.

THE ENTREPRENEURSHIP MAGNET?

GROWING UP, I NEVER WANTED to be an entrepreneur. Coming from a non-business family, the prevalent mental image of business was both negative and distant. It involved money, transactions and loans, things that were considered either contaminating or dangerous. Since business was the domain of a few communities, it was regarded as something inherent in others. You did not start a business, you merely came from a line of people whose nature it was to do business. In that sense, business and entrepreneurship, though seemingly highly related ideas, were actually experienced as two different concepts – business being an activity, entrepreunership a mindset.

There were few examples, even from within one's extended family, of people setting up businesses, and these examples reinforced one's instinctive distaste for business. Either there were those who seemed to struggle endlessly, moving forever from crisis to crisis, or those who did exceedingly well for a few years, and then inevitably met fates that were the stuff moral-science lessons are made of. The aura around business, and the stock market in particular, was deeply negative, and these were domains reserved for the hardened insiders who understood its convoluted, and often crooked, ways.

It is true that being an entrepreneur in India was excruciatingly difficult. The regulatory frameworks as well as the social ecosystem were actively hostile to business, and it was no place for starry-eyed novices. Business was a fixed insider's game, and individuals had little real chance of breaking in. Raising funds was exceedingly difficult and the consequences of even temporary setbacks could be devastating.

Clearly, a fundamental change is afoot. There is a new generation that regards entrepreneurship as their most favoured destination. Students from top-tier institutions aspire to starting something of their own. The heroes of the day are not industrialists from established business houses, but young gunslingers who have just ridden into town. Some of the most valuable businesses in the world have been started in the last couple of decades and virtually all of them by people young enough to be cutting classes in college.

A lot has changed otherwise, too. The lure of a steady job in a large stable company has waned over the last many decades. Over the years, the power equation between the employer and employees has become less skewed, and the job market has created opportunities that allow for people to change jobs with greater ease. The culture around employment has transformed beyond recognition as the regimented conformity expected of employees in an earlier era has given way to a much more informal and fluid working relationship. Globalization has accelerated mobility and enabled the widening of career horizons.

The younger generation today demands a level of independence and control over their time and their lives that conventional jobs struggle to provide in spite of all the changes that we have seen. The idea of being in charge of their destiny is a deeply attractive one.

The internet has brought about a dramatic change in the career landscape. It has dismantled many of the barriers that ensured that by and large status quo prevailed in business. At an earlier time, it was much easier for large established businesses to maintain their dominance. They had more money, better distribution, they could hire smarter people and reward their shareholders better. Today, money is available aplenty, distribution asymmetries have all but been wiped out in many categories, and the smarter people are keener to join an entrepreneurial venture.

The basis for creating wealth has changed. If, in an earlier time, capital and historical dominance were the biggest determinants of success, today ideas are the basis of wealth creation. The young have a great advantage here, for they understand the new business landscape much better than those steeped in the rules of a bygone time. The conventional advantages of age, experience and legacy have got devalued while the new codes of seamlessness, agility and fluidity feel uncomfortable to the old guard.

The overall ability to deal with risk has also increased. From a time when it was feared that the only change in one's economic status could be for the worse, there is, today, a greater belief in tomorrow. This change is gradual, but in the long run, inexorable. The younger generation, in particular those who come from more financially comfortable backgrounds, do not have the memory of scarcity of options that their parents experienced, and do not regard the future with the same nervousness that the earlier generation did. Also, starting out very early means that the opportunity cost of failure is low.

Besides, the idea of failure does not carry the kind of consequences that it once did. In an earlier generation, failure meant financial, social and psychological consequences of a kind that were difficult to recover from. In fact, the idea of being able to change the trajectory of life once it took a certain shape was in itself a fanciful thought. Not so anymore, which is why entrepreneurship is on the rise worldwide and in India, and is expected to become even more significant. Apart from the young, who are taking to starting up on their own, we see instances of women across the country too seeking to utilize their talents by taking the entrepreneurial plunge.

Even now, of course, there are a large number of young people who still prefer a steady job, preferably one offered by the government. The idea of risk-free, permanent white-collar comfort has an understandable pull in a poor country. But the conditions for a change in this mindset are ripe, ground up. Aspirations are changing, and the time when more young people look forward to being employers rather than employees is not as far as it might appear. What is needed is a corresponding effort to democratize access to entrepreneurial opportunities, vastly simplify regulatory frameworks, and provide the resources needed for more people to take up entrepreneurship.

THE CONTINUING POWER OF THE GOVERNMENT JOB

THE NUMBERS ARE STAGGERING. TWENTY-THREE lakh applicants for 368 peon's jobs in UP, 25 lakh vying for 6,000 Group D jobs in Bengal, 25 million applications for 90,000 jobs in the railways, 2 lakh for 1,137 vacancies for the post of police constables in Maharashtra. At one level, these numbers from the last few years highlight the scarcity of jobs in many parts of India, but at another, they speak to the continued power of the government job. In a growing economy, one would imagine that the choices of careers would be widening. We certainly see this happening in the larger cities, where private-sector jobs are usually preferred to government jobs, because of money, growth prospects and work culture.

But step outside into the larger India, as one had occasion to do as part of an ongoing project to make sense of what is changing in small-town India, and the picture changes completely. The private sector is viewed largely with suspicion, and with more than a little disdain. The private job is seen to be work at its most sweaty and unrewarding. One is answerable to the owner, there is no permanence, and the hours are long and hard. The exception is an IIT degree, which is seen as a passport to all kinds of opportunities; but even for many IIT aspirants, the eventual destination is a government job.

The reasons for the preference for a government job are easy to understand. The fact that a government job is permanent is a huge factor. It speaks volumes for the economy when stability is valued over everything else. The government job 'settles' one's life into a template of ever-after; anxiety about the future is substantially managed. And then there is the prospect of what is called 'oopar ki kamai' – the ability to make money on the side.

This is acknowledged in a matter-of-fact way without a trace of guilt, as if it were a legitimate perk that came along with the job. The government job is also seen to be much less taxing in terms of the effort that needs to be put in; the 'no tension' nature of employment is often spoken of.

But the real attraction of the government job is the power that is seen to come with it. In large parts of India, power is a stronger currency than money, for it is convertible into every other currency of note. The government job gives one a place in the 'official' social map of a region. One is somebody as per the caste one is born into, and then on the basis of the official designation one manages to acquire. Without such a fixed position, one floats without harness; one cannot do anything meaningful for others while anything can potentially be done to you. The intractability of the administrative system becomes the reason for its continued power – to crack it, one must be inside it. In small-town India, official power is a palpable presence; cars zoom around with designations on the number plate, names of municipal officers are common knowledge, transfers of key officers become headline news.

Which is why a government position, however menial, is often preferred to an objectively more attractive private sector or entrepreneurial option. We can see the evidence of this in the kind of people who apply for government jobs – CAs, MBAs, even PhDs can be found applying for jobs of peons and clerks – positions they would not dream of taking in the private sector. In the marriage market, which is the real test of what is socially valued, a person with a government job commands better terms. Getting into the government is a mammoth project by itself. Studying for a government job is thought of as much more of a job than actually working for the government. Taking up to three to four years preparing for a job is considered quite normal. For instance, in a state like Bihar, where towns are plastered with signs of people studying for these jobs, one comes across students slogging it out in special study groups, living away from home in terrible conditions, spending money that they can ill-afford, all to crack some government job. Being unemployed while preparing for a government job looks nothing like unemployment. There is a sense of purpose, great social support, an extremely busy day, and a thriving ecosystem that enables learning.

This results in a vast number of young people finding themselves trapped in a bubble of competitive exams, responding to a constructed reality of exams and interviews that bears little resemblance to real life. Subjects have to be mugged, arcane skills developed, purely for the purpose of landing the job. The learning here leaves little by way of residual knowledge; all of it gets consumed in the act of finding a job.

In a time of start-ups, influencers and Shark Tank, one would have thought that Newer Age opportunities would be what excited the young more than the stability of a government job. Given the growing importance of material comfort, the romance of being an entrepreneur should be what seduces the young. And while there are a few who are venturing out on their own even in the smallest towns in the country, it is still a small number, quite insignificant when compared to the number of people dying for a government position.

The intense demand for these jobs should mean that the government should get the best talent that is available. In the functioning of the government in most parts of the country, however, it is not immediately apparent that this is so. For most aspirants, the hard work stops at the doorstep of the job. What is being vied for is not work, but power. The government is dotted with extremely bright and committed people, but this is not a predictable pattern, simply a function of some individuals.

The attractiveness of the government job can, in theory, be very good news. It would indicate that that India is full of public-service-minded people who want to work to improve things on the ground. Sadly, the popularity of the government job is a sign, despite all the progress the country has made, of how static the interlocked social and economic systems have remained, and how administration gets decoded not as service, but as power. The preference for a government job in the current form is a vote for the past rather than the future.

THE MORE WE CONSUME, THE LESS IT'S MEANINGFUL

COME DIWALI, AND CONSUMPTION IS in the air. Bazaars are swollen with shiny merchandise, everything glitters in its thrall and everyone looks like mithai. And yet, the desire for things, while exhibiting an avidness that seems to keep growing, lacks something. Things lose lustre very quickly; we buy things and get bored, and as a way out of that boredom and as a way of passing time, buy some more things. This is true of many kinds of new things – traditional stuff like clothing or new technologies that come with frequent upgrades. The next big thing is awaited with anticipation, and gets absorbed into our lives virtually instantly, without creating a sense of satisfaction.

It is a strange paradox. Consumption is a much bigger factor in our lives today; we attach exaggerated significance to our own selves, and everything we buy is a tribute to our magnificence. Consumption is today an act of curating the self-building identity blocks bit by bit, as we define who we are through what we buy. Traditional sources of identity are being gradually hollowed out, and the new sources are those that can be acquired. The car we drive, the brand we wear, where we holiday – these are all things that add up to define who we are. The selfies we click are an anxious document of our own work, and we can never click enough selfies to satisfy ourselves.

But there used to be a joy about buying something, a sweetness in the act of putting one's heart into every act of purchase, that seems missing now. Scarcity created desire of a kind that burned slowly and long, eating up one's insides in a quiet way. Things burrowed their way into us by not being there, their absence creating a palpable space that cried out to be filled. By the time something was bought, it had already been consumed several times over in one's imagination. Things lived twice over, once as yawning absences and then as presences that were made to linger, till every last drop of juice was extracted from it.

The idea of the new had a magical quality – it was a miracle that needed to be preserved, nurtured, taken pleasure in for as long as one could. The new was a different state of being; it beamed with a sense of inner bliss, rubbing off its alchemic power on the proud owner. When consumption becomes a habit, things change. When was the last time someone said 'new pinch' to you? There is no need for inflicting compensatory pain in a world where the new is no big deal.

I don't know if other people do it, but I find myself putting myself in the shoes of my adolescent pre-liberalization self and seeing the world that I inhabit today with those wide eyes. This is the only way that consumption begins to become meaningful. How would those eyes see the way one lives today? If only one could extract the same kind of pleasure from consumption that one was able to earlier, then the greater ability to consume today would have some meaning. One recalls the pleasures of consumption without now being able to summon anywhere near the same intensity of feeling that it once evoked.

The pleasure of having a ten-rupee note in one's pocket, the heat that 'jeb-garmi' generated, the cornucopia of possibilities that nestled within one's grasp, cannot be recaptured in any way. No amount of actual money today can measure up to the feeling of wealth that was experienced then. For the middle-class children of this generation, money has material value, but they are equally aware of the limits of what it can buy. The ladder of desires today is far too high for any amount to be really meaningful, but in the days gone by, it took little for money to feel infinite. Consumption is a currency today, and the idea of an ascending array of choices makes it impossible for desire to be terminally quenched. One never has the latest, the best or the most expensive or most exclusive version of one's desired object or experience. In an earlier time, consumption was a terminal destination; for instance, once a car was bought, that was the end of that.

The idea of affluence in India is that state where every act of spending does not automatically need to be filtered through the lens of affordability, when one can spend without thinking about it. A little treat here, an impromptu vacation there, something that one 'picks up' on a whim, buying a spare set 'just in case' – these are the true luxuries for a generation that grew up worrying about spending any money whatsoever.

There is, of course, a vast section of society that is experiencing this new found ability to consume for the first time today. The lament of being jaded about consumption is the privilege of a fortunate few. For the rest, consumption is a vital force that courses through the lives of people, giving it energy and purpose. The power of consumption is that it is a universally accessible language, and is able to dot every day with a sense of progress. Every act of consumption becomes an affirmation of one's upward journey, a granular map of one's gradual ascent in life.

For those who have been consumers for a while, new games have to be invented for consumption to have meaning. We buy things not because of what they are but because of who we want to be. Increasingly, consumption is overtly about creating meaning. We buy brands that tell us stories about ourselves, and pay premiums to hear a good story told well. The irony is that the more we consume, the less its power to deliver meaning. When we barely consumed anything at all, consumption had the most meaning. Consumption today is the smoke that we blow at the mirror called the self.

IN PRAISE OF UNMARKETING

A FEW WEEKS AGO, I HAD the pleasure of eating what were, without question, the best idlis that I have ever had. This was at a small stall in Vijaywada going under the name of Shree Ganesh Idlis. This place is a little shack on a small road in a desultory residential colony, and is basic enough not to have any sign that displays its name. The idlis were divine, the upma even more so, but they had run out of dosas, which is what they were really famous for. Like many other stalls of this kind, there were clear codes to be followed – they were open only for breakfast; once they ran out of batter, they shut shop for the day; and idlis that became cold were not served to customers. They had been in operation for thirty years, were used to receiving guests from all over the world, but they couldn't be bothered to add a bench for people to sit down.

All over India, there are these wonderful places that serve absolutely brilliant food and they all have one thing in common – they know when to stop. Most of these places have no branches, little by way of marketing, and almost every single day, they run out of food to serve.

For anyone with a management degree or even the slightest exposure to the world of business, such behaviour seems to be nothing short of extraordinary. Why wouldn't the owner of a successful food stall aspire to be the owner of a restaurant, perhaps even a chain of restaurants? Why would he not make the most basic attempt to market himself, create a brand in a more conscious way, maybe advertise a little? Given that venture capital is so easily available today, why not monetize the value of the business that lies locked up otherwise?

In fact, in the dominant ethos of business today, it is not only mandatory to mop up all value that is embedded in any venture, but, if possible, one is encouraged to suck up future earnings in the name of valuations. The digital world serves as testimony to the appetite business has for earning today what a business might one day hope to earn over several years, if not a lifetime. So many financial instruments of the day collapse future potential into present profit.

The abiding idea that drives the world of business is that of scale. Success is replicated, scaled up, leveraged. The very idea of replication is that of dead multiplication, of things breeding and coming into being without having to come alive in any sense of the word. Scale comes from granting universality of access but taking away the grainy specificity of a particular experience. In doing so, ideas become products that deliver uniformity in a way that is easy to consume. This has always been true, but has become much more so today.

In a world of this kind, the idea that there are currencies of other kinds, that there could conceivably be room for people not to extract value but to let it lie unattended, fallow, would appear to be hopelessly dated. But for many ventures like Ganesh Idli, value takes on many forms – the appreciation of customers who hunt down this place and come from far and wide, the pride of maintaining quality, the feeling of successfully carrying on a legacy, and the cussed insistence on doing the precisely right thing, simply because that's how it should be done.

The quality of greatness, rather than that of serviceable sufficiency, comes from an ability to leave something on the table. Not every ounce of value is squeezed from a transaction; the price in this case bears no resemblance whatsoever to the value delivered. In this world, a product or experience cannot be fully described by what it costs – labels like high-end or premium get exposed for their poverty.

The difference is in the starting point – today we live in a world defined by the consumer; we begin with what we want to consume and work backwards, by stuffing things with the ingredients of success. This is as true of food as it is of management theory; we want to first find out what makes people consume more of some food or what the 7 signs of effective leaders are, and then go ahead and recreate those conditions to the best of our ability.

The world of Ganesh Idlis and its ilk, on the other hand, begins with the creator and caters first to his needs, and is constrained by the limits of his imagination as well as greed. The product is an expression of the creator's beliefs and abilities, and not a precis of consumer desires. It does both more and less than what is deemed ideal and creates its own ethos of consumption. By forgoing the value it could extract from the transaction, it rescues us from the act of consumption, by making us connoisseurs rather than mere consumers.

The world built around people who create, as against people who consume, is, fortunately, not a thing of nostalgia only. One of the great advantages of the internet is that in its purest form, it has little regard for scale. Interesting ideas generate their own currencies and, as a result, we are seeing an outbreak of creation – not only those that seek multi-billion-dollar valuations, but those that put their passion out on display for the world to appreciate. Small fashion labels, sites for food lovers, archivists of traditional forms of music and dance, collectors of knowledge about traditions and customs of specific communities, the internet is teeming with those who create because they want to and not because there is a market waiting for their efforts.

The opportunity of finding meaning in acts of creation is available much more freely today. The more we are to develop currencies other than money, the richer the fruits of affluence are likely to be.

CHAPTER 8

Outrage/Media

The Coming of Hot Democracy

India's new public sphere runs on heat.

Media, once a mirror, has become a magnifying glass – distorting, inflaming, consuming.

Outrage is now ambient, opinion is performance, and the line between citizen and mob has grown thin.

TOWARDS AN UNCIVIL SOCIETY?

WHENEVER ONE MOUNTS A CRITIQUE of the current state of media, one encounters a particular counter-argument. Where were you when the tilt was the other way around, when the liberal narrative held sway in almost all of media? No one complained about bias, or the quality of coverage, then, did they? The power has now moved decisively away from the traditional elite, and, along with social media, TV now speaks for the millions who were effectively silenced earlier, and this is what seems to be causing so much heartburn for a small section of commentators.

There is truth in this argument. There is no question that media was slanted the other way, particularly before 2014. Even if a debate was mounted and both sides represented, there was never any doubt as to where the channel stood, and what the 'right answer' was. And while the arrival of social media has changed things, it has done so for everyone. Is all the breast-beating about media today then just a sign of the once-powerful refusing to come to terms with a new reality?

It is important to make two vital distinctions. First, although there was an undeniable slant in the way media covered politics, it was by no means protected from severe criticism. The coverage of the Aarushi Talwar case was condemned in the strongest possible terms by so many of the same critics who were aghast at the way the Sushant Singh Rajput case was handled. The penetration of the market into media and the manner in which it transformed it also came under sustained scrutiny well before the change of the political guard.

Nor was the government of the day shielded from stinging criticism. The Bofors scandal, the CWG crisis and the Jan Lokpal movement are just some instances when the media went without any restraint against the government in power. Unlike today, when even the most egregious of the government's mistakes are defended by finding convoluted ways to attack the opposition, in earlier times, the government and its leaders were not deemed to be immune to criticism. There was an underlying sympathy for the ideology that the government represented (in its own confused and timid way), but it did not come in the way of the government getting rapped by the media.

The big difference today is in the manner in which the content is being presented. Every channel has a right to a political stance, and there is absolutely nothing wrong in leaning rightwards, as long as the essential codes of journalism are followed. The desire to seek out the truth, the discipline and rigour exercised in ensuring that one is dealing only in verifiable facts, the openness to being wrong, contrition when one makes a mistake, and the existence of a minimum level of civility in the discourse – all of these are conspicuous by their absence today, having been the norms in the past. The absence of such a discipline should worry everyone, regardless of their ideological leanings, for media transforms all of society, not just politics. We were witness to the absurd spectacle of our TV channels inventing outrageous lies in the brief conflict with Pakistan following the Pahalgam tragedy. The coverage bore no resemblance to anything remotely connected with journalism.

The role of social media complicates matters. While it is undoubtedly a democratizing force in its conception, the manner in which it is evolving is deeply troublesome for society as a whole. Apart from the kind of abuse that anonymity and access to a broadcasting channel fosters, much of what passes off as comment on social media is manufactured by an extensive network of professionals who generate hate and sow seeds of doubt as part of their job. Troll farms exist across the world, and use increasingly sophisticated techniques to shape large-scale public opinion and nudge us invisibly towards more extreme positions. A troll farm is not the exclusive preserve of any one side. Abuse has no ideology. Anyone can be harassed and discredited if one sets out to do so. Nothing is sacred – personal abuse, doctored quotes, photoshopped pictures, deepfake videos, attacks on family members, false news reports about alleged misdeeds – everything is easy to manufacture and circulate.

The new codes of propaganda are so powerful while being invisible that they are almost impossible to counter. The issue is much larger than the temporary advantage any one side of the political divide enjoys because of the so-called levelling of the playing field. What is being destroyed is reason itself. When we move away from a fact-based view of the world, and have at our disposal technologies that completely blur the difference between truth and falsehood, and transact in high-pitched, emotionally charged narratives, we construct a world where none of us will be able to find our bearings. A generation will grow up believing that the kind of language and behaviour they see on TV and social media is how arguments should be framed.

The problem about the one-sidedness of news coverage is a real one, but the manner in which news is being presented is what is truly dangerous. The descent into a primitive, tribal mindset is potentially irreversible. We are building a paranoid society, always alert to manufactured enemies, and quick to proactively attack in the name of defence. We are on the ground floor of change; imagine what kind of discourse will become the norm in a few decades. Whatever one's political inclinations might be, the idea of regressing into a world where the basest emotions rise to the top, and where we deploy our very worst side on the smallest of issues, is a deeply unappetizing one. Unless we act now, and find ways to restrain the cruder aspects of the current discourse, it will be too late.

THE POWER OF DISPROPORTION

ONE DOESN'T HAVE TO LIE to tell an untruth. Of course, lying is the most direct and efficient form of untruth, but there are other ways too. Over the last few years, the Indian state, and much of mainstream media, has been practising a different technique, one which does not depend on lying (although that doesn't stop it from doing so) but has a similar effect. It involves rescaling our sense of reality by exercising the power of disproportion. Simply put, it involves suppressing or ignoring certain facts and amplifying others. Make hitherto trivial events feel momentous and diminish the significance of others so that they feel unimportant. After all, there are no universal standards for judging what is important and what is not. So, powerful mainstream media can decide as to what reality it wants to make up for us. Not necessarily through fake news, but by a reinterpreted sense of what is important and what can be ignored or downplayed.

There are several elements to this strategy. Apart from selective suppression and magnification, it involves recharacterizing an issue so that its more troubling aspects are downplayed. The relatively insignificant aspects of an important issue are highlighted so as to give a sense that it is not being ignored, while avoiding discussing the more problematic areas. The emotional ante is upped for trivial issues to an extent that they start feeling like life-and-death issues. Media coverage is self-justifying, in that the more an issue gets covered, the more important it seems. The horrific Hathras rape and murder and the Sushant Singh Rajput–Rhea Chakraborty cases are excellent illustrations of how this technique works.

In the Hathras case, suppression by the state took on dimensions so monumental that even the usually servile media had to take note. To not allow the family a last glimpse of their daughter, to tap their phones and try and make them undergo a narco test, to threaten the family with dire consequences in case they spoke up, to ban any media interaction and cordon off the whole village and burn the girl's body in secret – the list of autocratic actions taken to deny the problem rather than address it bordered on the unbelievable, even in today's times. Then there was the attempt by some to acknowledge the problem but in terms that minimized it. It wasn't really rape, because no semen was found in the victim's body. It's not really about caste, but a problem faced by all women. It was terrible, but unless the problem of unemployment was fixed, men would get frustrated and commit these heinous crimes.

The other tactic is to try and present a small non-issue as the major problem. Why was a journalist trying to convince the parents of the victim to complain against the government? Wasn't this a clear sign of a conspiracy? Was the opposition trying to incite rioting and wasn't it imperative for the state government to act to prevent this from happening?

Presenting the Bollywood drug mafia as a defining issue for the country showed this technique at work in a sophisticated way. Since the only conceivable charge that could be placed at Rhea Chakraborty's doorstep had to do with her mention of recreational drug use, weed was presented as an unmentionable evil. This was patently absurd. For one, the use of weed and its variants cuts across all strata of society, from sadhus, Holi and Shivratri revellers, students, business executives, TV journalists, politicians, to people from Bollywood. It is sold in licensed shops in parts of the country and is part of our cultural fabric. Opium use is rampant in many parts of the country as part of community tradition. This doesn't justify any form of drug abuse, but one can hardly pretend that the mere mention of marijuana is a grievous crime. The frenzied emotional manner of presentation, which bordered on the psychotic, served to recalibrate our sense of reality. The power of disproportion, when used consistently, is that we lose our bearings. We start associating certain ideas and words with blasphemy and the mere invocation of these is enough to set us off, without regard to the issue at hand.

It has always been true that our sense of reality has been shaped by the media. There are only so many things that we can know through direct personal observation and experience, so we have to rely on someone else's account of what is happening in the world to make sense of it. It is obvious that anyone taking on this mantle of distilling events all around us into a few items of 'news', even when acting in good faith, will impose their own frames of what is important and what is not. The idea of news implies objectivity, some kind of capital-letter idea of Reality – mainstream media has traditionally relied on its accumulated capital to present itself as an exemplar of objectivity. But as the market has become more central to media, it has embraced the popular with gusto, and its sense of proportion has been increasingly guided by what is more market-friendly.

This does explain why a film actor's suicide would evoke such wall-to-wall coverage. One would expect that this case would hog headlines, but one would also expect that the coverage would examine all possible aspects of the case. After all, sensationalism doesn't care about what story is told, as long as it is titillating. What it does not explain is the manner in which the issue was framed and the deliberate attempt to fashion a pre-determined narrative, one that was punctured decisively by what should have been the basis of any reports in the first place – expert medical opinion. This was not an example of market-driven sensationalism but of agenda-driven narrative building.

Both Hathras and the SSR cases are examples of how the manner in which we process reality is being tampered with. A world where we lose our sense of proportion is one where we become infinitely malleable to any suggestion. We can be made to believe anything, outrage on demand, and ignore the worst calamity that may lie all around us.

THAT FEELING OF NUMBNESS?

IT WAS A MOMENT OF absurdity that seemed so right. A lady participating in India's loudest news show decided to eat lunch while others performed their usual rants. By the looks of it, she chewed every morsel the correct number of times, resulting no doubt in excellent digestion. If you happen to be one of the unfortunate residents of the little box-prisons that these shows put you in, and you are waiting endlessly for your 2 minutes of screaming time, eating a good meal is probably a productive way of spending time. And in this case, the panellist in question had the good sense to do something useful while engaging in something quite futile.

Our standards of watching TV news have sunk so low that we have become benumbed to farce. The idea of someone matter-of-factly masticating food on TV somehow captures the spirit of media today. Absurdity deserves absurdity, as numbness prevails. We have become numb in other ways too. When Covid rampaged through the country, there was a curious absence of analysis or a coherent critique as to what we might we doing wrong as a nation and what we could do better. For something that has such profound impact on our lives, it was strange to find such obvious indifference.

Contrast this with other countries, in particular the US, where Trump's handling of the pandemic was the primary subject under discussion. In India, the early days saw a lot of chest-thumping (and 'thali'-banging) about the Indian success in containing the virus. Once the virus hit India and the number of cases skyrocketed, instead of a critical appraisal of the Central and state governments' action, what we had was silence. The once laudatory WhatsApp groups moved on to other subjects. Instead, going by news channel headlines and social media trending subjects, issues relating to Bollywood seemed to be uppermost in our minds. Sushant Singh Rajput's tragic suicide spawned a mini-industry of vested interests that came to the fore, and, abetted by the media, hijacked the headlines on our TV channels. The case became ever more surreal by the day, and our news channels showed no compunction in making the wildest surmises, which changed frequently.

The other issue which met with muted responses is the border issue with China. By all accounts, China encroached on and occupied a significant tract of Indian territory. The government's response went through a bewildering series of denials, retractions, half-admissions, flashes of bravado, and obfuscations. Again, here, TV and social media warriors had little to say by way of critique or analysis. There was a lot of symbolic chest-thumping, fantasies of revenge and the mandatory Ajay Devgn film on the anvil, but little by way of substantive concern. The same pattern could be seen with respect to the economy. We were hardly in the best shape before Covid struck, and things have worsened since. Strangely, there was more pressure on the government before the crisis than there was afterwards.

Every election sees a spurt in interest on the part of the media. Here, too, it is interesting how we have become completely indifferent to the everyday phenomenon of the buying of legislators. In the last few years, we have seen numerous attempts, successful and unsuccessful, of toppling of governments by getting MLAs to switch sides. There was a time when such 'defections' (a word we never use anymore) excited strong critical comment; the phenomenon of Ayaram-Gayaram was seen to be a direct threat of democracy. Today, it is described in a completely different vocabulary – 'masterstroke', 'political genius' and 'Chankaya-niti' are some of the favoured descriptions. What has caused this large-scale passivity, this ability to accept so much without asking questions? We celebrate empty symbolic victories and brush aside substantive failures.

One can explain media pliability in political terms, but how does one make sense of societal indifference? The power of charismatic authoritarianism is that it overwhelms our critical faculties with symbolic reward. Banging 'thalis' to combat Covid and banning TikTok to show the Chinese their place are part of this new toolkit that substitutes substance with symbols, and facts with narratives. A new pantheon of heroes and enemies, concepts and ideals is constructed, which becomes our new yardstick. Institutions enable rather than regulate the powerful, and the media aggressively cheerleads this new direction.

For those critical of the government, numbness sets in, too – the sameness of the political reality, etc. Authoritarianism numbs and bores – that's how it works. This is not to make the case that governments must be criticized for everything that goes wrong in society, but for the need for sober reflection on the critical questions of the day. The National Education Policy, for instance, was a substantive move that called for measured analysis, but the subject was found to be too real to be discussed. Currently, the power of the dominant narrative is so strong that it sweeps everything that comes before it. As things stand, we could live in a state of permanent numbness, coming to life only as cheerleaders, blind followers or frustrated critics.

THE PERILS OF MEASUREMENT?

ONE OF THE REASONS WHY television news, and indeed most television programming in India, is substandard, has to do with the way its success is measured. Today, the only measure of quality is viewership and that, too, is measured on a minute-by-minute basis. Thanks to the measurement technology, which can record viewer attention at every moment, channels know exactly what keeps the audience watching. The urge is thus to load every second with something dramatic, lest the eyeball flicker elsewhere. Disinterest is television's greatest enemy, not distaste.

This sets in motion a domino effect whereby all channels chase the same formula regardless of whether they peddle news or entertainment. Constant stimulation is the name of the game. Truth, balance, intelligence, reflection, analysis become irrelevant. Which is why, while we might single out one or two channels as being especially guilty of the most egregious misdemeanours, virtually all of television follows the same codes in India, barring very few exceptions.

It is instructive that while this is true of newspapers, too, the degree to which it is so is of a substantially lower order. One of the key differences lies again in the method of measurement. While newspaper circulation and readership are measured just like TV viewership is, the metrics used are of an aggregate nature. We don't know for sure how much time who spent reading what part of a newspaper. The newspaper is measured in its entirety, and not through its individual parts. Had that been the case, most editorials and columns like this one would have disappeared long ago, considering their insignificant readership. While that may or may not be considered a significant loss, the fact that newspapers have more room to cover stories without having to deliver readership for every column inch gives them considerable breathing space as compared to TV.

The relationship between measurement technique and quality can be seen even more clearly when it comes to the OTT platforms. The kind of programming content that we see on these platforms is of a completely different texture. Free of the pressures of narrow measurement, at least for now, they can explore different kinds of stories, use interesting narrative techniques, and cater to very different tastes, without pandering to a single set formula. Their allegiance is of a longitudinal nature and of an aggregate kind. They want to serve all the needs of their viewers, by providing service over time.

The power of the subscription model is that it locates itself not in transactional time but in longitudinal time. Time is integrated, not atomized. Memory is restored to the market. Subscription is continued depending on the totality of the experience. Every individual event does not need to reek of anxiety and can afford not to pander to the lowest common denominator. Programmes can take some time to find their audience. As a result, even documentaries and unusual themes get reasonable traction. Interestingly, television in India has been, in theory, essentially a subscription service, but till recently, consumers did not have a real option in terms of choosing individual channels.

The subscription mindset works even where there might not be any subscription as such. Uber rates both drivers and passengers. It makes behaviour of both parties a variable in the future quality of service and patronage that one can hope to receive. It acts as a spur to quality on both sides, for everything is added up and allowed to play a role. The market mechanism works beyond pricing, and calibrating supply and demand, it now serves to shape the quality of one's experience by allocating a price-like mechanism to it. This is by no means a perfect system, and even if it were, the Indian mind would find a way to game it, but it does offer some improvement over the past. The same is true for food delivery sites. User ratings make and destroy reputations in an entirely new way. Unheralded places can become exceedingly popular if they provide a good-quality experience and well-known options can decline in no time.

Of course, while these new platforms and this mode of engagement has been created by the market, these are yet to be fully tested. These are lavishly funded by venture capitalists in the hope that these will become massively profitable businesses overall. The willingness to lose vast sums of money in the here and now is an important reason why we are seeing the quality that we are. It is interesting that this approach, which is rooted in a balance-sheet-inspired view of the world, where long-term assets are privileged over short-term profits, is itself a subscription-based view of the world. A more transactional view would have found it difficult to look beyond immediate losses and take a bet of this kind.

A subscription model is more closely aligned to our lived experiences. Relationships are a form of subscription; in fact, the very idea of relationships is based on a generalized form of reciprocity that unfolds over time rather than a more specific transactional version in the here-and-now. In any relationship, we are forever drawing on and building trust and goodwill, familiarity and understanding, experiencing emotions of a varied kind. A relationship is about something left over, something incomplete that gets deferred forever into the future.

Similarly, we look to the next Amazon Prime, Hotstar or Netflix show, as the platform tries to further understand what interests us. The mutual quest from both sides continues, both satisfied and yet unquenched. There is always the anticipation of what comes next as both programming and individual tastes evolve. There is an investment that both sides make into each other. With better data analytics, the sense of intimacy will deepen on both sides.

The current situation may not last. With time, as greater competition enters the fray, platforms will fragment and libraries will shrink and the pressure on measurement will grow. We can already see signs of this. But what has been demonstrated is that the more breathlessly and narrowly we measure things, the lower the incentive to build things of deeper and lasting value. Our impatience to be stimulated is the biggest enemy of our need to be satisfyingly informed or entertained.

AN ECOSYSTEM OF FEAR?

THE ARREST OF SEVERAL RIGHTS activists across the country on charges of having Maoist links or being anti-nationals, which has been going on for a while now, is reason for deep disquiet. There have been many labels that are used to demonize the dissenters – 'urban Naxals', 'anti-nationals', the 'Khan Market gang' – and media channels speak darkly about 'toolkits', all serving to build a narrative that any act of protest against the government is, in fact, aimed against the country.

And yet, there are those who argue that nothing dramatically new is happening. The law under which the action has been taken was strengthened by the UPA government, and some like Varavara Rao, Vernon Gonsalves and Arun Ferreira have been imprisoned even under previous regimes.

While it is true that previous governments also have a poor track record when it comes to dealing with dissent, there is no question that there is a difference today. That there is a clear attempt to create an atmosphere of fear is possible to discern when one examines all the actions taken by the NDA government. The production of fear at scale is being achieved not only through harsh punitive measures, but through a complex and elaborate network of actions, real and symbolic.

The case of media is illustrative. Media has been subject to pressure and arm-twisting before. But in recent years, the raid on NDTV and NewsClick apart, most other actions deemed coercive, including the removal of key voices critical of the government, have been taken by the owners of media platforms and not by the state directly. One can infer that the state was indirectly responsible for the same, but the question is, why should media owners, hardly unused to facing political pressure, give in this time around? There is no special leverage that this government has that previous regimes didn't. But the clear feeling among media circles is that this time around, the sense of threat is more palpable. This government is deemed capable of much more than what it has actually done; the fear is evoked by latent violence in the body language of the government rather than in its actions alone. 'Violence in the air' is a more effective way of fostering self-censorship than any direct method.

But there is another variable at work. In the case of media, the problem does not stem only from fear, but also from greed. The taming of media is largely a voluntary phenomenon, guided by a desire to cater to one's commercial self-interest by deferring to the needs of the market. When one outlet of the same media house can take an ideological line completely at odds with another, it is clear that fear alone is not at work. Market segmentation is. The state uses both levers, fear and greed, to get most of media in line.

And then there is social media, where keyboard warriors create a new vocabulary of fear with predictable regularity. Individuals are targeted, new labels are created, lists are generated and campaigns are launched to build a narrative of fear. The reward for these non-official soldiers is a dizzying rise from obscurity, and, in some cases, the promise of official recognition and rewards. Even bureaucrats and serving officers have an incentive to speak and act on behalf of the government. Celebrities become government spokespeople on social media, cricketers and actors parroting the same talking points. The differential treatment meted out to those who amplify the government's line and those who don't is stark.

The orchestration of fear is carried out with finesse. Fear reproduces itself thanks to the elegant design of the ecosystem of intimidation that is in place today. The more commentators connect the dots and discern larger intent from everyday actions, the more actively they participate in the production of fear. Showing signs of fear itself becomes proof – unless you are an anti-national, why should you be afraid?

The calibrated use of reward and punishment, the taking of action against victims rather than perpetrators, the penetration of virtually every institution that matters, the creation of voluntary and vocal cheerleaders for the actions of the state, the regular encouragement given from the highest level of the government to those who carry out intimidation, the periodic acts of brutal violence that indicate that the threats are not only symbolic in nature, the breeding of several kinds of private armies that publicly display their muscle, the succession of violently intemperate statements made by minor party leaders, and actions like the arrest of activists on charges that align with the larger narrative that is being built – these are all part of this ecosystem of fear.

The results of the 2024 elections seem to suggest that the old tropes do not seem to be resonating as well. The fear of 'urban Naxals' was unlikely to have galvanized a significant number of voters, for it is difficult to correlate this with any observed experiences in our everyday lives. The argument that the nation is under threat from such forces is one that might have great resonance with a small group of diehard supporters, but again looked unlikely to connect with a wider audience. The conspiracy outlined was far-fetched even by the standards of contemporary political discourse. From the perspective of voters, the 'enemies' identified have neither currency nor deep emotional resonance. As a political gambit, it was weak given that it leaves out most key opposition parties from this line of attack. The production of fear might have been carried out very effectively, but it failed to deliver great electoral effect.

Those who believe that things will change if the BJP is defeated might be deluding themselves. It does not matter who is in power; what matters is who sets the agenda. The power of a negative agenda is that even when one counters it, only more negativity is produced. The fear that has got manufactured does not come with an expiry date. That might well be the abiding legacy left by this government.

WE ARE NOT LIKE THIS ONLY!

THE DEMISE OF CHANNEL V was as much an occasion to reflect upon contemporary India as it was to think back about the time when the channel was at its peak. It is interesting that the channel's central quest – to find a new vocabulary of Indianness in the wake of economic liberalization and the embrace of globalization – continues to be relevant, but the shape it has taken today is of a completely different nature.

Apart from the economic opportunities it unlocked, liberalization and the emergence of a pan-Indian middle class also sparked off an attempt to find a common currency of Indianness that rose above the more traditional sources of identity. The attempt to constitute a 'we', that put some flesh on the idea of being Indian, featured television in its post-Asiad avatar as a key protagonist. As a medium, by virtue of its presence in homes across the country, it allowed everyone watching to experience the same reality at the same time. In doing so, it created a sense of community as it aggregated audiences in a way that cinema, for all its power, never could. For the young in particular, who lacked a distinctive voice they could call their own, Channel V scripted a new vision they could have about their own selves.

The search for a common 'we' in this era perhaps began with *Hum Log*, which collapsed the story of the Indian middle class into that of a single family, which the country adopted as a surrogate mirror. Advertising played its part, too, with the iconic 'Mile Sur Mera Tumhara' (1988) and the later 'Desh Raag' (early 1990s) too trying to give form to a 'we' that rose above caste and regional definitions. The highly influential 'Hamara Bajaj' ad captured a truth about the middle class and how it imagined itself. The sense of continuity embedded in the words 'Hamara

Kal, Hamara Aaj', became a blueprint for accommodating the past in the present.

The Indianness of Channel V had a very different quality – it was a blast of freshness, ironically made up of the sights, sounds and smells of our street selves. The careful enunciation of values, which was otherwise an important feature of the Indianness project, was tossed aside in favour of a more relaxed embrace of everyday behaviour. Neither shying away from it, nor explaining it in lofty civilizational terms, Channel V dealt with the strangeness of India by revelling in it. There was a madness about Channel V that set us free. It had a fiercely original take on all the things we were familiar with – it used material from everyday life and used it profanely. It eschewed any pious declarations of values, celebrating instead all that we scratched, sniffed, muttered and burped. It cheerfully made public what was otherwise private but all around us. It bent the familiar into the absurd, while never losing sight of its essential truth.

Regional stereotypes were not resisted, far from it. They were made to explode with gaseous glee. Lola Kutty, Udham Singh, Macho and Banjo, Quick Gun Murugan – these were stereotypes injected with a particularly potent hallucinogenic. The base was revelled in, the masala was the meal, the pajama nada spoke the truth. By exposing all that we were afraid to acknowledge about who we really were underneath the apparent 'sanskar and sabhyata', and finding reasons to like what we saw, Channel V took a burden off our shoulders. 'We are like this only' was a staggeringly self-confident statement that made the mirror our friend in the modern world. We were nuts, we were strange, we wore 'dhariwale' underwear, spoke eloquently from both ends of our bodies, and that made us cool.

But while Channel V took nothing seriously, it damaged nothing that we held as serious. The irreverence made us less self-righteous, but did not discard anything we held close to us; nothing valuable was harmed in the process of enjoying it. This was an easy form of Indianness, the least laboured face of the complexity and diversity that marks Indian reality.

In its first coming, the market was a freeing agent rather than a controlling one. It sparked off a real search for who we were and what we really wanted. Popular culture did not have to choose between statist mediocrity (Doordarshan) and formulaic escape (popular cinema). With time, however, as the market got its act together, it began to look for its own formula. It was more profitable to cater to the dominant rather than shape the emergent. The irreverence of Channel V became a pose, an 'attitude' that could be bought off the shelf.

In many ways, today we live in times that represent the mirror opposite of the 1990s. The mind is closing, rather than opening, we preach obeisance, not irreverence; from taking pleasure in offending all that was deemed proper, we are now terrified of causing any outrage. Everything either insults someone's honour or is deemed politically incorrect. The Channel V of the 1990s would today be unable to survive either those on the right or the left-liberals.

The sense of loss that one feels is not for Channel V, for it stopped being anything worthwhile long ago. And even at its peak, it spoke only to a small part of India. But for a brief period, it gave us the hope that we could find ways to like ourselves as we were, messy contradictions and all, and to find a way into the future with the past as a comfortable friend.

But hope today comes from new quarters. While mainstream media has become brain-dead, it is in the alternative media, which has grown to a sizeable proportion today, that we see that the spirit of Channel V is alive and kicking. Instagram Reels, YouTube, Twitter are all spaces where irreverence and defiance runs free.

ADVERTISING: NO LONGER A MIRROR

Hema, rekha, jaya and sushma. To a generation of Indians, these four names evoke instant memories. Part of an advertising jingle (for Nirma) that burrowed its way into our consciousness and took up permanent residence there, these names represent a kind of time stamp, compressing within them a picture of an era. Advertising has been, without our necessarily thinking of it as such, an important part of our emotional landscape. Most of us would remember different times in our life through some memories of the advertising prevalent at the time.

As a mode of communication, there is something quite unique about advertising, particularly on television. It is a compressed, highly stylized form of storytelling that implants desire directly and intrusively into our everyday lives. By associating consumption with the deeper motivations that drive us, it serves as a theatre where desire is enacted using dramatic fragments from our lives.

Advertising, seen one way, is a lie that speaks the truth. It exaggerates, embellishes and reframes reality in order to speak to desires that we are often unable or unwilling to articulate. It connects the banal with the lofty, embedding higher orders of meaning into small everyday actions of little consequence.

The choice of a bar of a soap cannot make a material difference to our lives, but advertising makes us invest this action with consequence; we connect the soap with a self-image that we covet. Its power lies in its unerring recognition of our desires and vanities; the solution it provides is most often transparently symbolic in nature, but by speaking to that part of us that we often live in denial of, it sets us free, even if that is through an act of artful illusion.

At any point in time, the advertising of an era helps articulate and frame the yearnings that animate it. It thus becomes a document of the times, a map that brings to the surface aggregate desires that are often hidden from view.

For an earlier generation, entertainment was a scarce commodity, and advertising often filled in, sprinkling the dreary hours watching Doordarshan with some semblance of animated energy. There are any number of advertising campaigns that resonated strongly, and looking back, one can see how some of these played a key role in shaping the ways in which we imagined ourselves.

'Hamara Bajaj' and its evocation of the idea of an imagined middle class 'we', VIP luggage with its 'Kal bhi, Aaj bhi' articulation of the idea of cultural continuity and timelessness of some cherished traditions, Nirma and its insistent and unapologetic announcement of the arrival of a new consuming class, Pepsi's *Yeh dil maange more*, that made perhaps the clearest statement about the hunger felt by the post-liberalization generation. Over the years, advertising slogans have become popular parlance, and have been used as titles of films, such has been their significance in popular culture.

Of late, something seems to be changing in our relationship with advertising, and in its ability to speak to our deeper motivations with a startling flash of insight. The odd example notwithstanding, it is not that easy to think of campaigns that capture the spirit of a generation or of this era. At one level, brands vie with each other to advertise their interest in all kinds of larger social issues – gender, sexual orientation, corruption, class discrimination – but at another, their ability to imprint themselves on the collective consciousness seems to be declining.

Part of the reason why this is happening lies in the changing nature of media. Unlike a time when all of us watched the same programmes, and had the same set of cultural references, today, in the digital era, we are all exposed to different stimuli at different points in time. Audiences are fragmenting in general, and the move towards greater personalization changes the social character of mass advertising. The young rarely encounter ads, since most media that they consume do not have ads in the same way that an earlier generation did.

As a source of entertainment, too, advertising is now a paler version of the kind of content we can find so easily digitally. The uniqueness of the advertising format, in terms of its ability to pluck out stories of all kinds in the name of selling products, now faces competition in the form of video content that uses far more disruptive modes of storytelling. In a larger sense, too, social media is now the primary chronicler of the times; it documents our desires in our own words and images that we cannot help but emit every minute of the day.

We have also changed as consumers. The top-down model of consumption is changing – today, we catch the contagion of desire from each other; we don't quite need the formalized ritual of someone exhorting us to do so. As consumers, we are growing in sophistication. Advertising is beginning to feel like a somewhat primitive form, full of easy-to-see-through contrivances.

As the world gets more data-driven, persuasion techniques will become far more personalized. The idea of collective and public manipulation of meaning, which is what advertising attempts today, gives way to more stealthy and individualized methods. Almost invisibly, the world comes to us slanted specially just for us, thanks to the data we bleed every single moment of the day.

The less we have in common to talk about and even disagree about, the more we drift away into our little islands of crystallized belief and set opinions. Advertising is a collective mirror, not of reality certainly, but of the reality of our dreams and fantasies. Without a common pool of references, it can become increasingly difficult to understand where the other person is coming from.

THE RISE OF THE OBNOXIOUS

There is good reason to believe that in the world of today, obnoxiousness is a legitimate virtue, made particularly attractive by the fact that being good at it involves arresting one's mental and emotional development at the age of four. One gets to throw tantrums, grab at whatever one wants, believe that one is the centre of the universe, make inflated promises and break them without a second thought, and, above all, call other people horrible names all the time. All this, far from making you universally despised and shunned, can build you up as a successful TV anchor, a social media star, a PR tycoon, or, if you are really lucky, Donald Trump.

Trump's obnoxiousness is well documented – one needs to be made of a special fibre to be able to make fun of the handicapped, ascribe a female journalist's tough questioning to her menstruating, insult the parents of a martyr, call people from a neighbouring country rapists and criminals and boast about the size of his equipment while trying to woo people to vote for him. To the bewilderment of about half of the US electorate and 95 per cent of every other living being on the planet, this actually helped him become the most powerful man in the world, not once but twice.

And he is not alone. In so many other parts of the world, obnoxiousness seems to resonate. Russia, the Philippines, Turkey, and even the UK all have prominent leaders whose lack of regard for maintaining civil appearances has actually helped rather than hinder their prospects. Social media, of course, is the place where the obnoxious from around the world gather and practise their own particular brand of honesty. Every single conversation has a good chance of turning into rabid abuse.

A key element at work is that what is being spoken of here is a form of performative obnoxiousness, a protocol of actions and statements that uses nastiness and grandiloquence in a pointed way in order to create a certain deliberate effect. Earlier, obnoxiousness was an involuntary overflow – the projectile vomiting of a diseased self into the world. It was that part of oneself that could not be contained, and most often came from an absence of self-awareness. The current mode of obnoxiousness has a better sense of itself, and grasps that there is enough oxygen available in the atmosphere for nastiness to become disproportionately productive as a strategy for personal advancement.

In a world that seems to many to have been made unbearably complex by the battle between the insufferably intelligent and the delusionally daft, there is a search for greater clarity. The extreme carries with it the virtue of not being confused for what lies adjacent to it, for in most cases, nothing does. The shallow ensures that one is always on firm ground, that one's feet do not have to flail about perpetually in nameless depths for some sense of certainty. Complexity gets seen as deliberate and vested obfuscation. Nastiness is the easiest disguise worn by those who wish to be seen as strong. The idea of truth has become so severely compromised that professed strength is seen to be a substitute for it. In a world where everyone is deemed corrupt, calling other people names without any restraint becomes decoded as a sign of honesty. Cursing everyone else puts them on the defensive, and, in most cases, the other side cannot muster up the obnoxiousness to respond in kind. When the obnoxious are attacked, they deny everything, concede not an inch of ground, and look to always stay on the attack. No conspiracy theory mounted in defence is too far-fetched, no claim too ridiculous, no allegation too fanciful.

Simultaneously, one's own greatness is trumpeted without any trace of modesty. Those who promote themselves hard actually do media a favour, for they can be picked up for coverage off-the-shelf. Even the search for greatness today is lazy – celebrities can simply claim to be so, and, in most cases, their bluff is not called. Criticism, disdain, sarcasm, all bounce off the individual – indeed, they serve to strengthen rather than deflate. Channels and news sites are full of people who are important for mysterious reasons – some claim to be film-makers, others are faded performers, and still others who are famous largely for appearing on television as famous and very loud people.

The great advantage in perpetually aggrandizing oneself is that the self-important lay down the terms of engagement with them. Eventually, the bloviating braggarts get our attention and become reference points; we follow them or hate them, but they become important enough for us to have a view on them. The strategy of saying, I am amazing, I am awesome, other people suck, is a form of behaviour-training – admiration, or, at the very least, a sense of their significance, is taught by employing the methods of repetition and amplification.

The self-promoting loudmouth is everywhere. In media, in business, in politics, speaking at conferences and festivals where they invariably get the loudest cheers. The notions of depth and quality are seen as strategies that have kept the elites in power, and there is a sense of liberation when a new kind of voice is heard. The directness, the uncomplicated self-absorption and the primitive nature of the promise combine to create a compelling force that we find easy to give in to. But by far the most important reason for the success of the obnoxious is that they are always entertaining. They are our reality shows in real life. We need to watch them compulsively even when they make our skin crawl. There is never a dull moment when they are around, and what can be more important than that today? Public attention is the most universally recognized currency of the time and nastiness trumps reason every time on this front. So, perhaps it is time to sit back and watch the show as it unfolds. It's going to be awesome, people. You have no idea. It's going to be so fantastic. Believe me.

THE DECLINE OF COLLECTIVE TRUST

Across the world, we have stumbled upon a truly vexing and quite a fundamental problem – we can't seem to be able to authoritatively separate the real from the fake, fact from opinion, expertise from motivated opinion. The world appears different depending on our belief system and every erstwhile fact is now merely someone's opinion, and all opinions seem to carry the same level of validity. The idea of balance now accommodates gross untruths of the most obvious kind, and objective standards are difficult to apply any more. The problem is not limited to news, but is about all instruments of collective certification.

Perplexingly, this is a new problem. We have, over the centuries, successfully built institutions that help manufacture collective trust. The judiciary, media, bureaucracy, academia – these were among several institutions that we reposed our faith in to act on our behalf. We believed in these institutions, more than on individuals who acted as their representatives. Who they were and what they believed in was not considered germane, although it is clear that like all human beings, they had their own views and feelings about many of the subjects they were adjudicating on. But we found it possible to grant them a neutrality of perspective, something we seem to have difficulty in doing today.

In truth, the belief in institutions is a little bit of a lie. We all know that institutions are not infallible, and that the opinions of individuals matter. But, in an earlier time, we chose to go along with this small act of self-deception for the sake of a bigger truth. However, once we start attributing motives to institutions, and start dismantling our own method of creating certification in a world where there is little that is self-evident, we start unravelling a system of order production, without having a way to put it together again.

Across the world, this process has been in the works for quite a while. The fact that Supreme Court judges in the US have, for quite some time now, been labelled as conservative or liberal, and that their ideological leaning has a substantial role to play in determining fundamental issues relating to personal freedom, is evidence of this. It is telling that some years ago, problems in the Indian Supreme Court arose on account of the controversy around how cases get assigned to individual judges. The abstract idea of justice should, in theory, be impervious to who the person pronouncing judgement is, but clearly that is far from being the case.

Experts of all kinds find that their opinion carries less weight than before. One's ideas become seen as a product of one's interests, ideals, or background, and thus have little legitimacy beyond that. Ideas lose power in such a scenario for they have little intrinsic worth, and the argument shifts to motivations behind the idea rather than the merits of the same. An idea becomes attached to its address rather than its destination.

The fact that the twice elected leader of the world's most powerful country could so blithely dismiss the dangers posed by global warming in spite of over 97 per cent of scientists agreeing on the issue, is a case in point. In the considerably less consequential but equally telling example of sport, a similar lack of faith in the human ability to certify events has been visible. Technology is now aiding, and in some cases replacing, human judgement. Part of the reason has to do with capability, but an important one has to do with our inability to place trust in another human being. The fact that in cricket, we use referees that are called 'neutral umpires' gives away what our real concern is. All umpires, once they wear their white coats, should be neutral, but it has become impossible to believe that this is possible.

There are reasons why this is happening. For one, the market mechanism, whose role in our lives has grown significantly over time, has put a price on any power that we might wield as certifiers. The media, judiciary, bureaucracy, auditors, teachers, academics, medical experts – none of these professions can escape the suspicion of being swayed by self-interest in order to express a certain opinion. The idea that everyone has a price has been demonstrated often enough for it become a default assumption.

Also, in the case of many institutions, there is a feeling among many that their power has been used only to certify a certain specific world-view, and the voice of a significant number of people has been delegitimized as being regressive or backward. Today, when new forms of media allow for those voices to be heard, the pent-up anger against some institutions, particularly the media, is on display for all to see. On the other side of the ideological spectrum, identity politics of a particularly unforgiving kind has surfaced of late, and any opinion expressed today has a good chance of being framed through the race, class, gender, caste and sexual orientation of the individual. In this construct, our ideas cannot escape our origins.

As a result, we find ourselves at an impasse that we have created for ourselves. The future looks bleaker, for both politics and technology are helping reinforce this trend. The distrust in institutions is getting popular sanction through democratic mechanisms in many parts of the world, as more politicians with extreme ideologies are elected into power. Technology is further helping blur the distinction between the doctored and the real. Conversely, there is talk that a technology like blockchain, which constructs trust not by building centralized institutions but by distributing over a scattered network, can potentially offer us a new mechanism of certification. It is possible that as we move to a world that is constructed around a newer set of conditions, we will need to imagine our social and administrative institutions differently. But, as things stand, we are heading towards a situation where we are discrediting the institutions that build collective trust, and creating conditions where only force determines who is right.

THE LAWLESSNESS OF THE LAW?

THE POLICE FORCE EXISTS TO maintain law and order, and to act decisively and impartially in order to do so. This is hardly a revelatory note to begin a column on. However, in the scheme of things these days, it needs to be said. For what we have been seeing in the last few years is that the police are playing a significant role in disturbing law and order and actually enabling trouble.

Innumerable videos are in circulation that document police excesses. A bunch of Muslims made to lie down on the ground and sing the national anthem punctuated by lathi blows (with one protester later succumbing to his injuries). Policemen storming the library of a university and attacking students indiscriminately. A group of policemen being caught destroying CCTV cameras in the same university, and in the troubled streets of Delhi. A group of policemen running amok, smashing cars in a Muslim neighbourhood in Uttar Pradesh. State-authorized encounters and the rampant use of bulldozers without any judicial oversight.

Excesses by police have always taken place. What is new is the impunity with which the police act. As a country, we are used to the incompetence of our public institutions. We know how government offices work and have adjusted to the difficulties of getting any bureaucratic body to simply do its job. Police incompetence is galling, but familiar. What we are seeing today, however, is a special kind of competence. The cops are selectively targeting who they go after, and this is a pattern that we see time and again. No action was taken in the 2020 JNU case where the right-wing perpetrators were not only caught on camera but had confessed to their actions. We have seen instances where the police have acted through their absence or their inaction.

Innumerable reports, including one by an NDA-partner MP, have documented the police's lack of response to urgent calls for intervention in the 2020 JNU case. In other cases, we have video evidence of the police ignoring attacks that were taking place right in front of their eyes, as in the instance of someone brandishing a gun and shooting a Jamia student in 2019. Overt violence, passive encouragement, strategic non-interference, total absence, erasure of evidence, torture in incarceration – a sophisticated array of techniques is being deployed to ensure that one section of the community faces the brunt of the consequences of the violence, no matter who was responsible for instigating it.

Admittedly, the cops have a difficult job when dealing with communally sensitive riots and there is no question that they are in the firing line of violence. They work under difficult conditions and face enormous pressure, suffering significant injuries and not a few casualties in the process. They have a right to use force, on occasion even of an extreme kind, in order to quell rioting and other acts of violence, but they are meant to act in a tightly controlled and calibrated way. Their excesses cannot be justified using the language of revenge. They cannot mirror the actions of lawbreakers; at all times, even when responding to the gravest provocation, the police have to act within the parameters set by the law. And at all times, their actions need to be even-handed. Anyone breaking the law, regardless of who they are, needs to be dealt with equally. The religion, caste or background of the lawbreakers should not be a factor of any kind.

Of all the egregious actions taken by the cops, none is perhaps as indicative of their strategy as the act of destroying CCTV cameras in Jamia and elsewhere in Delhi in 2019. Nothing, absolutely nothing, can justify this action. In the overall scheme of things, this might seem like a relatively minor infraction, but in terms of communicating their intent, it speaks the loudest. It shows forethought and deliberate planning, it signals that the cops are aware of the illegality of their actions, and are choosing to go ahead nevertheless. It is interesting that all those who have suddenly discovered the value of public property and use its destruction as a justification for police action, have nothing to say when the cops are caught coldly and deliberately destroying the same prized public property. Also, as is apparent to everyone, while the police can erase evidence of their actions once the video cameras are destroyed, the act of destroying them cannot be hidden. That they choose to go ahead regardless tells us how little they have to fear from anyone.

The support base of the government will cheer them on. The media will focus only on the violence perpetrated by the other side, working assiduously to build a narrative that absolves the government of any responsibility. The government, on its part, will support every action taken by the police.

While the use of the police as an extended political arm of the government is worrying, it is the judiciary that gives reason for an even deeper concern. As many newspaper editorials have pointed out, the courts are delivering judgments, or withholding any action as the case might be, in a manner that raises questions about the role it intends to play in keeping the state in check. Greater vigilance from the courts would go a long way in ensuring that the guardians of the law themselves operate within its ambit. The judiciary is the ultimate crucible that holds the very idea of law and order together. The edifice of the law is a wholly constructed one; unlike the physical world, nothing can happen unless by design. Every piece of action or inaction by the judiciary has consequences – it serves to either enable or circumscribe the actions of those in power. The exercise of the law depends on keeping alive the integrity of its core principles. If those are lost sight of, the judiciary can turn into the harshest and most repressive instrument of the state, for it has untrammelled powers. The lawlessness of the law and the disorder of order then becomes a real possibility, and while governments come and go, once our confidence in the rule of law is dismantled, it is very difficult to put it together again.

Today, Kohli is a genius. Not too long ago, Kohli was an arrogant jerk who needed to be sacked immediately. And Pujara is our only real Test batsman. Why are people like Pujara a fixture in the team when they deliver so rarely and so damn slowly? Playing a Test match without Ashwin is insanity. What a stroke of genius to play four fast bowlers! Shreyas Iyer is a self-absorbed, overrated player. How can we omit him from the Test team? Those following cricket on social media would be familiar with these kinds of opinions that routinely flood our timelines. On Twitter (now called X), the world can be described exclusively through exclamation marks.

On social media, the world changes every few minutes. Heroes become dastardly villains, discards become saviours, and dire predictions turn into delirious celebrations. In part, it is the nature of sport, for in this reality show, there really is no script, and so anything, no matter how topsy-turvy, can happen. It is, in fact, the reason why sports make for such compelling viewing – in a world where we know how most stories play out, when it comes to sports, every story comes with a possible twist in its ending. Fortunes change in an instant, and spectators hang on to this emotional roller-coaster by the white of their fingernails. The experience of swearing at someone on your TV screen in the choicest language one moment and then singing fulsome praises about the player or the team the next are experiences that are commonplace.

This hair-trigger volatility gets a residence on social media, where watching the timeline move is sometimes more entertaining than the game itself as supporters go into paroxysms of delight and anguish, venting themselves uninhibitedly as the game goes about its way. And this is not restricted to the significant moments of the game where extreme emotions are commonplace; the negativity here is atomized – every single delivery evokes strong and often unprintable reactions.

In a larger sense, too, it is a sign of the intense involvement that we have with whatever is current. The oversaturated coverage of current events, accompanied by an easy amnesia as things move off centrestage. Issues that blow up on social media usually have a shelf-life of a couple of weeks. The combination of intense wall-to-wall coverage for some time, followed by total forgetfulness, is a pattern that we have seen get repeated far too many times to keep count. Ironically, it also creates an opportunity for the intense emotion to be ignored altogether, since one knows that it will pass. Keeping one's head down and lying low is a reasonably effective strategy in many cases.

On the opposite end of the spectrum, we also live in a time where opinions are completely impervious to facts, where no amount of evidence will change the minds of those who have taken positions. We see this in the world of politics, where, having chosen a side, nothing will move people to even entertain another point of view. More surprisingly, we saw this at work when it came to vaccines and masks during Covid, when there was a concrete consequence to believing in the wrong bit of information. The ability to believe that scientists across the world were all part of a conspiracy to keep people ill would belong to the realm of demented fantasy if so many people were not ready to subscribe to it. Impassioned pleas by doctors in ICUs presenting first-hand evidence, or deathbed testimonies by the unvaccinated imploring others to get the shot – things that would ordinarily be considered chillingly persuasive bits of evidence – seemed to have little effect. People continue to believe what they do, till one day they stop having the ability to hold any opinion.

We seem to live simultaneously in two worlds – one that is a fast-flowing liquid one where currents sweep us with inexorable force before expending themselves and petering out, and another where everything is cast in stone-cold certitude, where all objects are immovable, and all opinions are implacable. In the former, we allow ourselves to be led by whatever is immediate and uppermost – social media allows every fleeting tiny impulse to get expressed instantly; our timeline is plugged into the shallowest part of our brains and twitches spasmodically with every new thought. We feel compelled to record our views on everything that happens around us – it is as if without our certifying stamp, events do not have the permission to pass into history. Our attention spans are small, the current of events is rapid, and our opinions are prodigious. Consistency of opinions is not a virtue, for really, no one really cares.

The other world comprises issues we use to define ourselves. Here, the labels we use to describe ourselves are extremely sticky. Liberal, conservative, 'bhakt', proud 'sickular', Trumpian, SSRian, social-justice warrior, woke-basher, anti-vaxxer, Thala fan, Virat-hater – whatever be our chosen self-description, we are dead serious about our world-view. Nothing, no fact, however self-evident, can shake us from what we believe to be true. That SSR was murdered, that masks are the biggest threat to personal freedom since gun control, that Modi can do nothing wrong, or nothing right, as the case might be, that Virat fans are jealous of Rohit and vice versa. Not all beliefs are false, but that doesn't matter, for even if they were, nothing would change.

The world does not exist outside but lives within us. What matters is not what happens out there, but what we want to feel in here. The relationship between individuals and the reality outside is in the process of getting inverted. How I want to feel is more important than the world outside. The seeming contradiction between two diametrically opposite modes of reaction – one that displays hair-trigger volatility and the other immovable constancy, are actually aspects of the same underlying desire – to see the world not as it is, but as a mirror image of what we want it to be.

THE COMING OF HOT DEMOCRACY

WHEN A RIGOROUS DEMOCRATIC PROCESS throws up someone like Donald Trump as the most powerful person in the world, it is natural to take another look at the concept itself. Over the last few years, the democratic process seems to have thrown up choices that would, some years earlier, have been possible only in the event of a coup. Something fundamental has changed about the way democracy is practised.

Democracy as a practice has always been a mediated one – the voice of the individual was heard directly once every few years and then relayed by an elected representative. The will of the people framed the politics of the day, but it was sought infrequently and worked within a larger constitutional framework, which was developed by a few for the many.

Opinion was regulated through a separate institution – the media, that strove to represent the ideals of democracy, without specifically worrying about representing the views of the public. The market, too, was meant to reflect the desires of consumers, but there were hardly any mechanisms to inject the voice of the consumer in business calculations; indeed, companies have to struggle to become 'consumer-centric', for it is not a natural instinct. The judiciary, of course, looked after the interests of the people from a lofty and deliberately detached perch – it was meant to pay no heed to public opinion or passions.

Almost all of the above has changed in some form. The increased role of the market in media has made the latter much more focused on leveraging its strengths for commercial purposes. The media uses the licence that it receives from society for its own purposes much more than it did in the past, where the idea of the larger good was more consciously a part of its mandate. Social media has given everyone with access to the internet a voice, and this has led to an unprecedented peek into the minds of people. Media is necessarily a two-way street today, with the audience having ample opportunities to respond to what is beamed out to them.

The democracy of today is thus a 'hot' democracy, an unmediated, volatile force that reacts quickly and responds sharply, with few restraints. Hot democracies are immediate, reactive, judgemental, demanding. Issues rise up like milk on the boil, and subside the same way. Issues get consumed through an intensely personal lens. Tantrums are frequent, as are orgasmic eulogies. People matter, not issues. Impatience becomes a big virtue, and passion becomes a highly valued idea, one that justifies everything. Desires demand satisfaction. Anger flashes, then aggregates.

Think of yesterday's 'cooler' democracy as a wire that transported energy from the public to the state, but one that came clad in protective insulation of many kinds. What we are seeing today is the gradual stripping of this protective insulation. The energy that is democracy is no longer applied purposively to a point of calibrated usefulness – it scatters in all directions unharnessed for the most part. In doing so, the institutions that were kept apart to provide scrutiny and oversight and that had an ability to intervene and take corrective action, are increasingly being fused together in a coalition of interests.

The judiciary, for instance, today adopts a much more populist view; it intervenes in all 'hot' issues with an avidness that is striking. Its positions seem to betray a greater anxiety to align with popular mood and it seeks out a more visible and central role in public life. The shift in the orientation of media has been spoken of far too often to bear repetition. It magnifies the 'hot' nature of democracy by jettisoning the ideals of detachment, balance and perspective – it chooses instead to both compress and amplify events.

Greater democratization has been a key characteristic of the digital era, and the impact of social media has been well documented, but the real change has been in the nature of this process of democratization. We are not only seeing more democracy, we are seeing more of a different kind of democracy. It is not only more direct, it is more fissile in nature. The idea of the public, too, has changed – it is now a multitude of privates, as every individual has the right to be heard. In some sense, everyone is out in the streets all the time, telling us what they think. And by seeing everyone else saying what they really feel, others are emboldened to express themselves with much less inhibition.

At one level, systems have to listen. In marketing, suddenly the voice of the consumer starts being heeded. Media gets off its high horse and starts tuning in to what its audience is interested in. Politicians become more publicly accountable. Individual injustices demand action, provided of course that they are deemed worthy of attention.

But equally, along with the ability to be heard, and the power to make a difference, comes the brute force of public will. Desire of any kind today is self-justifying by definition – it demands to be satisfied. Things that could not be said or even thought earlier can now be shouted. Idealism is being replaced by an honest acknowledgement of one's emotions – what matters is not that which must be professed but that which is genuinely desired.

Democracy is presumed to be a desirable idea because of the way in which it has been historically imagined. When controlled and guided by an overarching framework of ideals, democracy produces results of one kind. In a 'hot' democracy, however, the naked and unadorned will of the people has a better chance of being converted into state action. Along with that comes the great danger that we pose to ourselves, of electrocuting ourselves with our own energy. Donald Trump is a sign that the repressed instincts of a large number of people now has an address. And Trump is only a part of what might come to pass. If we really can get what we want, then it all boils down to what lies buried deep inside our hearts. And on that front, the news may not be so good.

OF HUNGRY, ANGRY PROGRESS

ON A CITY ROAD, THE smallest cars seem to have the most powerful engines, if the alacrity with which they zip between spaces – real and imaginary –, and the ominousness with which they breathe down the fenders of other cars is any indication. Traffic on Indian roads puts Messrs Higgledy and Piggledy to shame, as every vehicle strains to fulfil its highly individualistic dharma through unremitting acts of disorderly karma. To call the driving reckless would be inaccurate, for to be reckless one presumably needs to understand what the heck reck is in the first place, and there is no real evidence of that. Indian roads are full of angry, fuming beasts armed with too much power and too little sense, straining to get somewhere an inch early.

The combination of power and agility packed densely in vehicles of small sizes that the Japanese and the Koreans, in particular, have conferred upon us, has meant that speed of a frightening kind has been granted to us, people who neither have prior experience of it nor have the means or desire to learn how to control the new-found power at their command. Anyone can get a licence easily without actually learning how to drive decorously, or, in fact, learning how to drive at all, and there is virtually no effective policing or punishment once one gets behind the wheel and lets rip. The result is the creation of a loud, angry unregulated space where no rules are followed and the strong, aggressive and slightly unhinged have their way.

This set of circumstances is a larger pattern that we can see across many areas in India today. Media jumps to mind, particularly the relatively newer forms like OTT channels and social media, where the power of the medium is utilized at full throttle, its neck veins bulging all the 24 hours that it is awake. Our screens are an orgy of caffeine, consumed without sips, for that would mean a temporary lull. For things to work, it would seem that they need to be souped up, juiced up, hallucinogenically colourful, celebrity-infested, Yo-Yo-Honey-Singh-, Badshah- or -Mika Singh-soundtracked, eye-candy-peppered, masala-laden extravaganzas bulging with tautology. In other words, IPL.

Social media is another such space where the power to throw out one's opinion into the world, and particularly direct it at those who have got used to wielding the microphone, is a heady one. So heady that it has increasingly become a space where largely extreme and endemically nasty opinions abound. To be fair, this is true in many other parts of the world, but in India, this has spilled over into other facets of life where having an opinion is becoming synonymous with the closing of the mind to any other possible way of seeing things. The first reaction to an opinion one may disagree with is extreme and often abusive; things don't escalate, for they begin at the highest pitch.

Affluence, too, has powered the lives of those it has touched in ways that often take on an unseemly hue. Aggressive consumption, a lack of empathy for those without the means, a sense of entitlement that believes that the world must give way to all desires that they might become possessed of have become characteristics that can be seen all too often.

Democracy is the most powerful engine of all, and all it has to channelize its potent power is the political system as it exists today. Increasingly imagined through the lens of power rather than through what the power is meant to achieve, it has, in the last few years, become a self-serving instrument for those in or even around the driver's seat. The more democracy becomes about fulfilling the desires of those who can help form electoral majorities, rather than about connecting some larger ideals with the hopes and aspirations of people, the more it ends up reinforcing things as they are rather than fighting for things as they should be.

In times when change is discontinuously fast, the gap between the power available and the mechanisms created to govern its use become untenably large. A consequence of this is that this power, free from considerations of any obligations it might have to a larger collective, then tries to fix the system so that the absence of responsibility can become a permanent feature. The imbalance it creates becomes its primary justification, for it becomes virtually impossible to correct given that all elements of the system become subordinate.

Without investing in institutions that help convert power into meaningful performance, things cannot change. Top line growth provides energy but does not by itself distribute it across the system in a way that changes things in a fundamental way. It only increases the imbalances that exist. Given that the older mechanisms of self-regulation have either faded or been rendered irrelevant given the nature and speed of change, and the newer ones are thwarted by the interests of those with too much power, we now find ourselves in the midst of too much legislation without effective regulation.

A visit to a developed country was once a reason to get really depressed, so wide were the disparities between there and here. Much has changed, but there is something about the quietness of affluence there, the air of ease that surrounds everyday life, the certainty that pervades interactions with the smallest institution, and, of course, the relative sobriety on television that makes one more than a little envious. Not because India does not have those, but because it does not seem likely that India will have those any time soon. We could well match those countries in terms of power, affluence and influence, for conceptually, that is in our line of sight, but making peace with our progress seems a long way in the distance.

AN ODE TO INDIFFERENCE

Indifference might well be the best superpower we can have today. My father, for instance, cannot tell an Anil Kapoor from the Kapoor called Ranbir and wouldn't know either if they popped out of a birthday cake and sang 'Disco Station Disco,' and he is much happier for it. Not caring about celebrities begins with not knowing who they are. It is easy to look down upon celebrity culture and to vent about its ubiquity and uselessness, but one is still enmeshed in the matrix; one is simply on one side of the fence. The playground, however, is the same – a world infested by celebrities. In outraging against them, we acknowledge their power.

We get a sense of this power when we come across self-important influencers who we have no clue about. They might be extremely well known in their arena of involvement, but to the rest of the world, they are narcissistic freaks who are excessively in love with themselves as they make spectacles of themselves on some public street while shooting their latest reel. The power we feel at being able to dismiss them and think of them as jokes stems from our indifference. The ability to dismiss as drivel what one section of society thinks no end of is priceless. Who, for instance, is Elvish Yadav, and why should I care?

This came to mind during the endless discussions surrounding the Big Wedding. Everyone had a view, and those were enthusiastically shared, making it impossible to escape the subject. There were a lucky few who hadn't tuned into the event at all and seemed completely clueless about what happened, who attended and who didn't, who wore what, and how it stimulated the economy or didn't, whether it displayed India's clout or highlighted an abject lack of taste and imagination, what it said about us, India, our society, or the post social media world. It was a blissful form of ignorance, and, more importantly, of indifference.

I envy the people who do not follow cricket, particularly on occasions when our team is doing badly or when it contrives to lose a game it should have won. Looking at people who go nonchalantly about their work, not a crease on the forehead nor a burning desire to smash things – but a serene expression on their face that seems to communicate either a divine sense of bliss or musings about their next meal –, one is torn with envy.

Similarly, there are people who are not on social media, and contrary to what most of us would believe, they are able to breathe in and out, have their motor skills intact, and can string out words in a sentence coherently. Perhaps more so than the rest of us. Opting out, not as a mark of protest, for then one is constantly in awe of one's own nobility, but simply because it seems pointless and uninteresting, is so much more potent a weapon against a phenomenon that takes itself so seriously.

Politics, too, is an arena that has engulfed us and miniaturized us into labels that brook no deviation. Once we embrace a label, we are trapped in it and perform our duties as mandated. We must slant our views on all sensitive subjects, shut out evidence to the contrary, celebrate victories on our side with disproportionate glee, and spin our defeats expertly. It is our solemn duty to fight against a contrary opinion and to seek refuge in the banality of like-mindedness. We are convinced we are right, and that can be an exacting burden to carry.

Being apolitical may not be the answer, however tempting that might be, simply because one cannot escape the consequences of politics. But the ability to focus on other parts of life, to retain the ability to believe but do so with a sense of perspective, and not care about every little atomized bit of provocation that comes our way might ease mental health issues and provide a sense of perspective.

There are self-conscious opters out there, those who seek to 'live off the grid', by staying in remote places and eschewing technology and, more generally, the modern world. This is one way, of course, but it requires a lot of effort. It is a laboured and self-conscious form of freedom. One is as caught up in one's opposition as one would living 'on the grid'.

Indifference is different. It allows us to shrug our shoulders and refuse to take the world seriously. One follows the pursuits one enjoys but refuses to become part of a larger machine over which one has little control. A life steeped in the everyday, without arrogating to oneself any larger role or taking on responsibilities for the world beyond our immediate circle, might seem escapist, but there may be wisdom in it.

The fact is that we are being shaped by the tools we use and find ourselves inextricably tethered to a world without end or relief. Everything seems urgent and important in the world, and even the thought of opting out feels like an act of dereliction, of running away from the real world. But this is not the real world; it is an entirely fabricated universe with its own rules, which we are made to follow without knowing fully what we are signing up for. It has changed us in many fundamental ways and continues to do so. Fighting it from within isn't useful because any participation increases its power.

The problem, of course, is that for most of us, it is too late. We cannot feign indifference, for our thinking now is too deeply affected by the media we consume. We live in a symbolic world generated by electronic simulation and cannot extricate ourselves from its abstractions. We react constantly to stimuli and feel bereft in the absence of constant injections of dopamine. We feel most alive when outraged or angry. And there is always something that feeds our appetite.

CHAPTER 9

Politics

A Sense of Righteous Belonging

In post-mobile-phone India, politics is not just an ideology – it's a form of identity.

Digital citizens navigate love, hate, nostalgia and nationhood, often simultaneously.

Here, belonging is asserted with muscle, memory is a battleground, and certainty trumps nuance.

OF POLITICS AND CULTURE

Among the many possible explanations for the sustained rise of the BJP, and its growing ability to draw into its fold sections of the society that have historical reason to distrust it, is its ability to harness culture. The party has managed to blur the lines between politics and culture, and has presented itself as the natural choice for the majority community based on the fact it shares common values and a shared ethos.

It is clear that religion is an important component of the BJP's strategy, but a less commented-upon facet is its mobilization of culture. The ability of a wider swathe of people to see themselves as an extension of the world created by the BJP goes beyond active religious mobilization. If, on one hand, it has succeeded in weaponizing religious identity by creating a sense of perpetual victimhood in the majority community, it has also created a sense of affinity by presenting its case in culturally resonant terms.

The sense of identification with the party comes not only on account of its 'big' initiatives – Ram Mandir, the invention of the idea of 'love jihad', the criminalization of triple talaq, the abrogation of Article 370 and the like – but also because it uses more everyday motifs that are part of a more 'natural' sense of how Indianness is experienced by the majority community.

For decades, during the period when the Congress was ascendant, the separation of politics from cultural life was seen as a natural part of the prevailing political ideology. Notions of secularism and equity were ideas that were almost exclusively political rather than cultural in the manner in which they were framed. Steeped in this mental model of politics, the party did not overtly use cultural motifs nor did it employ any familiar iconography. The desire to speak to different communities meant that politics could not draw too deeply from cultural wells.

This helped electoral politics, at the national level at least, stay outside the perimeter of our social lives. Politics was either the full-time pursuit of a specific set of people or it was an activity that was performed once every few years, and then forgotten about. The majority thought of themselves as being apolitical and took some pride in that self-definition.

The BJP has changed that by bringing cultural issues to the political mainstream. It is a very particular view of culture, rooted in majoritarian impulses, but it does allow the party to speak effortlessly to a very large number of voters cutting across the many divisions that exist, except those of religion, of course. It presents its politics as an extension of our natural cultural impulses whereby the dominant blurs into the natural, and feels inevitable. As part of this strategy, the party exhibits a great comfort with existing social norms, and shows little interest in challenging these. It also understands the power of using cultural symbols in a potent way.

The use of the cow is a good example of the difference between two world views. If the reverence for the cow feels like a throwback to a primitive impulse that is wholly at odds with modern sensibilities to one side, it feels like the acceptance of a long-held and virtually incontrovertible belief to the other. Cows have been held sacred, not in a deity-in-a-temple kind of a way, but in the everyday feed-a-cow-on-the-street kind of a way. Opposing cow protection is an idea that is difficult to fathom. Of course, the BJP has successfully converted what is a relatively low-key cultural practice into a symbol of religious, and therefore national/cultural, belonging.

The banging of 'thalis' in support of the those on the frontlines of the battle against Covid might have felt ridiculous to a few, but it is another example of how culture becomes politics. By giving people a concrete action to perform, and by making participation a social performance, a powerful sense of a cultural collective acting in unison was constructed. The fact that such an action was deemed absurd by one group but enthusiastically participated in by so many others underlines the gulf in understanding that exists currently. The fact that in spite of having a not-too-impressive track record in its effort to contain the effects of the virus, this government enjoyed such popular support in the UP elections that followed, shows how well it understands how to connect with the mainstream in the country.

Apart from the more concrete symbols that can be deployed once culture becomes a part of politics, what it enables is a vocabulary that is effortless. The automatic ease in establishing an emotional bond with the audience that Narendra Modi enjoys is a function of the fact that the language that he uses is replete with culturally familiar expressions. The sense that 'he understands us' comes not only from the content of his speeches but from the manner in which he invokes a culturally comfortable world. His 'Mann Ki Baat' speeches are an explicit example of how the idea of a paternalistic figure, who is concerned about people who share his values, has been constructed.

Social media has also made politics much more cultural in nature. It becomes possible to make everything political by providing a running commentary on every moment of our lives in terms that are political. Small issues, like an ad that allegedly offends Hindu sensibilities, can become ones of national import, and succeed in sending a strong message about the power wielded by those dominant today. Things that lay outside the political domain, largely because political conversation did not have any regular platforms nor extended reach, are now easy to include. The grammar of politics has changed beyond recognition. If there has to be a serious counterpoint to the dominant political force in the country, then it needs a completely fresh mental model of politics. New concepts, a new language, new modes of engaging people, and, at the top of the list, new leadership.

THE RIGHTEOUSNESS OF HATE?

There was an incident a few years ago when an Uber driver decided to take his passengers to the police station because they were coming from an anti-Citizenship Amendment Act (CAA) protest and were discussing the same in the vehicle. It is an understandably scary prospect when individual citizens decide to don the role of vigilantes and sit in judgement on what constitutes an anti-national act.

Viewed from the Uber driver's perspective, however, he probably thought that he was doing a good thing, something truly noble. In his scheme of things, the people in the car were traitors, anti-nationals bent on dismantling the country. It is possible, at the risk of being presumptuous, that this was one of the most significant achievements of his life, this willingness to step up for the cause at some risk to his means of livelihood. There might have been some doubt in his mind about what action to take, and, by his own admission, he contemplated a fate far worse than merely taking them to a police station, but he hadn't the slightest doubt that he was in the right. That the party in government and responsible for the maintenance of the rule of law chose to felicitate him would only crystallize this belief.

This is true of many of those who are willing to commit acts of violence in the name of the nation or in defence of their religion. For most of them, it is not a self-serving pursuit involving any significant material gain. There would be those who are cynically and knowingly manipulating the truth for political ends, as also those who have a commercial interest in toeing this line, but there is a large mass of supporters who are true believers. The strength of this belief can even make them willingly accept an obvious lie as the truth; since they know the larger truth, the smaller lie is deemed inconsequential.

All around the country, a virulent form of nationalism is being weaponized, and, more importantly, being internalized as a duty. The media is playing a huge role in normalizing this. In his statement framing the results of the Delhi exit polls, a leading TV anchor described the citizens of Delhi who seemed set on voting for the AAP as having no interest in an issue like the abrogation of Article 370, nor in the CAA, and were thus not interested in safeguarding the interests of the nation. To his mind, the entire population of Delhi was treacherous because in a state election, they apparently chose to vote for the party that offered a better everyday life in concrete and measurable terms. Some might have thought of it as the BJP's failure, but to this gentleman it was clear than an entire city had turned rogue.

Till some time ago, we had dog whistles of many kinds – sly and artful references that cast Muslims and liberals as anti-national. Now we have blaring foghorns. It becomes possible to characterize a gathering of women and children in the heart of the capital, a gathering that had stayed resolutely peaceful in the wake of many provocations, as being the nerve centre of a terrorist plot. Just uttering the name Shaheen Bagh was enough, for it evoked images that did not need to adhere to or derive from any form of reality.

While it is true that the role of the media in normalizing this discourse cannot be overstated, it would be delusional to believe that nationalism does not work at a much deeper level. The appeal of nationalism, particularly among the young, needs to be better understood. Given the economic situation of the country and the looming crisis of employment, there is a growing anxiety and a simmering sense of anger that is looking for an address, a destination that it can direct itself at. One would have thought that the most likely target of this anger should have been the government, which is the primary agent responsible of ensuring that it is creating enough jobs. But the BJP's success has been in making nationalism a much more pressing and immediate issue than those that would otherwise have been considered pressing and immediate – the small matter of findings jobs, earning good livelihoods, and meeting the many aspirations that have been activated in post-reform India. All of us look for our basic needs to be met but we also look for a sense of purpose, an assurance that we are significant and that our actions count for something, and this is what the ruling party is so effectively speaking to.

To find meaningful employment is difficult, but to be an activist for a right-wing nationalistic cause is so easy. All that one needs to do is settle back into an identity that one was born with. It needs no additional effort, no striving of any kind, and little risk. One is part of the dominant majority, one has numbers and the backing of the state on one's side, which will protect one if one does commit any acts of violence. One can simply, by deciding to become part of the movement, exercise real power over one's immediate surroundings. One also experiences a heady sense of belonging, an elevating feeling of being part of some martial mission to cleanse the country of its ills. Those who oppose this are, by definition, the enemy. And as everyone who is right-minded knows, it is the majority that is under threat, and that its actions are proactively defensive. As a prominent ruling party leader has asserted, if we don't beat back the minority today, Mughal Raj is not far from coming.

The change is real and is likely to be irreversible. For a lot of Indians, the case has been closed. The lines have been drawn. Hate is not a choice, but a duty. And it gives hope, succour and a true sense of purpose to people who think of themselves as good and righteous human beings.

THE FUTURE OF THE PAST

WHAT IS IT ABOUT THE past that produces wisdom? Why is it so easy to believe that the ancients held all the keys to truly deep wisdom? For civilizations to locate an essential form of truth this far back in time is interesting. Why are so many battles of today based on knowledge created in contexts far removed from our own? What is it about our own age that we distrust or disdain? It is interesting that the medieval age is not credited with any great wisdom; we have to go back to the ancients to plumb those timeless depths. Something about the idea of the ancient seems to be synonymous with having deep reservoirs of insight that subsequent ages cannot rival.

To be sure, there exists evidence of great wisdom that resided in the past. A lot of it is both profound and timeless. But why should the knowledge gathered in any era be enshrined as being definitive? Just as our ancestors left us some deeply profound philosophical precepts that have timeless value, quite clearly there are a whole lot of other areas where the modern age knows much more. The need to assert that everything that was conceived of in the past must necessarily be true because it was conceived of in the past is dogma. Things must have a source, and the idea of having a fixed point of origin anchors us in a world where things seem to move too fast. To go back to the source for understanding and comfort is understandable, but since the past is largely a product of the way in which we construct it, our sense of it is necessarily limited. We look at the past through the lens of the present, which is, in some ways, nothing more than the present looked at through the wrong end of binoculars. We value those things in our past that we fear we lack today. Our claim to the greatness that we wish to locate in ourselves gets strengthened if we are to establish that we have greatness implanted in us from the very beginning.

The idea that our present gets legitimized by our past is a widespread one, but that in no way makes it correct. The paradox is that at one level, we are convinced that we are more advanced than our preceding generations, that we know more and understand even more. At the same time, we do not back the wisdom of our times; for that we need to go back several centuries to a time which, at one level, was nothing like ours, but equally, was imbued with no special qualities either. In fact, we do not think of our own era as possessing any wisdom – the progress made is seen through the lens of advancements. The present is merely the skin of time, while the past is seen as a residue, a repository of wisdom. The truth is, it was just another era with its own set of circumstances, its own contemporary concerns and its own modes of knowledge and storytelling. Individuals, then too, tried to interpret the world around them, some with deep insight and others much less memorably.

Why is it so easy to discount the value of today's wisdom? Why is the present fractured into alcoves of competing ideas but the past imagined as one monolithic flat landscape?

The trouble with ideologies that venerate an idealized past is that they have little interest in using those ideas to shape the present. This would involve a process of continuous evolution, modification and rejection in order to creatively use the knowledge of the past. If Western knowledge systems enjoy dominance, it is partly because of the geopolitical pre-eminence of the West in recent centuries, but also because they have kept pace with the times. Western science and philosophy continue to reference the past but have found ways to think of knowledge as a living system, that is constantly adding to itself by acts of adaptation and challenge. The old is built on ceaselessly, knowledge is added and updated.

Movements like Hindutva, which are apparently rooted in a desire to reconnect with the wisdom of the past, are in reality far less ambitious. Hindutva today has less to do with the desire to find an Indian way of thought and more as a way to find resentments rooted in the past. There is little visible attempt to build contemporary modes of knowledge using the frameworks of the past. The mainstream political discourse focuses not on ideas, but on a few token cultural symbols. It is a car that has one gear – the reverse, and instead of a windshield it sports a giant rear-view mirror. There is undeniable value in looking back and retrieving the wisdom that is on offer there, but the real opportunity is to then project it forward, after adjusting for the changed context. Ideas that are alive do not fear change, and the true value of wisdom is that its principles can be adapted for new circumstances. To cite the loftiness of the past but to use it only as a tool to harness repressed anger is a gross underutilization of a powerful instrument.

The argument that Indian knowledge systems have been suppressed for centuries because of a skewed geopolitical order is a powerful one. The need to look at the world through an Indian lens, using concepts and frameworks that are locally produced, is not only a correction of an epistemic imbalance, but also something that will add value to a world that is struggling to find new perspectives. The possibilities that an Indian way of thinking can unleash are endless, but for those to be realized, the country needs to get over its resentful and petulant obsession with its minorities. The project to revitalize traditional Indian wisdom needs to be more intellectually ambitious. Currently, the past is being used as a source of identity alone, and that belittles it. We are the primitives of a future civilization, as poet Gary Snyder reminds us, and some day our ideas will be regarded as timeless wisdom. That is, if we have any.

DISTRUSTING THE YOUNG

Does THE MODI GOVERNMENT HAVE a fundamental problem with universities and the young people studying there? The recurring episodes of unrest at different university campuses seem to point in that direction. The specific causes that spark off the problem might be different in each case, but, by now, a pattern is emerging in the way in which the state reacts to these incidents.

Often, what triggers unrest has a strong political dimension. In the case of JNU, the stoking of the unrest that we saw a few years ago may have been deliberate for it helped serve the party's strategic ends in adding flesh to the nationalism discourse. But in PhD scholar Rohith Vemula's case, the party, through its response to the suicide, tied itself in knots, trying all kinds of manoeuvres – bullying, bluster, obfuscation, counter-attacking, denial (challenging Vemula's caste) – and ended up with a protracted and extremely messy fall out.

But beyond politics, there is a deeper discomfort. Nobody can claim that BHU is a hotbed of communists, but the fact that a case of molestation ballooned into a confrontation between students and the authorities a few years ago reveals something about the kind of attitude that this regime harbours when it comes to the youth. At its core, beyond the specific political dimensions of these episodes, there lies a more fundamental disconnect that the party has with the idea that young people have a mind of their own.

The paternalistic grounding of the Sangh cannot but show itself in such situations. The young are meant to learn and obey. They should study, follow rules and respect tradition. Young people cannot be trusted to take decisions about their lives. Parents are right and know better. If the young make mistakes, they need to be punished. If elders do something wrong, it must be respectfully ignored. Young followers who add muscle to the cause are welcome, but the idea that they can ask any kind of questions is a source of great discomfort.

The attempted recasting of Valentine's Day as 'Parents' Respect Day' was particularly telling. It sought to replace the fantasies of the young with those of the old. A world where children revere and pay ritual obeisance to their parents, head bowed in supplication. Initiatives like the anti-Romeo squads are another manifestation of the suspicion with which the desires of the young are viewed – the idea being that those who seek the freedom to mingle with the other sex outside the institution of marriage or the supervision of elders are fair game for self-appointed guardians of morality.

The situation becomes even more pronounced when it comes to young women, as could be seen from the words uttered by none else than the then vice chancellor of BHU, who said, in the aftermath of the molestation case mentioned earlier, that in trying to talk about sexual harassment, the girl students 'have put their modesty in the market'. The fear of female independence and the desire to exercise control over their movements and speech is visible in the words and actions of many different party and Sangh functionaries.

The BJP lives in a world of paternalistic certitude. Even within the cabinet, the code is of unquestioning obedience and frequent invocation of loyalty to the leader. There is little room for dialogue, and feedback, too, is sought within a tightly regulated space. The PM's unwillingness to answer questions but otherwise communicate profusely in one direction only comes from this mindset. A device like 'Mann ki Baat', which is again kindly and avuncular in tone, underlines the fact that the dispensing of wisdom to those who don't know better is seen to be a key part of the role that leaders must play.

But if this is so, what explains the fact that PM Modi and the BJP are, in general, quite popular with the youth? How does this hypothesis sit with the fact that this government is an avowed believer in technology and the answers it can provide? Its use of digital media has been pioneering, not just as a way to communicate but also in planning and organizing elections. Does talk of a disconnect with the youth carry any real weight?

This is the paradox at the heart of the issue. The current regime has a problem with young people. Even though young people, by and large, may not have a problem with this government. The party cannot handle even the slightest sign of youthful independence and comes down with disproportionate force whenever that happens. If a widespread movement against the government gets triggered by such repeated state overreactions, the responsibility for the same will lie entirely at the government's doorstep.

But there are reasons why this has not happened so far. Foremost would be Modi's personal popularity and his ability to speak in the idiom of the new by embracing the symbols of progress. The use of technology and social media, the reaching out to the world, a great comfort with branding and marketing – he has managed to present an old mindset in a dramatically new form.

The other reason is that the prevalent mood of the young in India is that of pragmatic docility; they are not particularly keen to rebel. They are looking to be led, and in successive elections, Modi's promises created a pathway for their burgeoning aspirations. Besides, the respect for the older generation is genuine and deep, and there is no intrinsic urge to buck tradition. But that does not mean that they will not resent attempts to control them beyond a point.

Given this and the fact that prospects of employment in the future look very gloomy, the chance of a dramatic shift in the mood of the youth is a real possibility at some stage. In Modi, the BJP has someone who has given them cover and bought them time, but the RSS-driven party cannot change in a hurry – perhaps it cannot change at all – and that might turn out to have material consequences in the future.

THE MUSCLE ECONOMY

Every once in a while, we see stories of various misdeeds of influential and well-connected young men. Abductions, rapes, brawls, road rage – a wide spectrum of criminal behaviour has been on display. After some initial outrage, in most cases, these crimes get papered over and equilibrium returns. To be well-connected, all one needs is access to some position of power, even if it was in the distant past. To be the nephew of an ex-councillor is enough.

It would seem that once any politician, major or minor, in power or not, past or present, living or dead, has enjoyed a position of power, then automatically all those who are in proximity and claim some connection, become immune from the laws of the land. That India has a VIP culture is well known, but that the definition of a VIP has become so democratized, is significant. Today, effective power is wielded by those who are, at best, very minor VIPs. There is an entire section of society, hidden from the view of media for the most part, that is at the forefront of the power-as-immunity culture. Rich builders, contractors, magistrates, corporators, councillors, lawyers – and their relatives, friends and well-wishers – are part of this group that can be loosely classified as the muscle economy.

What is interesting is that for a significant section of this group, bad behaviour is not an aberration, an accidental outpouring of excess animal spirits of some 'enthusiastic youngsters'. It is a necessary demonstration of power. The public flouting of rules is institutionalized by the many exemptions that this group routinely gets – in addition, the need is to visibly break a few more rules so as to underline the difference in status enjoyed by the powerful as well as those who choose to support them. The state actively participates in this process, not only creating a parallel structure of rules and facilities but by giving it additional legitimacy and, indeed, equipping it in its pursuit of such displays. Criminalization of politics leads leaders to become targets for their rivals, which earns them the right to protection by the state, which, in turn, allows them to harbour a private-army-at-large that they can deploy to further their interests. The state not only tolerates criminality but subsidizes it. To make sure, the state doubles down on the protection offered to the muscle economy by actively harassing anyone attempting to take any punitive action against these transgressions.

For this government, a radical overhaul of the political culture is not a priority (in a small but telling sign, among the three vehicle lanes that go through security checkpoints at Ahmedabad airport, one is designated as the VIP lane). It is exceedingly difficult for any mainstream party to take up this cause as it would attack what is the primary perk of being a politician – the ability to get things done without fear of consequences, at least from the law. No party takes action against its own members when they behave badly. The callousness with which politicians have been mouthing off on sensitive issues, including threatening rivals with rape, has never invited any action, barring a token apology and that, too, in rare cases. This is what politicians do, is the tacit understanding. The truth is that parties depend on the muscle economy far too much for them to want to do anything very seriously about curbing its influence.

The muscle economy becomes much more naked as we move away from the centre towards the periphery, but it is far from absent anywhere. Get involved in an accident or try and register a case against someone, and you will see its force getting unleashed. One quickly enters a parallel universe where seemingly obscure people can get someone influential on the line, where policemen turn into middlemen broking power for large sums of money and where one's personal safety gets threatened in a very believable way. All the apparent means of recourse at one's disposal dry up suddenly and one feels vulnerable, exposed and very afraid. Till a simple and basic right like being able to file a police complaint is something no citizen can take for granted, talk of a rule of law in any real sense is laughable.

The fact that power gets so easily distributed among those who have some proximity to the powerful is a sign that power in India does not accrue to a role but is awarded almost in perpetuity to an individual. The railing against dynastic politics is not real unless it attacks this ingrained form of familial power sharing. Getting elected today is like a benediction received by all members and associates of an individual, which is then collectively exercised. The impunity with which this power is flaunted is, in part, what drove the anger in evidence during the Anna Hazare-led movement. The AAP, which attempted to harness this anger, has fallen on difficult times, but it needs only one ghastly incident to get things boiling all over again. And given the ways of our muscle-bound bonsai VIPs, chances are that this is only a matter of time.

A JIHAD AGAINST LOVE?

That a term like love jihad can become such a legitimate part of serious conversation is a fact that needs to be better understood. It is either a testimony to a fevered media circus that latches on to any catchy formulation and then recirculates it furiously till it seems to take on the appearance of news, or it is actually part of a concerted campaign of some kind.

At one level, there are always fringe elements in the political space that espouse extreme views, and the 'beware of Muslim men who cast covetous glances and think impure thoughts about our women' idea is hardly a new one among the more radical Hindu groups. This kind of thinking is not limited to those from a particular religious denomination, and concerns about 'contamination' and 'conquest' can be found in most closed ethnic or racial groups.

The issue of love jihad itself is a curious one. If, indeed, the fears are true and there is a concerted effort to make young Hindu women fall in love with Muslim men so as to convert them to Islam, there is precious little that the law should be able to do about it. As long as an individual gets married of her own free will, and there is no criminal misrepresentation involved, the motivation behind the union is not material. If any coercion is involved or if the woman faces harassment after getting married, then, in any case, she has the full protection of the law, regardless of her religion. And as 7,100 dowry deaths in 2019 testify, violence against women seems hardly limited to any community.

What do anxieties about love jihad translate into in terms of action on the ground, assuming that there is such a conspiracy? Cases of abduction/coercion clearly fall into the purview of existing laws and hence don't need any extra action. The need to ensure that Hindu girls are not 'misled' into falling in love with love jihadists would mean that they would need to be watched over and prevented from being attracted to the 'other side'. Public spaces of all kinds would need to be patrolled so that families and so-called community leaders could intervene early enough to prevent such a possibility.

The problem is compounded by the fact that the so-called love jihadists sometimes pretend to be Hindus and take on misleading names just to fool impressionable young Hindu girls. The alleged deception of a girl called Tara Shahdeo by someone claiming to be Ranjit Kumar Kohli (but actually Rakibul Hasan) has actually been the case which has triggered this renewed anxiety about love jihad. This means that all love affairs are presumptively suspect, since an apparently Hindu boy may actually be a love-toting jihadist. Which, in turn, means that the only way that love jihad can be thwarted is by launching a jihad against love, and by ensuring that 'our' women stay secure under the protection of community norms and male elders who know better. For all the protestations that are made about love jihad being separate from love marriages, the very nature of the former makes it impossible for it to separated from the latter. Let us take a moment to appreciate just how strange this formulation is. An entire community is essentially confessing that it is unable to attract 'its' women and that another community is better at it. This fear of the lack of adequate masculine qualities is at the heart of so much of resentment against the Muslim.

The anxiety about love jihad, which, on the surface, appears to be an attempt to deepen religious polarization, ends up effectively being nothing but a dressed-up dread of female free will. The narrative goes thus – if women are given too much freedom, they will misuse it for, of all things, getting married to Muslims. The idea of love jihad, in practical terms, translates into no possible action, works purely at the level of the mind, and puts existing authority structures more securely in a position of power over women. In that sense, it deepens anxieties about two fundamental fault lines in society – religion and gender – simultaneously. This is why, in spite of its manic wild-eyed appearance, the phrase touches a chord among some. It crystallizes fears and makes a more permanent home for prejudice in our everyday lives.

As a party, the BJP needs to tread carefully here, for what appears to be an attempt to ride polarization for electoral gains could turn into an agenda of such dramatic conservativeness that it could seriously hurt the party. At this point of time, an attempt to go back in time and curtail everyday freedoms of young women, in the name of protecting them from the nefarious designs of love jihadists, makes little sense. Modi's constituency is socially conservative but it is in search for change that is not disruptive; it is not for a return to medieval restrictions. Love jihad may seem to be about religion, but it ends up being about reversing the fragile freedoms that young women have eked out for themselves. More than anyone else, it is in the BJP's interest to stop the love jihad issue from defining its agenda.

THE PHYSICAL AND THE POLITICAL

F OR SOMEONE WHO IS NOT really an early-morning person, occasional forays into the dawn and its immediate neighbourhood are always revealing. People of all ages, sizes and genders are running, walking, exercising, cycling and belly-laughing purposefully everywhere one looks. For a country that thought of physical exertion largely as a product of bad fate, this is a real transformation.

The need for some kind of physical activity is clearly linked to a growing consciousness about health and fitness. There is a new determination that lines our jaws, a new destination that our bodies strive to attain. Gyms across the country bear testimony to this need, as new parts of the body begin to acquire names. Abs, triceps, quads, hams and other abbreviations that bristle with concentrated purpose have begun to grow out of our bodies, with us intent on toning them and giving them shape.

At one level, as our bodies no longer need to work, in a world made soft by technology, they need to work out. We punish our bodies, because otherwise they would rot from disuse. Physical exercise serves many purposes, but a fundamental need that it satisfies is for us to experience our bodies in a state of stress. Additionally, the sense of purpose and a feeling of belonging that one derives from collective physical exertion is difficult to substitute by any other action.

This is an insight that plays a significant role in many arenas. Business certainly understands this – the sport and fitness industry has been growing worldwide as more people start taking physical exercise more seriously. The other arena, which may not, at first glance, seem to be a candidate for exploiting this human need, is politics.

A big difference between the right and the liberal-left in India is the extent to which the physical is part of the efforts to mobilize popular support. The left is high on language and ideas, but low on the physical, barring the occasional protest march and candlelight vigil. Leaders have, down the years, embarked on padyatras, with Rahul Gandhi's Bharat Jodo Yatra being the latest, but these are largely built around the individual and do not usually represent an attempt to mobilize people on a larger scale.

The right, on the other hand, has a much deeper understanding of the power of getting people to do something as a sign of their belief. There is a reason why the 'shakha' is so central to the RSS way of life. Even a minimal form of physical activity carried out in a group binds one to the collective. Combined with a distinctive uniform and a specific set of rituals, the feeling of being part of a cadre wedded to a cause gets instilled. There is also a strong element of the martial, which aims to signify a more aggressive resolve on part of the majority community. Physical exertion serves as a concrete form of investment into a belief system. It hardens intention – making it tangible. You're not just fighting for what you believe, you're preparing for the fight itself.

For the young in particular, activities are instruments through which ideals get implanted. Religious practice is a good place to see this understanding at work. The organizing of any festival in the neighbourhood, be it a Vishal Bhagwati Jagran or Ganesh Chaturthi, involves a whole set of actions that allow for the physical mobilization of a group of people. One signals one's belonging to a group not necessarily by buying into its beliefs, but by participating in its activities. The need for these occasions when one can submerge one's individual identity into something larger can be seen in the frenzied masses of people that pour out of trucks and buses, drenched in sweat and swooning to the hypnotic beats of the music that blares out at each such event.

Be it a group of 'gau rakshaks', the kawadias who set off on an arduous journey in large groups, or the self-appointed guardians who patrol the moral borders of society by identifying and challenging instances of 'love jihad', a lot of political mobilization is, in fact, some form of physical activity wrapped up in a political or cultural cause. In some way, these are versions of picnics, however aggressive their intent might be, where a group of people get to exercise their surplus anger and energy in the name of a larger cause.

The link between the idleness that is on evidence as one travels across the country and the growth of these private forces that find something to do in a way that appears meaningful to them, is difficult to miss. The gap that exists in the lives of the underemployed youth in the country needs to get filled. Physical activity that is laced with an undercurrent of anger is an ideal fit with the sense of marginalization that significant sections of the country are experiencing today. There is a sense of doing something, of making a difference, whatever its nature might be, that animates the participation of the young in such collective actions.

The importance of harnessing the physical is not new. The politics of physical activity has had a rich tradition in the country, particularly during India's freedom struggle. The Gandhian practice of politics emphasized the importance of the physical, beginning with acts of sanitation and encompassing several modes of action, including marches, the burning of imported clothes and the use of the 'charkha'. The sense of belonging to a vibrant movement needs to be translated into physical experience, something demonstrated well during the Jan Lokpal movement.

Today, however, it is largely one side of the political fence that seems to grasp the power of physical mobilization, and the need to convert political leaning into physical participation. Organized politics has gone off the streets, into the bylanes of social media and the TV studio. Which is why many pressing issues often do not translate into political movements on the ground. The politics of words perhaps needs to be accompanied by the politics of physical action.

AN INEVITABILITY ABOUT IT?

IT WAS LIKE WATCHING A statue topple in slow motion. You knew it was going to happen, and happen soon, but the sight was still a little surprising. Arvind Kejriwal and the AAP's fall had already been scripted, and as one by one the pieces fell in place, it was the consummation of a demise foretold.

Several factors played into this, with the party being both victim and protagonist. There is no question that the Centre targeted Kejriwal, his key associates, and the party. It handcuffed the local government to a lieutenant governor determined to thwart it at every instance, and fundamentally made the task of providing any meaningful governance extremely difficult. This was a completely transparent ploy, and in any country with a functioning media, it would have been difficult to pull off, but we are well past that theoretical possibility now.

For the AAP, this was a body blow. After it evolved from its activist roots into being a political party in every sense of the word, the basis of its connection with voters was its brand of welfarism, with free and affordable basic facilities such as electricity and water, as well as a much greater focus on providing quality services in the areas of education and healthcare even to the poorest. Kejriwal himself embodied the common man, and the iconography he surrounded himself with – the muffler and the 'jhadoo' – helped complete the picture of a grassroots-minded political formation.

Not being allowed to deliver anything new to his constituency has meant that for AAP voters, it is rational today to vote for the party in power at the Centre. It makes little sense to continue to support a government that is unable to act on its behalf, whatever the reasons might be. For many voters, it does not matter who is right or wrong, but who is in a better position to help them.

The corruption cases against Manish Sisodia and Kejriwal haven't helped either. While critics of the Centre also label this as a purely political move devoid of any judicial merit, the truth might be a little more complex. There is no way of knowing, but it is not out of the realm of possibility that the urgent need to generate funds for campaigns might have led the party into actions that could legitimately invite punishment. And while virtually every political party has found its own mechanisms of finding this source of funds, the AAP was particularly vulnerable, since it was constantly in the crosshairs of the Centre.

One doesn't know how much this has dented Kejriwal's image as an anti-corruption crusader, but arguably that was no longer his calling card. What is interesting is that there was no major grassroots reaction to his arrest, and that perhaps speaks of the diminution of his brand even before the court case and the arrest.

Over the years, the politician Kejriwal has perhaps become far too politically supple for his own good. He began by accreting power to himself, getting rid of the brand names who could compete with him. Although this did not hurt him too badly, it knocked a big hole into the party's claim over the idea that it was out to cleanse politics in India. He proved himself as a canny street fighter and was soon seen as perhaps the only challenger to the brand of politics practiced by the BJP. But that sense that here was a different politician practising a new brand of politics was fading.

After the 2019 elections, the party made a strategic decision to stop targeting Modi personally and to play what a lot of observers have called the 'soft Hindutva' card. He promised free tirth yatras, and his recitation of the Hanuman Chalisa, and carefully calibrated statements on immigration, marked this shift.

To what extent has the soft pedalling of religious polarization hurt him? Many commentators argue that this made him indistinguishable from the BJP and gave voters no reason to vote for him if they wanted an alternative. There is possibly some truth in this, but for the AAP, this gambit always seemed defensive in nature, to prevent the BJP from being able to attack it on that front.

It seems likelier that the voters rejected Kejriwal not because he was not distinct enough from the BJP, but because he stopped being useful. He simply did not seem to have either the gumption or the resources, physical and mental, to overcome the challenge posed by the Centre to deliver anything of value anymore. The trust that was placed in him, the belief that he was the strongest champion they could have on their side, has been replaced by a dawning recognition that he, like other politicians, was primarily interested in taking any position that would keep him in power. However, unlike other politicians from the ruling party, he did not have the means to do something for the voters in a meaningful way. It is noteworthy that in the entire time, not a single thing that he said went viral or struck a resonant chord. He was another politician making another political speech.

There is a lesson here somewhere, but it is not easy to find. One could argue that had he maintained greater integrity to his cause and shown less interest in survival, perhaps this would not have come to pass. It is equally possible that without the cunningness and political agility he has shown, he would have already been erased from our consciousness. The reality is the BJP has just too many weapons in its arsenal, and for Kejriwal and the AAP, it was just a matter of time.

THE MARKET FOR SIMPLICITY

IT IS TELLING THAT THE deeply entangled issue of extricating Britain from the EU was decided on the basis of a referendum. Yes or No. In or Out. It is perhaps even more telling that the whole issue went under the fetching brand called Brexit, leading, of course, to a rash of other such morbidly simple reductions of complex questions – Rexit, for one, dealing with the departure of the head of the central bank of a country, and then we have the as yet unexplored but nevertheless fascinating possibilities presented by Grexit, Frexit, and so on.

It is no coincidence that Donald Trump, too, sees the world in crayon. According to an article by Jack Shaper in *Politico*, 'Run through the Flesch-Kincaid grade-level test, his text of responses score at the 4th-grade reading level.' He himself is 'amazing' and 'fantastic' and his enemies are 'idiots', 'losers' and 'morons'. The world presents itself to him through an intensely personal lens – everything is, in some ways, a validation of Donald Trump. He makes the world simple, and proposes answers that, to his supporters, ring out with the truth that no one else tells.

The simple is, at its simplest, an argument that is the shortest distance from an immediate emotion arising out of a direct experience of the world. When what you feel is what is right, the world becomes so much easier to deal with. Brexit and Trump both connect with an emotional truth that precedes logic. That doesn't mean that both lack any logic in their positions, but only that the support for their positions is not dependent on whatever logical arguments accompany them. This is why, in the face of the most obvious, repeated and brazen lying, one of the major reasons that his supporters cite for their support for Trump is that he speaks the truth. In a sense, this is true – Trump says things that his supporters already 'know' to be true.

The referendum, the online poll, the objective-type question paper, the show of hands in a studio audience, these are all devices that all display their rejection of complexity. The referendum reduces democracy from an ecological process to a binary event by transferring responsibility and sidestepping the mandate given to those in power. While it is true that the Brexit vote reflects the will of the people, it is worth noting that there is a reason why the referendum is not an instrument of choice for most democracies.

The democratic process accounts for the fact that its constituents are arrayed across a spectrum of abilities and interests – not everyone is equally interested in issues of governance, and some understand and engage with complex questions better than others. By creating an intermediate level between the electorate and the state, the democratic process accommodates and absorbs the varying intensities of involvement that its citizens are capable of. Even the administration itself is organized in a way that people closest to a decision are meant to have greater ability to take a view on it. Not every MP, for instance, needs to be capable of engaging with trade policy, but those involved in the issue certainly need to. The democratic system uses the will of the people as a guide, while giving itself the ability not to be overwhelmed by it. The referendum forces people to reduce questions to their simplest form, which, in turn, is an invitation for them to fall back on their primary impulses.

In a larger sense, there is a reason why the exaggeratedly simple strikes such a chord today. The dominant intellectual constructs of recent times imposed a standard of behaviour that rendered illegitimate a lot of concerns that many had about their immediate surroundings. The reason why Trump gets such a response when he rails against political correctness is because he is seen to speak a truth that is in plain sight but which no one else is willing to articulate. Political correctness is the dead skin of idealism, it is the lie that pretends that change has happened when it has not; it challenges reality with a new vision that is never seriously pursued, it deflates idealism even as it apparently celebrates it. It makes virtue out of deafness and blindness and uses absolute yardsticks that it judges others by.

With political correctness, what becomes important is the reaction to what is said, displayed, or professed and the focus is on maintaining an appearance of a just world. Time or effort is not spent trying to convert people to a new world-view, they are simply asked to shut up and toe the line. Liberal values come from a vision of a world that needs work from everyone, for it asks people to rise above some natural instincts. By making the doubts that arise when dealing with these questions seem illegitimate, and by creating an alternative vocabulary of concerns that bear little relationship with the more basic questions that most people grapple with, the mutterings against the liberal cultural narrative are driven underground. Only to erupt with great force as they have now.

Fear of large-scale immigration, of being overrun by people with a different way of life who would change the fabric of one's society irretrievably, for instance, is presented by the liberal elite as an outdated anxiety that cannot be heard or responded to, only attacked and disdained. Another factor is the overweening dominance of the financial world, one which increasingly operates using mechanisms and scales that bear little relationship to reality as it is commonly understood. The world moves by rules made by the few for themselves and everyone else bears the consequences. The market for radical simplicity and of 'natural' clarity has its roots in the unwillingness that the intellectual elites have displayed in acknowledging the legitimacy of the fears that such a world evokes.

The cultural mainstream is fighting back. What is popular is the truth. What is felt instinctively is legitimate. What is feared will come true. What is complex is a conspiracy. And the past is a safer place than the future.

MANN KI BAAT AND BRAND MODIJI

IF THERE IS ONE THING that all commentators, including even the critics of this government, agree upon, it is that Narendra Modi is an extremely popular leader, who generates a level of trust and respect that borders on superstition. His actions are presumed to come from a place of sincerity, something that was in stark evidence in the reactions to his demonetization initiative. All criticism of the government – whether relating to the slowdown in economic growth post-demonetization, its perplexing interest in all things bovine, or its risky efforts to intrude into people's kitchens –- seemed to lack the power to make any dent in his image. In a time when faith in politicians is at an all-time low, what explains Modi's extraordinary ability to evoke this kind of presumptive trust?

There are many elements that go into the making of a brand like Modi. He strikes a deep chord with his aura of clarity and strength, speaks simultaneously to anxieties and aspirations, communicates using emotionally resonant metaphors, understands the power of branding key initiatives to generate a sense of activity and purpose, and knows the power of enigmatic silence. But there is one specific note in his persona that is particularly interesting – his ability to convey a sense of empathy and intimacy while in most other ways behaving like the Great Leader. In the comprehensive communication mix that he uses, there is one that stands out for its intelligence and restraint – 'Mann ki Baat', his fortnightly address to the nation, where we get a clear glimpse into this aspect of Modi.

An interesting combination of narrative strategies is used, apparently unselfconsciously. The overall sense is that of a comforting soundtrack that locates his government in our daily lives; an audio murmur that reinforces, without making heavy weather of it, some key themes of interest to Modi. The tonality is that of a kind, concerned family elder, who is sharing ideas, hopes and even doubts with his extended family. Modi speaks about subjects connected with government programmes, with cleanliness being a recurring theme, as well as general life advice, the need to try new things – learn a language, travel in an unreserved second-class compartment for 24 hours, learn to ride an auto-rickshaw or cycle rickshaw, not just a two- or four-wheeler, utilize the summer vacation well, and so on. Even when government programmes are spoken of, the vantage point used is that of the ground level, with individual stories being the focus.

Audience feedback is woven into the narrative at many levels, and suggestions are played back. Not everything is agreed to, but a sense of listening to what is being said does get communicated. Modi uses a lot of open-ended statements, including some that convey doubt and uncertainty. 'Sometimes, I think,' 'But then I came to some new realization,' serve to humanize the content, and give it an introspective personal touch. The sense is that of someone confiding in little old you, of all people, talking as he is thinking, rather than that of a prefabricated script. The content is loosely packed, with enough mention of the insubstantial – the weather, some references to sports, a lot of talk of festivals, so as not to feel too pointed and purposeful.

While advice is offered, usually there is little offered by way of direct intervention. The temptation to wave magic wands and confer individual favours is avoided, and this helps the broadcast rise above the transactional. This is not a 'raj darbar', where complaints are heard and justice dispensed, but a 'pravachan', where folksy wisdom is shared.

Unlike most other communication that comes out of this government, there is little by way of pointed attack or hyperbolic self-congratulation; indeed, political language is avoided, by and large. There are some references to the self in third person, but otherwise successes of the government are framed in terms of changes in people's mindset rather than through delivered outcomes.

Hindutva rhetoric is largely absent in an overt sense, but religious practice as a part of everyday life is woven into the narrative. The broadcast is replete with references to Hindu saints, festivals as well homages to the right-wing pantheon of past leaders, but this is one place where festivals and key figures of other religions find significant mention. The Christmas broadcast, for instance, began with a reference to Christmas as well as a quote from the Gospel of St Luke, before going on to mention the birthdays of Madan Mohan Malaviya and Atal Bihari Vajpayee in that order.

Radio is the ideal medium for this kind of a fireside chat. Warm, intimate, with a voice that reaches out and fills space without any visual distraction. Radio creates the experiential illusion of community, a circle of trust, better than any other medium, and 'Mann Ki Baat' finds an ideal vehicle for its ambitions in this form.

Admittedly, it can never be a primary tool that gives results of a dramatic kind, and this is not even intended, but it is invaluable in creating the overall persona.

Modi virtually rediscovers radio as a tool for soft propaganda, by making it do what it is capable of doing. Governance is broken down into its uncapitalized form; it becomes a more human endeavour, full of relatable purpose and sincere intention. This is a patient seeping, the irrigation of deep roots, the tending to and nurturing of a feeling. It communicates the confidence that the leader is in it for the long haul, that the time horizon at work is much longer than five years. 'Mann Ki Baat' helps create a dimension to the Modi persona that rises above the din and clamour of the political, and it does so by going small rather than big. A low-key slow-burn radio programme is one of the reasons why Brand Modi is now Brand Modiji – a subtle shift that carries with it emotional equity that critics find hard to shake.

THE GANDHI PARADOX?

Every time any event involving Mahatma Gandhi takes place, the Modi government is fulsome in its tributes. Through all formal means of communication, Gandhi is treated with due reverence and is accorded the appropriate ceremonial endorsement in line with what successive governments have done. But things are not what they seem, for this valorization of Gandhi is skin-deep, and it takes little, particularly from the BJP's support base, for the more real feelings about the man to emerge.

To illustrate, on the death anniversary of the Mahatma, very often we find that Nathuram Godse also trends on Twitter (now called X), where many florid tributes are forthcoming. A leader from the Hindu Mahasabha mock-enacted the shooting of Gandhi, while celebrating the actions of Godse. Posts attacking Gandhi in graphic terms, including justifying his killing, were plentiful in number. And, in keeping with tradition, many of these voices were 'fortunate enough to be followed on social media by the prime minister'.

On the government's part, it is a strategic move to attack Nehru without restraint, but to leave Gandhi out of the firing line, at least formally. Attacking Nehru has several advantages, not the least of which is that he serves as a surrogate for his descendants. Attacking both Gandhi and Nehru would also expose the party to the oft-repeated charge that it played a marginal role in the freedom movement, which is why it is demonizing both its heroes. Focusing anger on Nehru, while ritually celebrating Gandhi, allows for the subtle distancing of the freedom movement from Nehru. Apart from being a tactic, the dislike for Nehru is, in any case, visceral, and finds expression so often that it has become a running joke.

But in many ways, Gandhi is the real figure of distaste. Nehru might be the easier target, but Gandhi is no less the enemy. A recurring theme in the imagination of those on the right is the sense of loss felt as a result of the partition of the country, for which Gandhi is held squarely responsible. The government on its part communicates its aversion in thinly veiled codes – speaking of Gandhi and Savarkar in the same breath, for instance, which is a dead giveaway of their true feelings about the man.

The nostalgia for undivided India is easy to understand at an abstract level, but the truth is that had Pakistan, and later Bangladesh, not become independent, then the religious composition of India would have looked significantly different. Instead of constituting 14 per cent of the population, Muslims would have made up nearly 25 per cent of the country, making the prospect of a Hindu nation that much dimmer. Wanting Pakistan as part of India is, in effect, a demand by the right to want more Muslims, and this is mystifying. All the anxieties about the size of the Muslim population would have got magnified, and, politically, too, Muslim representation would have made it difficult for this section of the voters to be ignored.

As is the case in Kashmir, the tendency is to see territory as 'belonging to us', while disowning the people that go with it. But if the current Pakistan and Bangladesh were to be part of India, then the ability to control three different tracts of territory through military would have been much more difficult. The idea of Akhand Bharat 'belonging' to 'us' becomes less meaningful when the definition of 'us' itself changes. The insider/outsider classification that is at work today would have been rendered null and void had the country not been partitioned. Put simply, there would be no Pakistan to send Muslims and 'anti-nationals' to.

The implicit mental model at work seems to be rooted in the idea of conquest in a medieval kingdom rather than that of inclusion in a modern democracy. The urge to reverse history ignores the fact that in many ways, the kind of erasure sought is simply not possible. Keeping today's Pakistan and Bangladesh within the folds of India would not be tantamount to conquest, but a redefinition of India itself.

The demand for a unified India should, on the other hand, translate into comfort with the idea of unity and equality. If we are indeed part of the same fabric of nationhood, then why the need to demonize the other side? Today, the impulse is to ask all those that do not toe the government's line to 'go to Pakistan'; Akhand Bharat is, in effect, the idea of all of Pakistan coming to India. You cannot want an entire people to become of a part of who you are, while finding every way to disdain them.

The other puzzling aspect of the reaction of the right is its aversion to the idea of Hindu terror. To nuance this a little, it is easy to see why the label 'terrorist' is objected to. The effort is to make it synonymous with Muslims, and hyphenating Hindu with terrorism clearly militates against that need. But otherwise, the idea that the once-timid Hindu is now capable of anger, and even violence, is an important part of how the right narrativizes itself. The idea of Hindu terror gives form to that desire. The label 'terror' might be seen as undesirable but the idea underlying this description should not cause the kind of anger that it does. The desire to hang on to the idea of the accommodative Hindu is unquestionably a deep instinct, even when the opposite impulse, that of being taken seriously and feared, is perhaps even stronger.

Gandhi will continue to be an object of faux-reverence, while being systematically undermined. His ideas have never been easy to adopt, but for the current regime they are anathema. He himself is more useful.

CAUGHT BETWEEN REWARD AND GUILT

A TRUTH THAT PERPLEXES AND VEXES the critics of the NDA government is how Narendra Modi and his party continue to not only win elections but enjoy widespread popular support. More importantly, Mr Modi somehow seems to effortlessly elude any criticism for his government's actions or the lack thereof.

It helps, of course, that that the media often works as a force multiplier for the government, in large part because its viewers like and respond to the tenor of its coverage. It is extremely unlikely that the media would be so strongly aligned with the government had there been a stronger undercurrent of anger against it. Supporting the government suits it, which is why what we see on display is not grudging acceptance of the government's diktats but a militant espousal of its preferred narrative.

The problem with the critics of this government is that the frameworks and mental models they are using are outmoded. The issues that are of primary concern to this group have little mainstream resonance, and, hence, are condemned to be consigned to the periphery of the political process. Real understanding is substituted by a form of self-righteous name-calling. Bigoted, regressive, divisive, fascist, misogynistic, repressive, authoritarian – these are the kind of labels that fly around in profusion from the liberal camp. While these might offer some succour to a closed group of like-minded liberals, they have virtually no impact on the people who are supporting Modi.

The fundamental difference between the two sides is that what the right offers today is a system of reward and validation, while the liberal side offers flagellation and guilt. The key to understanding the appeal of the right is that it makes people comfortable as they are and does not demand that they change in order to feel good about themselves. The past is legitimized, society as it exists is celebrated, natural impulses that drive people are held up as ideal. What is demonized are the forces of disquiet, which destabilize the status quo, which are constantly carping about what is wrong with the way things are.

The nation becomes a very important rallying point for the right, for it allows people an identity that rises above their origins, and is deemed widely to be beyond any criticism. It is possible to inculcate a sense of community that collaborates for a common cause. There is a very real sense of being part of something important, of every individual mattering. It also allows for all criticism of the government to be characterized as being against the interests of the nation, which, in turn, allows supporters to feel self-righteous as they bask in the patriotic glow that they confer on themselves. The sense of community, of being part of something larger than themselves, is what allows people to overlook the hardships that they have to face when the government's actions impact them adversely. The persona of Modi as a decisive, caring leader who means well, and one who is constantly under attack by people who do not have the larger interests of the nation at heart, adds to this narrative.

The Ram Mandir is another example of using a popular deity as a rallying point for the majority community. Since the courts have, in their wisdom, ruled on the Babri Masjid issue, which Hindu will have strong objections to the establishment of a Ram temple in Ayodhya? One doesn't need to be a bigot to feel rewarded by the temple.

When critics made fun of people banging 'thalis' to fight Covid, they failed to grasp the emotional power of a sense of participation that such symbolic actions evoke. The big difference between the two sides might well be the degree to which they grasp the centrality of symbolic emotional reward when it comes to politics. What is counter-intuitive is that on the surface, the right feeds off anger and bitterness. The TV anchors who bat for the government are spittle-spraying dementors, social media is full of targeted abuse and hate, and the political discourse is in constant search for enemies to demonize, if not imprison. This is vital in order to create a sense of legitimacy for the ruling narrative, for it needs to work less hard to prove its relevance. It doesn't matter if many of these fears about being besieged are contrived or transparently false. The power of fake news is that it is seen to speak a higher truth.

But important though this whipping up of bitterness is, the real power comes from the positive feelings that are generated. The invocation of past humiliations, imagined and real, and a sense that these will be avenged is a reward by itself, but the larger reward lies in a sense of righteous belonging that the ruling party has managed to evoke. That's why support for this government transcends its actions, and even ideology. The sense of comfort, of belonging, of one's deepest desires being acknowledged, is what makes Modi's government impregnable, at least for now. The liberals market dissatisfaction, the right offers validation. As the right sees it, the former constantly point to differences, division and discrimination in their quest for equality and justice. What the liberals see as an attempt to redress injustices, the right sees as an all-out effort to delegitimize everything they hold dear. The problem with those opposing this government is that they have no alternative rewards to offer. The liberal discourse has very few takers, and serves largely to mobilize the supporters of the government. The traditional levers of caste and sub-regional aspirations have been stripped of their potency. Unless a new political vocabulary emerges, there is little hope of a viable political alternative to the BJP. For that to happen, there is a lot of unlearning that those opposed to the government have to do.

THE NEED FOR SOFT INFRASTRUCTURE

SOME TIME AGO, A MAN called Manoj Kathuria was put in jail and denied bail. His fault? While navigating knee-deep water in his SUV, he unwittingly pushed water into a basement, where three students who were trapped died. There is no possible way he could have known that the simple act of driving on waterlogged streets would result in such a tragedy. Our police and judiciary are capable of some daft things, but to hold him responsible is truly world-class idiocy.

The problem is, what is at work is not stupidity but a patented way of defusing crises whenever the system is challenged. Take immediate and visible action, find a scapegoat, however improbable, and shield those who are truly responsible till the controversy dies down. Go back to life as usual.

And as it happens, we have seen a procession of things going wrong. The new Parliament building leaking. Parts of airports caving in or flooding. Train accidents galore. Bridges collapsing. Cities drowning. Exam papers leaking. Questions are being asked of the governments in power, as they should be. But there is a deeper malaise that we don't really discuss – one that implicates all governments, whatever their political hue.

We are deeply involved with the question of infrastructure. It is an area that has received attention from successive governments, both at the central and state levels. We applaud the building of new highways, the overhauling of airports, the construction of flyovers and underpasses, and the refurbishment of railway stations as signs of our development, and indeed they are.

What is rarely discussed is the reason why all these infrastructural advances don't quite translate into a sustained sense of well-being. There is a reason why bridges are so prone to collapsing, why new roads disappear at the drop of rain, why young kids drown in a basement because of flooding, and why rich people keep driving over innocent bystanders with impunity.

What we lack is attention towards soft infrastructure – the protocols of administration, regulations, healthcare, education, and financial services, as well as judicial and police action. Beyond a point, the difference between developed countries and others does not lie in hard infrastructure but in all that supports this infrastructure and keeps it going.

None of our institutions work in the manner intended. The process for choosing the best partner is deeply suspect. A favoured party wins the contract by putting in a low bid, which is subsequently revised. The quality of construction is abysmal. The average life of a highway internationally is supposed to be 28.2 years; I don't know the corresponding number in India, but we have all seen pictures of potholes in the roads of our major metropolises. And as one travels to smaller towns, roads are spray-painted on rather than built, and every monsoon means a fresh refurbishment of the roads designed to last no more than a few months. The same goes as far as maintenance is concerned. And the less said about accountability, the better.

Corruption has infiltrated every possible aspect of our lives. Every rule can be broken or bypassed, and every safeguard can be ignored. Any major accident brings forth a flurry of action designed to quell controversy, but only in the immediate vicinity of the problem and for a limited period. Corruption is not only monetary but also exists under the guise of influence. No action can be taken against someone who is rich or important (or has been important once).

Corruption is not only a moral problem or an issue of some people making money illegally; it works to dismantle the entire logic on which the idea of administration rests. For things to work, individuals playing an official role need to work in a manner divorced from any personal interest. An auditor needs to audit, a fire safety inspector needs to pull up those who are violating guidelines, a purchase officer chooses the best option in an impartial way, and so on. In a corrupt system, none of this happens; every step is compromised, tainted by some personal interest or another.

Until we recognize that our administrative structure is essentially defunct and needs a drastic overhaul, nothing in India will work like it is meant to. No government has shown an interest in this, and it is admittedly a mammoth task. The problem is not that governments don't understand the need for doing this, but that they have developed a vested interest in keeping things the way they are.

Control over institutions is desired; elections must be funded; and local politicians must be appeased by giving them money-making opportunities.

It is not as if things cannot work in India. UPI is a great example. It helps that there is no need for human intervention or adjudication here. Our airports, too, are, on the whole, success stories. They can compete with airports anywhere in the world, and the immigration experience is far superior to that of most developed countries. Even here, some of the problems outlined earlier do exist, but by and large, things work. The reason for that is that here the intention is clear and has, for the most part, been translated into action.

It is customary to blame people for a lot of this mess. We complain about the lack of a civic sense and a 'chalta-hai' attitude in our public behaviour. There is truth in this, but it is also a consequence of living in a system that doesn't work. One must look out for oneself because following the rules will only mean that one will be left behind. Which is why the same people who migrate overseas have no trouble following the rules.

Development is not about the height of our skyscrapers or the speed of our trains. It lies in making life predictable and comfortable, in knowing that things will work and then that when they don't, they will get fixed on their own.

POSTSCRIPT

I**NDIA SEEMS TORN BETWEEN OPPOSITE** impulses. It seeks progress but avoids fundamental change, is in a hurry to be admired by the world but feels frustrated when its internal reality does not match its self-image.

It is tempting to read the present as a moment of unravelling. The rise of polarizing politics, the slow corrosion of institutions, the performative aggression that passes for identity – these are evident features of the current Indian reality. But to stop there would be to miss something equally vital: the deep and undeniable energy that pulses from below.

This is not an energy that has yet found a consistent expression. It is often scattered, sometimes misguided, and frequently co-opted. But it exists. In small towns bursting with first-time entrepreneurs, in teenagers coding apps on their phones, in local creators building global audiences, and in citizens demanding better – however clumsily –, there is a yearning for more.

India today is both more centralized and more decentralized than ever before. While power consolidates at the top, agency is bubbling at the bottom. While narratives are being created, counter-narratives are being imagined. The same digital networks that spread misinformation also enable mobilization, creativity, and dissent.

This is not really about choosing to be pessimistic or optimistic, but in understanding what the new rules of engagement are. India is being changed by strong forces that are non-linear, and it is furiously negotiating with each of these in a way that only it can. Looking back, we might see this as a time of reckoning – between a past that we refuse to leave behind and a future that is gatecrashing into our lives. Perhaps the churn we see today will turn out to be a necessary prerequisite for something more elevated, something that takes us to a destination that more of us can agree on.

This book is not a conclusion but a pause. Even as we are absorbing the cascading impact of one technology, another is breathing down our necks, promising to change everything yet again. There are still choices to be made, paths to be chosen, imaginations to be reawakened. And if the future is uncertain, it is also – for that very reason – still open.

ABOUT THE AUTHOR

Santosh Desai, author of the book *Mother Pious Lady: Making Sense of Everyday India* and the columnist behind the long-running column 'City City Bang Bang' in *The Times of India*, is regarded as one of India's leading social commentators. His work documents the changes India is going through, viewed from the lens of everyday life. In another life, he is one of India's foremost brand thinkers, having spent over two decades in advertising and eighteen years in brand consulting. He is also a founder at Think9 Consumer Technologies, a company that helps early-stage start-ups to scale up. He is a graduate in economics and a management graduate from IIM-Ahmedabad.